D0828162

EST Marathon 1994

One-Act Plays

EST Marathon 1994
One-Act Plays

Edited by Marisa Smith

Contemporary Playwrights Series

SK
A Smith and Kraus Book

A Smith and Kraus Book
Published by Smith and Kraus, Inc.

Copyright © 1995 by Smith and Kraus, Inc.
All rights reserved

Manufactured in the United States of America

Cover and Text Design by Julia Hill
Cover Photo ©1994 by Thomas McHugh

First Edition: May 1995
10 9 8 7 6 5 4 3 2 1

CAUTION: Professionals and amateurs are hereby warned that the plays represented in this book are subject to a royalty. They are fully protected under the copyright laws of the United States of America, and of all countries covered by the International Copyright Union (including the Dominion of Canada and the rest of the British Commonwealth), and of all countries covered by the Pan-American Copyright Convention and the Universal Copyright Convention, and of all countries with which the United States has reciprocal copyright relations. All rights, including professional, amateur, motion picture, recitation, lecturing, public reading, radio broadcasting, television, video or sound taping, all other forms of mechanical or electronic reproductions such as information storage and retrieval systems and photocopying, and the rights of translation into foreign languages, are strictly reserved. See individual plays for contact information.

Library of Congress Cataloguing-in-Publication Data

EST Marathon '94 : the one-act plays / edited by Marisa Smith. --1st ed.
        p. cm. -- (Contemporary playwrights series)
        ISBN 1-880399-83-0

        1. One-act plays, American. 2. American drama--20th century. 3. Ensemble Studio Theater. I. Smith, Marisa. II. Series.

        PS627.053E88   1995
        812'.04108--dc20   95-2287
                                                              CIP

To Helené and Stephen Gordon
whose true philanthropy has sustained
the Ensemble Studio Theatre's yearly Marathon Festival
of One-Act Plays.

And to the playwrights, actors, directors,
designers, and technicians
who have brought the Marathon plays
to life over eighteen seasons.

Contents

FOREWORD

The Ensemble Studio Theatre's One-Act Marathon of 1994, the subject of this exciting volume, was a banner year in the history of this unique series. Selected from more than one thousand entries, the plays here reflect the main components of artistic life at EST by representing established veterans, emerging writers and brand new voices in American theatre.

By producing the Marathon each year we pay homage to the oft-neglected short play form and give writers a chance to flex their one-act muscles in a national forum. Since its inception the Marathon has spawned scores of one-act festivals in New York and all across the country. Even commercial producers have taken note and recent Marathon plays by Arthur Miller, Christopher Durang, and David Ives have emerged this season in commercial contexts. It is safe to say that as a result of being rescued by EST in 1976, the one-act in America is alive and well.

The career of every major American writer can be traced back to early success in the short form—Arthur Miller, Tennessee Williams, Eugene O'Neill, Wendy Wasserstein, Lanford Wilson, Romulus Linney, Horton Foote, Edward Albee, Marsha Norman, John Guare, Sam Shepard, and David Mamet, to name a few. The one-act play is crucial to the growth of a playwright. This adventurous publication will help insure that these fine Marathon plays will reach a wider audience and that the power of the one-act will be felt far across our artistic landscape.

On behalf of our board of directors and all our members at Ensemble Studio Theatre in New York and California, I thank Smith and Kraus for their innovation and commitment in producing this collection. And I urge the reader to browse, select, and enjoy these one-acts and hopefully, to produce them.

Curt Dempster
Artistic Director
Ensemble Studio Theatre

EST Marathon 1994
One-Act Plays

Rosemary With Ginger

by Edward Allan Baker

To Joel "riley" Schapira for clearing the pasture
so I could run with this Rosemary With Ginger

ROSEMARY WITH GINGER was directed by Ron Stetson and stage managed
by Judith Sostek with the following cast:

Rosemary . . . . Kristen Griffith
Ginger . . . . Michaela Murphy

ROSEMARY WITH GINGER by Edward Allan Baker. © 1994 by Edward Allan Baker. All rights reserved.
Reprinted by permission of the playwright. All inquiries should be addressed to the playwright's
agent, Ms. Elyse Kroll, The Gersh Agency NY, Inc., Suite 2400, 130 West 42nd Street, New York, NY
10036. No amateur or professional performance or reading of the play may be given without obtaining, in advance, the written permission.

EDWARD ALLAN BAKER: ROSEMARY WITH GINGER was Mr. Baker's 6th EST Marathon Experience joining DOLORES, NORTH OF PROVIDENCE, FACE DIVIDED, A PUBLIC STREET MARRIAGE, and LADY OF FADIMA, and his newest play, A DEAD MAN'S APARTMENT, has been chosen for Marathon '95. Other plays include PRAIRIE AVENUE, THE BRIDE OF OLNEYVILLE SQUARE, THE BUFFER, 27 BENEDICT STREET, and he co-authored IN THE SPIRIT with Chuka Lokoli (Native American Ensemble). DOLORES (produced worldwide) is included in the edition of BEST SHORT PLAYS, 1988-89, and made into an award-winning short film that starred Judith Ivey. He was invited to The Sundance Film Institute in 1990 with his screenplay PRAIRIE AVENUE, and is currently writing a feature film for Showtime titled JUST NORTH OF PROVIDENCE, and is an Adjunct Instructor of Playwriting at the University of Hartford.

AUTHOR'S NOTE

One afternoon in Providence Rhode Island around 1973 when I was all of twenty-three, I was doing one of my favorite things: having a warm piece of apple pie, a cup of coffee, and smoking an unfiltered camel cigarette in a downtown diner. It was just after noon. Place was hopping. Jukebox blared Elvis singing "Love Me Tender." All was fine in Providence this day when a woman's voice drowned out Elvis with "YOU CAN'T JUST TAKE MY KIDS GOD DAMN IT!" Most of us turned to see a young woman, early 20's, screaming into the receiver of the pay phone. "I LOVE MY KIDS, DON'T THAT COUNT FOR SOMETHIN?!" I stayed glued to her as most of the patrons turned away. "THEY'RE ALL I GOT, OH GOD PLEASE DON'T TAKE 'EM...I'LL — I'LL FIND WORK, I'LL WORK THREE JOBS, JUST DON'T TAKE 'EM FROM ME..." Feeling self-conscious she turned around and we locked eyes and I felt her ask me for help. She yelled into the phone "I'M NOT A BAD PERSON, I'M GOOD...I AM GOOD..." A middle-age guy at the counter, visibly annoyed, said: "if you're so good, you wouldn't be losin ya kids." A general feeling of agreement passed from one end of the counter to the other when a head-cook or manager or somebody took the phone from her, hung it up, and said: "take your problems outta here. C'mon, out, out, goodbye, outta here, les go, use the phone on the street ta do your cryin." He (at least) opened the door for her and a blast of cold air entered the diner. I remember. I cried watching her leave. I couldn't help it. The diner was loose now. They (patrons) got away without having to feel anything. And I think most were proud of that. "Ha! Didn't get pulled in. I'll have another coffee." Little did they know, that they, along with the broken-hearted woman, played a part in the creation of a playwright! I now have one purpose: to make people feel compassion for one another regardless of differences in class. That purpose was seeded in a diner in Providence and since then I've merged my purpose with a brief passage from THUS SPAKE ZARATHUSTRA by Nietzsche: "of all that is written, I love only what a person hath written with his blood. Write with blood and thou wilt find that blood is spirit."

—Edward Allan Baker

"there's no need to watch the bridges that we're burnin'"

—al green

CHARACTERS

Ginger — 37
Rosemary — 40

TIME

A Friday afternoon in October of 1993

LOCATION

Peter Pan Diner, Providence, Rhode Island

ROSEMARY WITH GINGER

*The shell of a diner that prospered in the 50s and 60s and now
there's one booth left that's downright and the large window (that
looks out to Elmwood Avenue) has a huge X taped to it, bullet holes
visible above and below the X. Stage-left is the counter and among
the many things piled atop it include a coffee-maker with fresh coffee, and in the center a small counter-top jukebox. Door to the outside is up-right, clump of keys hang from the lock, and up-left is the
entrance to rest rooms and kitchen. A payphone is by the entrance—*

*Boxes of diner paraphernalia are piled in different areas of the
space mixed in with chairs, tables, and counter stools. Menus are
strewn about the tiled floor—*

*The Peter Pan Diner is down to its last booth, its last waitress,
its last song—*

*Scene: In the darkness is heard the ending of the song—"For
The Good Times" sung by Al Green then a phone ring—beat—
Lights up on Ginger on the payphone.*

GINGER: ...cause we're closed...for good...don't matta since when...Mrs.
Guertin, listen to me...I can't give you the soup-of-the-day cause
there is none...that's right...so you have to stop callin an...no-no
I'm not foolin you...I'm here just cleanin up an...
(Knocking heard on the front door. Ginger turns to look.)
Uh listen Mrs. Guertin you take care a yaself...I will uh-huh bye...
*(Ginger hangs up and proceeds to the door. She's clad in a skirt,
fishnet stockings, sneakers, and a plain-looking blouse. She turns
the clump of keys and lets in Rosemary.)*
GINGER: *(continued)* Where you been?
ROSEMARY: *(walks by Ginger)* You gotta be outta ya fucken mind still
bein here...
GINGER: I been callin an...
ROSEMARY: I don't believe I drove my Barretta through this shit neigh-
borhood...

GINGER: 'Bout time you got in touch with me don't ya think?

ROSEMARY: Every corna, every fucken corna packs-a-guys holdin their crotches an eyein me an forget stoppin for stop signs...I had one hand on my gun an the...

GINGER: *(quickly)* You brought a gun?

ROSEMARY: Oh please, somebody got you pinned an pullin off your jeans there'll be two words comin outta ya mouth... "fucken shoot him!"

GINGER: You been drinkin, haven't you?

ROSEMARY: This area's been taken over by the Hu-Mong honey, an this diner is closed an you wanna know why?

GINGER: I can smell the blackberry brandy, Rose...

ROSEMARY: Fuck you and listen.

GINGER: I don't wanna listen if you're on one of your drinkin binges an...

ROSEMARY: This diner is closed cause the Hu-Mong don't eat meatloaf specials an don't have English muffins in their diet and hate American chop suey!

GINGER: Now I know why you didn't get back to me when I...

ROSEMARY: The Hu-Mong eat people!

GINGER: Oh god you're in that asshole mood.

ROSEMARY: Yeah well...

(Rosemary is clad in tight jeans, small white boots and a jazzed up jean jacket over a loose-fitting blouse.)

Me and Raymond the oran-ga-tan man got into this big fight an he's like screamin in my face not lettin me talk so he goes like "yeah well you're outta here!" So I busted every mirra in the house...

GINGER: Look if you don't wanna do this then...

ROSEMARY: Get me a coffee, girl, if ya not too busy...

GINGER: Don't take it out on me cause Raymond...

ROSEMARY: Get me a coffee, Miss, half a cup, black...

GINGER: *(at the counter)* Really if you don't wanna do this with me then...

ROSEMARY: *(by the booth)* I'm here! *(beat)* I'm here...

(Rosemary slides in the booth while Ginger gets the coffee. Rosemary removes her coat.)

GINGER: I thought we should do somethin for Ma, yunno, cause lately she's been gettin depressed an nothin goes good for her...then there's you.

(Rosemary picks up a piece of paper from the table and reads.)

ROSEMARY: "Unsung Mother of the Month Award."

(Ginger walks to the booth with cup of coffee.)

GINGER: If she wins they'll give her a five hundred dollar gift certificate to the Shoppers World.

ROSEMARY: You do most of the writin it, I'm just hidin from the oranga-tan man whose gotta be losin his mind about now with no mirras an I flushed his diet pills down the toilet an just for the hell of it I beat the shit outta his mailbox!

GINGER: Are you gonna help me?

ROSEMARY: "Are you gonna help me?" *(Rosemary removes a pint of brandy from her pocketbook and adds some to her coffee.)*

GINGER: *(beat)* So you did drop outta A-A...

ROSEMARY: Goddamn people with their sob stories an—an everybody wants to hug an hug an pray an pray, it's like my worst nightmare. Rememba when Dad used to say—there's nothin worse than bein around reformed drunks?

GINGER: You're just like 'im, it's unbelievable.

ROSEMARY: An that's bad?

GINGER: Yeah he's dead.

ROSEMARY: Oh cut it out, will ya?

GINGER: How soon you forget the horrors you went through an how you almost died an how you couldn't stop throwin up, Jesus Rose!

ROSEMARY: It's unda control... *(drinks)* An I don't want to talk about it. *(finishes drink)* I'm here at the fucken Peter Pan Diner riskin my life, my car, my vagina, so lets do this fucken thing an get out...

GINGER: You got a way a puttin things that's like so crude...

ROSEMARY: Speakin a crude, you an Harry talkin yet since the Madonna thing happened?

GINGER: *(looks down to paper)* Lets start this thing...

ROSEMARY: You still on the couch?

GINGER: Rose!

ROSEMARY: I'm just catchin up on the news.

GINGER: YES I'm still on the couch!

ROSEMARY: I woulda thrown his ass out if it was...

GINGER: I got three kids an no money an nowheres to go so what am I gonna do?

ROSEMARY: I'd sleep in a shelter before I'd...

GINGER: I put it past me cause...I—I have to, okay?

ROSEMARY: Good.

GINGER: I can't leave him right now.

ROSEMARY: Fine don't leave him.

GINGER: I'm dealin with it.

ROSEMARY: I got it Ginger, I got it.

GINGER: I don't have to breathe inta the bag no more.

ROSEMARY: Breathin on your own, good for you.

GINGER: You haven't told anybody, have you?

ROSEMARY: Nobody would believe it so why bother an fuck it. Look, sorry I brought it up. Lets get started. We grew up here, I don't wanna die here.

GINGER: Yeah...

(Rosemary is looking over the application.)

ROSEMARY: Play a coupla tunes.

GINGER: There's only one song in the jukebox.

ROSEMARY: It's not Madonna, is it?

GINGER: Fuck you Rose...

ROSEMARY: *(reading then looks up)* Says it's due on the ninth.

GINGER: Right.

ROSEMARY: That's like...

GINGER: Today.

ROSEMARY: *(drops application)* So whadda we do? I don't get what we're supposed to do. How do we even start the fucken thing?

GINGER: *(picks up the application)* Says here they want to know about her past, her childhood and a profile on what she done for her family to deserve this recognition...

ROSEMARY: Where do you pick up these things?

GINGER: TV. So...she was born in September...

ROSEMARY: The tenth.

GINGER: What year?

ROSEMARY: Well she's sixty so sixty from ninety-three...

GINGER: Um nineteen thirty-three...

ROSEMARY: *(rises)* In a house.

GINGER: Really?

ROSEMARY: On Federal Hill.

GINGER: In a house?

ROSEMARY: That's what she said.

GINGER: Never knew that.

ROSEMARY: Now you know. *(Rosemary is behind the counter looking to make more coffee.)*

GINGER: *(writing)* In a house September tenth nineteen thirty-three my mother was born in a house on Federal Hill to the parents of...

ROSEMARY: Uh Raffi-ella and...what was Ma's Dad's name?

GINGER: Oh uh...shit, it was...

ROSEMARY: Died in a gutter...

GINGER: I know I know...I think, John...

ROSEMARY: John what?

GINGER: Ma's maiden name is Walsh...

ROSEMARY: But she hated that, rememba? So use Nana's maiden name which was Jackavone.

GINGER: *(writes)* Born to the parents of John and Raffi-ella Jackavone.

ROSEMARY: Probly not gonna check it anyway...

GINGER: Okay, afta she was born, then what?

ROSEMARY: *(snaps)* Ray that fat fucken mother-fucka givin me shit! Cocksucka thinkin he can push me around anytime somethin don't go his way, yunno, the prick thinks I'm like Miss yunno Carmella Castration, yunno, like I want these things to happen mother fucka! *(beat)* THINGS HAVE BEEN VERY ROUGH ON ME LATELY!

GINGER: *(turns to Rosemary)* All right, all right...

ROSEMARY: *(bangs on the counter)* Coffee! I need more coffee! Where's the fucken help in this place?!

(Ginger rises. Rosemary proceeds back to the booth.)

Coffee, half way...Miss...

(Ginger is behind the counter getting more coffee as Rosemary takes out her cigarettes.)

ROSEMARY: Can I smoke in here?

GINGER: A course. It's the Peter Pan Diner. *(beat)* I woulda been here twenty years this December.

ROSEMARY: *(smokes)* The ladies room. I just rememba the ladies room an everybody fixin their underwear cause this is where we'd all come afta makin out in the park...

GINGER: Me and Harry sat right over there decidin where we—we wanted to...

ROSEMARY: Do it? You can say it.

GINGER: You told me not to do-it.

ROSEMARY: I told you—it hurts to do-it, if you remromba right.

GINGER: An it did.

ROSEMARY: Afta that it hurts in different places.

(Ginger returns to the booth with more coffee. Sits. Looks back down to the application.)

GINGER: So uh...I guess we should go to when she was sickly...

ROSEMARY: Yeah sure...

GINGER: When she had Saint Vincents disease...

ROSEMARY: What?

GINGER: Shit, was it Saint Vincents or Saint Francis?

ROSEMARY: What was what?

GINGER: Oh it's a sickness of the nerves but I don't rememba which Saint it is.

ROSEMARY: Ma had that?

GINGER: Still has it.

ROSEMARY: No shit...

GINGER: They named it afta a Saint in those days but I can't for the life of me rememba uh...

ROSEMARY: So this Saint was a nervous bastard?

GINGER: I don't know but rememba when Ma would start to lose it, usually when you pissed her off like the time she found the book on sex unda your bed an...she'd... *(Ginger stands and does Ma.)* "How I got somebody like you, a kid like you, I-I just don't know what I did to deserve thiiiis! Why do you torture me like thiiiiis?!"

ROSEMARY: *(beat)* That stinks Gin...was more like... *(Rosemary stands and does Ma.)* "You're a pig! You're no good! You come from Hell! You're the curse my mother put on me!"

GINGER: Oh right right I forgot about the curse thing...

ROSEMARY: Fucken spit be comin outta her mouth, eyes bulgin like a fucken frog and you're tellin me that—that some Saint acted that way?

GINGER: I don't know 'bout the Saint havin it uh but don't matta...okay, where are we? Um...

ROSEMARY: *(sits)* What a life...

GINGER: *(writing)* So she was sickly an very skinny from bein sickly an afta that...uh...her father was found dead drunk or—or just dead in a gutta on the corna of...

ROSEMARY: Down the street. Corna of Peace an Broad.

GINGER: Froze to death.

ROSEMARY: They found him with no shoes on.

GINGER: So I should say someone stole his shoes?

ROSEMARY: Someone did.

GINGER: So I should write it?

ROSEMARY: Write it for chrissakes!

GINGER: I don't know, Jesus!

ROSEMARY: "So I should write it?" "I should write it...?"

GINGER: I was askin a simple lit...

ROSEMARY: You been on the couch too long, girl!

GINGER: Okay okay an Ma was how old then?

Rosemary He gets the bed an you get the couch?

GINGER: I think she was around eight. I'll write eight.

ROSEMARY: Eight's when everythin starts to go bad so say eight.

GINGER: I wrote it.

ROSEMARY: I know.

GINGER: So at eight...

ROSEMARY: Eight.

GINGER: She went through this.

ROSEMARY: Dead father.

GINGER: No father at eight.

ROSEMARY: He was an asshole.

GINGER: I don't put that down.

ROSEMARY: No shit.

GINGER: Just—he died when she was eight.

ROSEMARY: Froze to death.

GINGER: I did put that in.

ROSEMARY: Ma said he was an asshole.

GINGER: I never heard Ma say asshole.

ROSEMARY: Actually she said prick.

GINGER: Ma said prick?

ROSEMARY: "Ma said prick?"

GINGER: (moves from booth) I hate it when you drink, I really do. You get that look in your eyes that's nothin but trouble.

ROSEMARY: I—I just don't know why we're doing this—this thing cause it's not gonna affect the way Ma deals with me anyways so...

GINGER: So you think by raggin on me is gonna...what? Me an Harry got a problem an I made the big mistake a tellin you an then you think you can throw it up in my face anytime you want—with—with that fucken smirk that goes with it!

ROSEMARY: I can't help it, okay, every time I see the piture a you comin in your house an seein him with his pants down an—an...

GINGER: I don't feel like re-livin this right now!

ROSEMARY: *(rises)* When you look at him, his hands, his face, his eyes, don't you like get fucken repulsed?

GINGER: We got a problem!

ROSEMARY: Uh-huh, fine...

GINGER: We're gonna deal with it when...when we can an which is more than you're doin...

ROSEMARY: *(looking out window)* I deal.

GINGER: *(back in booth)* Yeah yeah right yeah you deal...

ROSEMARY: I do. I don't let nothin slide.

GINGER: Yeah dealin for you is bustin mirras in your boyfriend's house an—an back to drinkin afta almost dyin and fightin with your first husband an his new wife over the kids you... *(Stops short. Beat-beat.)*

ROSEMARY: That I what?

GINGER: That you yunno just...just not bein stable somewhere, I don't know...

ROSEMARY: I love my kids. You sayin I don't love my kids?

GINGER: I would never say that, god...

ROSEMARY: Never?

GINGER: No!

ROSEMARY: Cause I love my kids cause they're my kids.

(Pause)

GINGER: *(looks back to application)* Ma was eight when her father died...where do we go from there? *(beat)* When she met Dad an...an she was sixteen, right?

ROSEMARY: *(looking out window)* Yup.

GINGER: Okay um an he was....

ROSEMARY: Probly eighteen. Ma's mother wanted to kill him.

GINGER: So she's sixteen an livin alone with her mother an meets Joe Quinn, gets pregnant an then what? They married then....

ROSEMARY: Ran away to Boston.

GINGER: Really.

ROSEMARY: Really. Ran away. Lived there. Had me. Came back. With me. Moved to Althea Street. He drove a cab. She was makin potato chips for the A&P...

GINGER: Should I put in about Ma goin through some tough times yunno an havin all those miscarriages afta—havin me and you by the time she was uh twenty-three, twenty-four....

ROSEMARY: You gonna put stuff in 'bout Dad smackin the shit out of her whenever things didn't go his way?

GINGER: *(beat)* Oh. Should I put that um...she was abused?

ROSEMARY: *(approaches booth)* Oh married an pregnant at sixteen, worked at A&P, had two kids and a bunch of miscarriages and was an abused woman! Hey, give that lady a closetful-a-clothes! She is truly amazing!

(Silence. Rosemary goes to the counter and sits facing Ginger.)

GINGER: You wanna keep goin?

ROSEMARY: I ask that to myself every day.

GINGER: You know what I'm talkin about.

ROSEMARY: Do you know what I'm talkin about?

GINGER: You know what I'm talkin about.

ROSEMARY: Do you know what I'm talkin about?

GINGER: Jesus! Are you on those stupid pills again?!

ROSEMARY: No I'm off. One day I just couldn't stop playin with myself so I stopped takin 'em.

GINGER: The things you say...

ROSEMARY: It's the truth. I always tell the truth. *(beat)* How 'bout you? You always tell the truth?

GINGER: You got that look on your face again. That Dad look.

ROSEMARY: You tell the truth, don't you?

GINGER: You wanna keep doin this or not?

ROSEMARY: I'm here, aren't I?

GINGER: I—I really thought for a minute yunno that it'd be kinda nice...me and you in our old neighborhood an—an away from kids an men an just...just together alone for a change in this place where we'd done stuff...me askin you my big sista for advice on guys an...

ROSEMARY: Told ya not to marry Harry, didn't I?

GINGER: *(beat)* Maybe you did. *(beat)* I thought that I'd put in how Ma was...well how everybody came to her with their problems that our house was an open house.

ROSEMARY: Our house was a dirty house.

GINGER: No you know what I mean, right?

ROSEMARY: Our house wasn't even a house, it was an apartment.

GINGER: Oh right right.

ROSEMARY: Other people had houses.

GINGER: That's good... *(writes)* Always...lived...in...an... apartment...

ROSEMARY: Could hear everythin an everybody up an down an all around. Would go to sleep to "Leo, now Leo!" And Leo would yell "Wait Flo, I gotta find it first!"

GINGER: An Mrs. Auerbach downstairs with the polio... *(beat)* Oh that's great! Ma helped her walk!

ROSEMARY: Put in how Ma was on my back day in an day out an how she tortured me an...

GINGER: I can't put that in here...she'd lose.

ROSEMARY: Fuck it. I can't get inta this. I'm gettin hungry. Menu please, Miss...

GINGER: *(writing)* There's nothin to eat.

ROSEMARY: I want a turkey club with tomatoes and mayo on the side, french fries well done and the bacon too but not black an spare my sandwich from the toothpicks, I hate the fucken toothpicks an oh yeah to drink I'll have a coffee cabinet an don't forget to bring the vinegar for the fries!

GINGER: Only have crackers.

ROSEMARY: Well that sucks! *(turns quickly to Ginger)* One time! One time I pulled Laurie's hair and it was only cause I was grabbin for her arm an she like moved an I got her hair instead yunno it was a mistake...I wouldn't pull her hair, an—an....

GINGER: Okay, okay...

ROSEMARY: An that bitch of a bitch wife a Brad's—Betsy that cow— makin it like I messed up when Little Brad cracked open his head cause I didn't make sure he was wearin a bike helmet! I mean since when did this become a law, this bike helmet thing?!

GINGER: I...

ROSEMARY: *(quickly)* They're my kids! Not Betsy's, they're mine!

GINGER: I know, I know...

ROSEMARY: *(goes to booth)* Wait, just wait till she hears that me an Brad screwed only like about two months ago! They wanna fuck with me then I'll fuck right back!

GINGER: You're kiddin me...

ROSEMARY: I bumped inta him at Memories this one night the Five Satins were playin an wham out in the parkin lot an in his truck we did-n't stop for an hour!

GINGER: Oh.

ROSEMARY: *(has a drink)* And it was great too an he was sayin all kinds shit 'bout how he still loves me and misses me an wishes there was a way, yunno, you shoulda heard 'im, right?

GINGER: You did it in the parkin lot of Memories with Ray in the Club?

ROSEMARY: The oran-ga-tan man was too busy kissin up to the Five Satins an tryin to jew-em-outta their askin price...

He didn't even know I was gone, the fat fuck!

GINGER: God...

ROSEMARY: *(beat)* Fuck you "god" fuck you.

GINGER: Wait a....

ROSEMARY: Like I'm some pervert for doin it, fuck you too. Your husband's got his lips to the TV an his cock in hand an there's somethin wrong with me?!

GINGER: I didn't say there was....

ROSEMARY: *(moves from booth)* Tend to your own garden 'fore you start comin down on what I do!

GINGER: I wasn't comin down on....

ROSEMARY: Least I was dealin with flesh!

GINGER: Oh god what are you....?!

ROSEMARY: The time was right an—an maybe the moon was right an it's not like I...yunno didn't do it with him before...it was familiar and it was real...

GINGER: *(stands)* You done attacking me?

ROSEMARY: *(sits at counter)* I'm not attacking you. I didn't like your tone, that's all.

GINGER: I mean I got enough bullshit in my life an one day I daydreamed me and you with Ma at The Shoppers World pickin out clothes for her an—an earrins an...but you got a way a turnin it all around cause you don't give a shit 'bout nothin but...then seein you back to drinkin is depressin enough...

ROSEMARY: Yeah. Like you talkin to Brad.

GINGER: What?

ROSEMARY: Like you talkin to Brad.

GINGER: What are...?

ROSEMARY: Like you an Brad havin a little talk about Rosemary. *(Rosemary pulls out an official-looking letter from her pocketbook.)*

GINGER: I...we...

ROSEMARY: I woke up this mornin to a sheriff servin me with an affidavit from Brad.... *(looking at the letter)* Um... "an my ex-sista in-law Ginger Willis is in agreement with my decision to pursue custody of the children. In our phone conversations she agrees with me that the children's safety and well-being is in danger if my ex-wife is drinking."

GINGER: Oh god....

ROSEMARY: "...my ex-sista-in-law spoke at length of Rosemary's past drinkin problems stating to me that her sister's mental condition has gotten worse since being with Raymond Perretti, her live-in boyfriend who owns the nightclub Memories and likes to drink and party..."

(Rosemary pauses then crosses to the booth.)

ROSEMARY: I'm gonna scratch out Raymond Perretti and put "..since being with the oran-ga-tan man..."

GINGER: *(takes a step to Rosemary)* Rose, he's really worried an—an....

ROSEMARY: Fuck you.

GINGER: He called an I...

ROSEMARY: I'm outta here....

(Rosemary putting stuff back in her pocketbook. Ginger gets closer to her.)

GINGER: Listen to me Rose....Rosemary look at me!

(Rosemary looks at Ginger.)

I...Brad called me an we talked or he did most a the talkin an I don't know what you got in your head about it but it was...he talked about a temporary custody thing an wondrin when you're gonna get help. I—I think he is really worried, uh I don't think he's tryin to be mean or....anyway...um...

(Ginger sits. Stares down at the application. Pause.)

ROSEMARY: I...I...keep hearin...my my kids' voices...

GINGER: I know...

ROSEMARY: "Mommy, where are we goin?" "Mommy, why are you drivin so fast?" "Mommy, please don't drive so fast."

GINGER: Rose...

ROSEMARY: "Just be quiet an—an Laurie make sure your seat belt is on tight..."

GINGER: What are you....?

ROSEMARY: "Mommy, it's scary...you're scarin me..." "mommy, why'd you take us outta school, mommy please we want daddy..."

GINGER: This happened?

ROSEMARY: "We're goin to Rocky Point Cliffs kids. Daddy says I never do anythin with you kids so we're going to Rocky Point Cliffs an look out over the ocean, okay?"

GINGER: *(nervously)* When did this happen?

ROSEMARY: "Even Auntie Ginger says I'm not a good mother."

GINGER: *(stands)* What are you talkin about?!

ROSEMARY: "But mommy we go to school today, we got masks to make for Halloween an...mommy bring us back!"

GINGER: Are they in the car?! *(Ginger runs to the window and looks out.)*

ROSEMARY: "You sit down Laurie! I am your mother so you listen to me, now sit before I..."

GINGER: Stop it Rose!

ROSEMARY: "I am your mother....I am your mother..."

GINGER: You stop it goddamn it!

ROSEMARY: "It's too windy up here mommy...the water is so...is so gray..."

(Ginger grabs a coin from the counter then runs to the payphone.) "I'm your mother, kids...don't be afraid of me, no need to be afraid of me..."

(Ginger is dialing.) "Just look out, okay, not down...look straight out."

GINGER: *(on phone)* C'mon, pick up, pick up...

ROSEMARY: "Okay, now hold hands kids...an—an I'm gonna step over here..."

GINGER: Hello! Brad!

ROSEMARY: "...cause I wanna take your piture..."

GINGER: Listen, where are the kids?

ROSEMARY: "Laurie...step back hon...you're still too close to mommy..."

GINGER: Call the school then call me at the diner! *(hangs up the phone)*

ROSEMARY: "...now c'mon back up for your mother...I want the best piture I can get to show people my kids..."

GINGER: You cut it out Rose!

ROSEMARY: "Nice one, now I want ya to turn around so I get a piture a you both lookin out over the ocean..."

GINGER: I never said those things!

ROSEMARY: "I'm gettin closer okay, but don't turn around an look at me..."

GINGER: He just put that stuff in there!

ROSEMARY: "Laurie, don't look at Mommy I said!"

(Ginger turns to face the phone.)

GINGER: Please god no don't let this happen oh god, oh god I....

ROSEMARY: "I'm right behind you now don't move an don't look back an...."

(Phone rings. Ginger gets it.)

GINGER: Yeah!

ROSEMARY: "Here we go, ready?"

GINGER: *(listens, calmer)* Okay....yeah....nothin I...

(Ginger turns to look at Rosemary. Rosemary picks up her drink and drinks.)

ROSEMARY: Ah, that hit the spot...

GINGER: *(on phone)* ...sure bye...

ROSEMARY: Well, fuck you Ginger.

GINGER: Doin that...makes you feel, what? Happy?

ROSEMARY: I'll be happy as soon as that turkey club gets here.

GINGER: I don't believe what you just did!

ROSEMARY: You're helpin 'im take my kids from me.

GINGER: No!

ROSEMARY: You turned against me...

GINGER: *(suddenly)* WHO was at your house when you couldn't stop throwin up and WHO called the rescue squad an WHO cleaned up the blood you was spittin up?! *(Ginger steps closer to Rosemary.)* It was me who stopped you from jumpin out the winda an it was me who sat on you screamin for the nurse while you spit in my face an afta three days a that I stood back an saw you gettin all the flowers an everybody loves Rosemary an Rosemary says "Ginger put these over there" an "Ginger watch for the nurses while I sneak a smoke" an I did it but deep down I was there waitin for a hey-by-the-way-thanks-for-what-you-did-for-me but Rosemary was too busy flirtin with the doctors to notice her only sister who as usual took time from her own family to be with Rosemary cause Rosemary needed me...

(Rosemary is preparing herself to leave.)

"No Harry I can't, I gotta help Rosemary move..." "I'll be right back, I gotta pick up Rose's kids..." "Harry, nobody can find Rose so I gotta go..."

(Rosemary straightens up.)

Then that day that stupid thing with Harry happened...

ROSEMARY: Open the fucken door Ginger...

GINGER: I...I walk into my house and...

ROSEMARY: An Harry's pants are down an he's up to the Madonna video, beatin off to the beat, guys do that shit...

GINGER: I DON'T LIKE IT OKAY!

ROSEMARY: I really have to go so if...

GINGER: Like I'm a fucken tard for bein old-fashioned an what is everythin comin to?! Why is everybody goin fucken mental?!

(Rosemary starts for the door but Ginger gets there first and takes out the keys from the lock.)

ROSEMARY: *(walks back to the booth)* Oh great. Held hostage in the Peter Pan Diner.

GINGER: So...we're we're standin there—like two people separated by a winda...

ROSEMARY: Oh shit...

GINGER: An lookin at him I got right there...I don't love this guy an probly never really did.... An I been doin houseshit for seventeen years, seventeen years a—a him drivin his oil truck an me shovin food in front a people an as a wife I had nothin...an it galled me knowin you told me not to marry him—it galled me an I....

ROSEMARY: Whaddaya want me to say about all this?!

GINGER: If I leave him where do I go? An—an what about the kids an—an Ma...shit, I—I go out there an what? Look for a guy an say save-me-please an oh by the way I got three kids an I been...I been havin anxiety attacks an oh yeah oh yeah...I—I...I was told that I got uh two lumps...in my right breast...

(Rosemary looks up at Ginger.)

That's where I was before I...I was at the uh Doctor Ferrante an...I even joked with him cause his hands felt so warm on my...an I said somethin like um...Jesus maybe I shoulda picked up a bottle of wine 'fore I came, right, an uh he didn't seem to hear me...he just kept pressin this one spot an I could see in his eyes that uh-oh...what's a matta? An he told me...not one lump...but two an I cried right there an he he was nice enough to um hold me for a minute an I...all I was thinkin was about my kids an wantin to be in my house with my family an I somehow managed to drive an I walk in feelin uh light-headed an I catch Harry an un...

(Rosemary is visibly upset. Ginger steps closer to her.)

And Rosemary....fuck you too.

(With that Ginger sits. Wipes her eyes with a napkin. Rosemary stares at her. Silence.)

ROSEMARY: *(finally)* All a lie?

GINGER: My life with Harry stinks an the Madonna thing happened.

ROSEMARY: No lumps?

GINGER: Just wanted to see if you gave a shit is all.

ROSEMARY: *(beat)* That was good.

GINGER: Good teacher, don't ya think?

ROSEMARY: Guess.

GINGER: Rose, I'm just gonna say it. You're a real real shitty mother an you're a drunk that's made you into a maniac but you know what? I'm gonna tell you somethin right here an it probly goes back to when we was kids when you would hum a song close to my ear when mom and dad were fighting so I wouldn't hear 'em but I love you as much as I love my kids, I'd give you my last breath an... *(sits back)* Sorry for gettin sappy here an I would never turn against you. Never. I said things to Brad that well I shoulda been sayin to you but I chickened out cause in your way you can make people afraid to say what should be said. Like Dad was. *(beat)* I won't hug you or nothin cause I know you hate that... *(beat)* You all right?

ROSEMARY: Yeah—yeah... *(beat)* I'm just...yunno I'm afraid...

GINGER: Makes two of us....but hey Ma went through some tough times, right?

(Rosemary nods. Beat.)

I gotta pee.

(Ginger rises and proceeds to the rest room but stops at the counter and bangs the side of the jukebox then exits into the bathroom. A couple of beats of silence then Al Green's song "For the Good Times" fills the Peter Pan Diner. Rosemary is crying. Pause. Ginger exits the bathroom. Rosemary gathers herself and even manages a smile—

ROSEMARY: My turkey club ready yet?

GINGER: Sorry Miss...the kitchen is closed. *(She sits across from Rosemary.)*

ROSEMARY: Let's do the thing for Ma someplace else.

GINGER: Where?

ROSEMARY: Memories?

(Ginger can't believe it.)

I'm kiddin, I'm kiddin. *(Rosemary laughs. Beat.)* Brad's probly gonna get custody, huh?

GINGER: Yeah Rose, probly. But it's a temporary thing.

ROSEMARY: Yeah. *(beat)* I'll bounce back.

GINGER: You always do.

(Beat. Rosemary extends her hand out to her sister.)

ROSEMARY: Hang on Ginger...

(Ginger grabs hold of her sister's hand.)

GINGER: I'm hangin on Rosemary....

(They face each other as lights fade and the song increases in volume and continues through the curtain call.)

END

For Whom the Southern Belle Tolls

by Christopher Durang

FOR WHOM THE SOUTHERN BELLE TOLLS was directed by Walter Bobbie and stage managed by Michele A. Kay with the following cast:

Amanda . . . . Lizbeth Mackay
Lawrence . . . . Keith Reddin
Tom . . . . David Aaron Baker
Ginny . . . . Patricia Randell

(Note: A showcase presentation preceded this EST production. Its cast was Laura Waterbury as Amanda, John Money as Lawrence, Timothy Kivel as Tom, and Julie Knight as Ginny.)

FOR WHOM THE SOUTHERN BELLE TOLLS by Christopher Durang. © 1993 by Christopher Durang. All rights reserved. Reprinted by permission of the playwright. All inquiries should be addressed to the playwright's agent, Helen Merrill, Helen Merrill Ltd., 435 West 23rd Street, Suite 1A, New York, NY 10011. No amateur or professional performance or reading of the play may be given without obtaining, in advance, the written permission of Helen Merrill, Ltd.

CHRISTOPHER DURANG has had two other plays in past Marathons: SISTER MARY IGNATIUS EXPLAINS IT ALL FOR YOU (Obie Award) and NAOMI IN THE LIVING ROOM. Other plays include BEYOND THERAPY, A HISTORY OF AMERICAN FILM, and THE MARRIAGE OF BETTE AND BOO. He performed with Julie Andrews in Sondheim's PUTTING IT TOGETHER at Manhattan Theatre Club. He's acted in films including HOUSESITTER, BUTCHER'S WIFE and MR. NORTH. He's on the council of the Dramatists Guild.

AUTHOR'S NOTE

I've always had a strong reaction to the play "The Glass Menagerie." I think it's quite a wonderful play. I first was captivated by the play when I took home a recording of it from the library, which featured the stellar cast of Jessica Tandy as Amanda, Montgomery Clift as Tom, Julie Harris as Laura, and David Wayne as the Gentleman Caller. Tom's feeling trapped, Laura's feeling overwhelmed by the world (and typing class), and Amanda's trying to force them both to be other than they are—these themes reverberated with me.

In graduate school at Yale School of Drama, I first discovered that as I got older there was something in me that was starting to find the Amanda-Laura relationship funny—these two souls stuck together, one hopelessly trying to change the other one, who couldn't and wouldn't budge.

My fellow playwright Albert Innaurato and I ended up writing a strange sketch based on "Menagerie" when we were asked in our first year to do a mock poetry presentation at the Yale Art Gallery, regarding William Blake and Thomas Gray.

Albert and I, on a similar crackpot wavelength, both came up with the silly fiction that William Blake and Thomas Gray met while performing in a summer stock production of "The Glass Menagerie." And without too much further discussion about it, Albert played an overbearing, vulgar Amanda, and I played a withering, sensitive-souled Laura having to deal with this terrifying force-of-nature mother. We did not dress as women to do this sketch. We dressed as priests—Albert in a white, High Mass robe (grand and dominant), me in a black monk's robe (simple and subservient). (Albert and I were both raised Catholic—and in Albert's plays he often wrote about violent, angry

Italian nuns; and in my plays I often wrote about repressed and repressive Irish nuns. And so to dress as priests as a means of playing women seemed somehow extremely logical to me and Albert.)

Albert's Amanda picked on Laura mercilessly and kept maliciously calling her a cripple. ("Mama, don't use that bad word beginning with 'cr,' " my Laura would say. "What bad word is that, Laura honey?" Albert's Amanda would bray back. "Crocus? Crumpet? Crunnilingus?")

Anyway, this co-authored and co-performed sketch was quite lunatic, and became part of a cabaret called "I Don't Generally Like Poetry But Have You Read Trees?" that Albert and I performed in the mid-70s, both at the Yale Cabaret and at the Manhattan Theatre Club.

Then in the late 80s, I saw yet another production of "The Glass Menagerie." Between the various movie and TV versions, a couple of high school productions, and some stage ones, I felt overexposed to the play. And though I still admired the play quite genuinely, I seemed to have reached that place where I found it hard to respond to it normally because I knew it too well.

And though I as a child always felt sympathy for Laura, as an adult I started to find Laura's sensitivity frustrating. In my youth, I found Laura's interest in her glass animals to be sweet and otherworldly (with the appropriately perfect symbolism of her loving her glass unicorn the best of all her collection). But now, as an adult, I felt restless with her little hobby. Come on, now—did she actually spend hours and hours staring at them? Why didn't she go out bowling, or make prank phone calls, or get drunk on a good bottle of bourbon?

Anyway, I started to find Laura annoying and frustrating.

It's out of this irritation with Laura's sensitivity—a feeling greatly at odd with the Williams original—that I seem to have written this parody, "For Whom the Southern Belle Tolls."

I've been happy when some of the critics have described this parody as "affectionate." I do feel affectionate toward the original play. But there is something about sweet, sensitive Laura that seems to have gotten on my nerves.

—Christopher Durang

CHARACTERS

Amanda — the mother
Lawrence — the son
Tom — the other son
Ginny

FOR WHOM THE
SOUTHERN BELLE TOLLS

Lights up on a fussy living room setting. Enter Amanda, the Southern belle Mother.

AMANDA: Rise and shine! Rise and shine! *(calls off)* Lawrence, honey, come on out and here and let me have a look at you!
(Enter Lawrence, who limps across the room. He is very sensitive, and is wearing what are clearly his dress clothes. Amanda fiddles with his bow tie and stands back to admire him.)

AMANDA: Lawrence honey, you look lovely.

LAWRENCE: No, I don't, mama. I have a pimple on the back of my neck.

AMANDA: Don't say the word "pimple," honey, it's common. Now your brother Tom is bringing home a girl from the warehouse for you to meet, and I want you to make a good impression, honey.

LAWRENCE: It upsets my stomach to meet people, mama.

AMANDA: Oh, Lawrence honey, you're so sensitive it makes me want to hit you.

LAWRENCE: I don't need to meet people, mama. I'm happy just by myself, playing with my collection of glass cocktail stirrers.
(Lawrence limps over to a table on top of which sits a glass jar filled with glass swizzle sticks.)

AMANDA: Lawrence, you are a caution. Only retarded people and alcoholics are interested in glass cocktail stirrers.

LAWRENCE: *(picking up some of them)* Each one of them has a special name, mama. This one is called Stringbean because it's long and thin; and this one is called Stringbean because it's long and thin; and this one is called Blue because it's blue.

AMANDA: All my children have such imagination, why was I so blessed? Oh, Lawrence honey, how are you going to get on in the world if you just stay home all day, year after year, playing with your collection of glass cocktail stirrers?

LAWRENCE: I don't like the world, mama. I like it here in this room.

AMANDA: I know you do, Lawrence honey, that's part of your charm. Some days. But, honey, what about making a living?

LAWRENCE: I can't work, mama. I'm crippled. *(He limps over to the couch and sits.)*

AMANDA: There is nothing wrong with your leg, Lawrence honey, all the doctors have told you that. This limping thing is an *affectation.*

LAWRENCE: I only know how I feel, mama.

AMANDA: Oh if only I had connections in the Mafia, I'd have someone come and break *both* your legs.

LAWRENCE: Don't try to make me laugh, mama. You know I have asthma.

AMANDA: Your asthma, your leg, your eczema. You're just a mess, Lawrence.

LAWRENCE: I have scabs from the itching, mama.

AMANDA: That's lovely, Lawrence. You must tell us more over dinner.

LAWRENCE: Alright.

AMANDA: That was a *joke*, Lawrence.

LAWRENCE: Don't try to make me laugh, mama. My asthma.

AMANDA: Now, Lawrence, I don't want you talking about your ailments to the feminine caller your brother Tom is bringing home from the warehouse, honey. No nice-bred young lady likes to hear a young man discussing his eczema, Lawrence.

LAWRENCE: What else can I talk about, mama?

AMANDA: Talk about the weather. Or Red China.

LAWRENCE: Or my collection of glass cocktail stirrers?

AMANDA: I suppose so, honey, if the conversation's comes to some god-awful standstill. Otherwise, I'd shut up about it. Conversation is an art, Lawrence. Back at Blue Mountain, when I had seventeen gentlemen callers, I was able to converse with charm and vivacity for six hours without stop and never once mention eczema or bone cancer or vivisection. Try to emulate me, Lawrence, honey. Charm and vivacity. And charm. And vivacity. And charm.

LAWRENCE: Well, I'll try, but I doubt it.

AMANDA: Me too, honey. But we'll go through the motions anyway, won't we?

LAWRENCE: I don't know if I want to meet some girl who works in a warehouse, mama.

AMANDA: Your brother Tom says she's a lovely girl with a nice personality.

And where else does he meet girls except the few who work at the warehouse? He only seems to meet men at the movies. Your brother goes to the movies entirely too much. I must speak to him about it.

LAWRENCE: It's unfeminine for a girl to work in a warehouse.

AMANDA: Now Lawrence, if you can't go out the door without getting an upset stomach or an attack of vertigo, then we got to find some nice girl who's willing to *support* you. Otherwise, how am I ever going to get you out of this house and off my hands?

LAWRENCE: Why do you want to be rid of me, mama?

AMANDA: I suppose it's unmotherly of me, dear, but you really get on my nerves. Limping around the apartment, pretending to have asthma. If only some nice girl would marry you and I knew you were taken care of, then I'd feel free to start to live again. I'd join Parents without Partners, I'd go to dinner dances. I'd have a life again. Rather than just watch you mope about this stupid apartment. I'm not bitter, dear, it's just that I hate my life.

LAWRENCE: I understand, mama.

AMANDA: Do you, dear? Oh, you're cute. Oh, listen, I think I hear them.

TOM: (*from off-stage*) Mother, I forgot my key.

LAWRENCE: I'll be in the other room. (*starts to limp away*)

AMANDA: I want you to let them in, Lawrence.

LAWRENCE: Oh, I couldn't, mama. She'd see I limp.

AMANDA: Then don't limp, damn it.

TOM: (*from off*) Mother, are you there?

AMANDA: Just a minute, Tom, honey. Now, Lawrence, you march over to that door or I'm going to break all your swizzle sticks.

LAWRENCE: Mama, I can't.

AMANDA: Lawrence, you're a grown boy. Now you answer that door like any normal person.

LAWRENCE: I can't.

TOM: Mother, I'm going to break the door down in a minute.

AMANDA: Just be patient, Tom. Now you're causing a scene, Lawrence. I want you to answer that door.

LAWRENCE: My eczema itches.

AMANDA: I'll itch it for you in a second, Lawrence.

TOM: Alright, I'm breaking it down.

(*Sound of door breaking down. Enter Tom and Ginny Bennett, a vivacious girl dressed in factory clothes.*)

AMANDA: Oh, Tom, you got in.

TOM: Why must we go through this every night? You know the stupid fuck won't open the door, so why don't you let him alone about it? *(to Ginny)* My kid brother has a thing about answering doors. He thinks people will notice his limp and his asthma and his eczema.

LAWRENCE: Excuse me. I think I hear someone calling me in the other room. *(calls)* Coming! *(exits, upset)*

AMANDA: Now see what you've done. He's probably going to refuse to come to the table due to your insensitivity. Oh, was any woman as cursed as I? With one son who's too sensitive and another one who's this big lox. I'm sorry, how rude of me. I'm Amanda Wingvalley. You must be Virginia Bennett from the warehouse. Tom has spoken so much about you I feel you're almost one of the family, preferably a daughter-in-law. Welcome, Virginia.

GINNY: *(speaking very loudly)* Call me Ginny or Gin. But just don't call me late for dinner! *(roars with laughter)*

AMANDA: Oh, how amusing. *(whispers to Tom)* Why is she shouting? Is she deaf?

GINNY: You're asking why I am speaking loudly. It's so that I can be heard! I am taking a course in public speaking, and so far we've covered organizing your thoughts and speaking good and loud so the people in the back of the room can hear you.

AMANDA: Public speaking. How impressive. You must be interested in improving yourself.

GINNY: *(truly not having heard)* What?

AMANDA: *(loudly)* YOU MUST BE INTERESTED IN IMPROVING YOUR-SELF.

GINNY: *(loudly and happily)* YES I AM!

TOM: When's dinner? I want to get this over with fast if everyone's going to shout all evening.

GINNY: What?

AMANDA: *(to Ginny)* Dinner is almost ready.

GINNY: Who's Freddy?

AMANDA: Oh, Lord. No, dear. DINNER IS READY.

GINNY: Oh good. I'm as hungry as a bear! *(growls enthusiastically)*

AMANDA: You must be very popular at the warehouse, Ginny.

GINNY: No popsicle for me, ma'am, although I will take you up on some gin.

AMANDA: *(confused)* What?

GINNY: *(loudly)* I WOULD LIKE SOME GIN.

AMANDA: Well, fine. I think I'd like to get drunk too. Tom, why don't you go and make two Southern ladies some nice summer gin and tonics? And see if sister would like a lemonade.

TOM: Sister?

AMANDA: I'm sorry, did I say sister? I meant brother.

TOM: *(calling as he exits)* Hey, four eyes, you wanna lemonade?

AMANDA: Tom's so amusing. He calls Lawrence four eyes even though he doesn't wear glasses.

GINNY: And does Lawrence wear glasses?

AMANDA: *(confused)* What?

GINNY: You said Tom called Lawrence four eyes even though he doesn't wear glasses, and I wondered if *Lawrence* wore glasses. Because that would, you see, explain it.

AMANDA: *(looks at her with despair)* Ah. I don't know. I'll have to ask Lawrence someday. Speaking of Lawrence, let me go check on the supper and see if I can convince him to come out here and make conversation with you.

GINNY: No, thank you, ma'am. I'll just have the gin.

AMANDA: What?

GINNY: What?

AMANDA: Never mind. I'll be back. Or with luck I won't.

(Amanda exits. Ginny looks around uncomfortably, and crosses to the table with the collection of glass cocktail stirrers.)

GINNY: *(looking at stirrers)* They must drink a lot here.

(Enter Tom with a glass of gin for Ginny.)

TOM: Here's some gin for Ginny.

GINNY: What?

TOM: Here's your poison.

GINNY: No, thanks, I'll just wait here.

TOM: Have you ever thought that your hearing is being affected by all the loud machinery at the warehouse?

GINNY: Scenery? You mean, like trees? Yeah, I like trees.

TOM: I like trees too.

AMANDA: *(from offstage)* Now you get out of that bed this minute, Lawrence Wingvalley, or I'm going to give that overbearing girl your *entire* collection of glass gobbledygook—is that clear?

(Amanda pushes in Lawrence, who is wearing a nightshirt.)

AMANDA: I believe Lawrence would like to visit with you, Ginny.

GINNY: *(shows her drink)* Tom brought me my drink already, thank you, Mrs. Wingvalley.

AMANDA: You know a *hearing aid* isn't really all that expensive, dear, you might look into that.

GINNY: No, if I have the gin, I don't really want any Gatorade. Never liked the stuff anyway. But you feel free.

AMANDA: Thank you, dear. I will. Come, Tom, come to the kitchen and help me prepare the supper. And we'll let the two young people converse. Remember, Lawrence. Charm and vivacity.

TOM: I hope this dinner won't take long, mother. I don't want to get to the movies too late.

AMANDA: Oh shut up about the movies.

(Amanda and Tom exit. Lawrence stands still, uncomfortably. Ginny looks at him pleasantly. Silence for a while.)

GINNY: Hi.

LAWRENCE: Hi. *(pause)* I'd gone to bed.

GINNY: I never eat bread. It's too fattening. I have to watch my figure if I want to get ahead in the world. Why are you wearing that nightshirt?

LAWRENCE: I'd gone to bed. I wasn't feeling well. My leg hurts, and I have a headache, and I have palpitations of the heart.

GINNY: I don't know. Hum a few bars, and I'll see.

LAWRENCE: We've met before, you know.

GINNY: Uh huh.

LAWRENCE: We were in high school together. You were voted Girl Most Likely to Succeed. We sat next to one another in glee club.

GINNY: I'm sorry, I really can't hear you. You're talking too softly.

LAWRENCE: *(louder)* You used to call me BLUE ROSES.

GINNY: Blue roses? Oh yes, I remember, sort of. Why did I do that?

LAWRENCE: I had been absent from school for several months, and when I came back, you asked me where I'd been, and I said I'd been sick with viral pneumonia, but you thought I said "blue roses."

GINNY: I didn't get much of that, but I remember you now. You used to make a spectacle of yourself every day in glee class, clumping up the aisle with this great big noisy leg brace on your leg. God, you made a racket.

LAWRENCE: I was always so afraid people were looking at me, and pointing. But then eventually mama wouldn't let me wear the leg brace anymore. She gave it to the Salvation Army.

GINNY: I've never been in the army. How long were you in for?

LAWRENCE: I've never been in the army. I have asthma.

GINNY: You do? May I see it?

LAWRENCE: *(confused)* See it?

GINNY: Well, sure, unless you don't want to.

LAWRENCE: Maybe you want to see my collection of glass cocktail stirrers.

(He limps to the table, and limps back to her, holding his collection.)

LAWRENCE: *(holds up a stick)* I call this one Stringbean, because it's long and thin.

GINNY: Thank you. *(puts it in her glass and stirs it)*

LAWRENCE: *(fairly appalled)* They're not for *use.* *(takes it back from her)* They're a collection.

GINNY: Well I guess I stirred it enough.

LAWRENCE: They're my favorite thing in the world. *(holds up another one)* I call this one Q-tip, because I realized it looks like a Q-tip, except it's made out of glass and doesn't have little cotton swabs at the end of it. *(She looks blank.)* Q-TIP.

GINNY: Really? *(She takes it and puts it in her ear.)*

LAWRENCE: No! Don't put it in your ear. *(takes it back)* Now it's disgusting.

GINNY: Well, I didn't think it was a Q-tip, but that's what you said it was.

LAWRENCE: I call it that. I think I'm going to throw it out now. *(holds up another one)* I call this one Pinocchio because if you hold it perpendicular to your nose it makes your nose look long. *(He holds it to his nose.)*

GINNY: Uh huh.

LAWRENCE: And I call this one Henry Kissinger, because he wears glasses and it's made of glass.

GINNY: Uh huh. *(takes it and stirs her drink)*

LAWRENCE: No! They're just for looking, not for stirring. Mama, she's making a mess with my collection.

AMANDA: *(from off)* Oh shut up about your collection, honey, you're probably driving the poor girl bananas.

GINNY: No banana, thank you! My nutritionist says I should avoid potassium. You know what I take your trouble to be, Lawrence?

LAWRENCE: Mama says I'm retarded.

GINNY: I know you're tired, I figured that's why you put on the night-shirt, but this won't take long. I judge you to be lacking in self-confidence. Am I right?

LAWRENCE: Well, I am afraid of people and things, and I have a lot of ailments.

GINNY: But that makes you special, Lawrence.

LAWRENCE: What does?

GINNY: I don't know. Whatever you said. And that's why you should present yourself with more confidence. Throw back your shoulders, and say, "HI! HOW YA DOIN'?" Now you try it.

LAWRENCE: *(unenthusiastically, softly)* Hello. How are you?

GINNY: *(looking at watch, in response to his supposed question)* I don't know, it's about 8:30, but this won't take long and then you can go to bed. Alright, now try it. *(booming)* "HI! HOW YA DOIN'?"

LAWRENCE: Hi. How ya doin'?

GINNY: Now swagger a bit. *(kinda butch)* HI. HOW YA DOIN'?

LAWRENCE: *(imitates her fairly successfully)* HI. HOW YA DOIN'?

GINNY: Good, Lawrence. That's much better. Again.

(Amanda and Tom enter from behind them and watch this.)

GINNY: *(continued)* HI! HOW YA DOIN'?

LAWRENCE: HI! HOW YA DOIN'?

GINNY: THE BRAVES PLAYED A HELLUVA GAME, DON'TCHA THINK?

LAWRENCE: THE BRAVES PLAYED A HELLUVA GAME, DON'TCHA THINK?

AMANDA: Oh God I feel sorry for their children. Is this the *only* girl who works at the warehouse, Tom?

GINNY: HI, MRS. WINGVALLEY. YOUR SON LAWRENCE AND I ARE GETTING ON JUST FINE, AREN'T WE, LAWRENCE?

AMANDA: Please, no need to shout, I'm not deaf, even if you are.

GINNY: What?

AMANDA: I'm glad you like Lawrence.

GINNY: What?

AMANDA: I'M GLAD YOU LIKE LAWRENCE.

GINNY: What?

AMANDA: WHY DON'T YOU MARRY LAWRENCE?

GINNY: *(looks shocked; has heard this)* Oh.

LAWRENCE: Oh, mama.

GINNY: Oh dear, I see. So that's why Shakespeare asked me here.

AMANDA: *(to Tom)* Shakespeare?

TOM: The first day of work she asked me my name, and I said Tom Wingvalley, and she thought I said Shakespeare.

GINNY: Oh dear. Mrs. Wingvalley, if I had a young brother as nice and as special as Lawrence is, I'd invite girls from the warehouse home to meet him too.

AMANDA: I'm sure I don't know what you mean.

GINNY: And you're probably hoping I'll say that I'll call again.

AMANDA: Really, we haven't even had dinner yet. Tom, shouldn't you be checkin' on the roast pigs feet?

TOM: I guess so. If anything interesting happens, call me. *(exits)*

GINNY: But I'm afraid I won't be calling on Lawrence again.

LAWRENCE: This is so embarrassing. I told you I wanted to stay in my room.

AMANDA: Hush up, Lawrence.

GINNY: But, Lawrence, I don't want you to think that I won't be calling because I don't like you. I do like you.

LAWRENCE: You do?

GINNY: Sure. I like everybody. But I got two time clocks to punch, Mrs. Wingvalley. One at the warehouse, and one at night.

AMANDA: At night? You have a second job? That *is* ambitious.

GINNY: Not a second job, ma'am. Betty.

AMANDA: Pardon?

GINNY: Now who's deaf, eh what? Betty. I'm involved with a girl named Betty. We've been going together for about a year. We're saving money so that we can buy a farmhouse and a tractor together. So you can see why I can't visit your son, though I wish I could. *(to Lawrence)* No hard feelings, Lawrence. You're a good kid.

LAWRENCE: *(offers her another swizzle stick)* I want you to keep this. It's my favorite one. I call it thermometer because it looks like a thermometer.

GINNY: You want me to have this?

LAWRENCE: Yes, as a souvenir.

GINNY: *(offended)* Well, there's no need to call me a queer. Fuck you and your stupid swizzle sticks. *(throws the offered gift upstage)*

LAWRENCE: *(very upset)* You've broken it!

GINNY: What?

LAWRENCE: You've broken it!

GINNY: What?

LAWRENCE: You've broken it. YOU'VE BROKEN IT.

GINNY: So I've broken it. Big fuckin' deal. You have twenty more of them here.

AMANDA: Well, I'm so sorry you have to be going.

GINNY: What?

AMANDA: Hadn't you better be going?

GINNY: What?

AMANDA: Go away!

GINNY: Well I guess I can tell when I'm not wanted. I guess I'll go now.

AMANDA: You and Betty must come over some evening. Preferably when we're out.

GINNY: I wasn't shouting. *(calls off)* So long, Shakespeare. See you at the warehouse. *(to Lawrence)* So long, Lawrence. I hope your rash gets better.

LAWRENCE: *(saddened, holding the broken swizzle stick)* You broke thermometer.

GINNY: What?

LAWRENCE: YOU BROKE THERMOMETER!

GINNY: Well, what was a thermometer doing in with the swizzle sticks anyway?

LAWRENCE: Its *name* was thermometer, you nitwit!

AMANDA: Let it go, Lawrence. There'll be other swizzle sticks. Goodbye, Virginia.

GINNY: I sure am hungry. Any chance I might be able to take a sandwich with me?

AMANDA: Certainly you can shake hands with me, if that will make you happy.

GINNY: I said I'm *hungry*.

AMANDA: Really, dear? What part of Hungary are you from?

GINNY: Oh never mind. I guess I'll go.

AMANDA: That's right. You have two time clocks. It must be getting near to when you punch in Betty.

GINNY: Well, so long, everybody. I had a nice time. *(exits)*

AMANDA: Tom, will you come in here please? Lawrence, I don't believe I would play the Victrola right now.

LAWRENCE: What Victrola?

AMANDA: Any Victrola.

(Enter Tom.)

TOM: Yes, mother? Where's Ginny?

AMANDA: The feminine caller made a hasty departure.

TOM: Old four eyes bored her to death, huh?

LAWRENCE: Oh, drop dead.

TOM: We should have you institutionalized.

AMANDA: That's the first helpful thing you've said all evening, but first things first. You played a little joke on us, Tom.

TOM: What are you talking about?

AMANDA: You didn't mention that your friend is already spoken for.

TOM: Really? I didn't even think she liked men.

AMANDA: Yes, well. It seems odd that you know so little about a person you see everyday at the warehouse.

TOM: The warehouse is where I work, not where I know things about people.

AMANDA: The disgrace. The expense of the pigs feet, a new tie for Lawrence. And you—bringing a lesbian into this house. Why, we haven't had a lesbian in this house since your grandmother died, and now you have the audacity to bring in that... that...

LAWRENCE: Dyke.

AMANDA: Thank you, Lawrence. That overbearing, booming-voiced bull dyke. Into a Christian home.

TOM: Oh look, who cares? No one in their right mind would marry four eyes here.

AMANDA: You have no Christian charity, or filial devotion, or fraternal affection.

TOM: I don't want to listen to this. I'm going to the movies.

AMANDA: You go to the movies to excess, Tom. It isn't healthy.

LAWRENCE: While you're out, could you stop at the liquor store and get me some more cocktail stirrers? She broke thermometer, and she put Q-tip in her ear.

AMANDA: Listen to your brother, Tom. He's pathetic. How are we going to support ourselves once you go? And I know you want to leave. I've seen the brochure for the merchant marines in your underwear drawer. And the application to the air force. And your letter of inquiry to the Ballet Trockadero. So I'm not unaware of what you're thinking. But don't leave us until you fulfill your duties here, Tom. Help brother find a wife, or a job, or a doctor. Or consider euthanasia. But don't leave me here all alone, saddled with him.

LAWRENCE: Mama, don't you like me?

AMANDA: Of course, dear. I'm just making jokes.

LAWRENCE: Be careful of my asthma.

AMANDA: I'll try, dear. Now why don't you hold your breath in case you get a case of terminal hiccups?

LAWRENCE: Alright. *(holds his breath)*

TOM: I'm leaving.

AMANDA: Where are you going?

TOM: I'm going to the movies.

AMANDA: I don't believe you go to the movies. What did you see last night?

TOM: Hyapatia Lee in "Beaver City."

AMANDA: And the night before that?

TOM: I don't remember. "Humpy Bus Boys" or something.

AMANDA: Humpy what?

TOM: Nothing. Leave me alone.

AMANDA: These are not mainstream movies, Tom. Why can't you see a normal movie like "The Philadelphia Story." Or "The Bitter Tea of General Yen"?

TOM: Those movies were made in the 1930s.

AMANDA: They're still good today.

TOM: I don't want to have this conversation. I'm going to the movies.

AMANDA: That's right, go to the movies! Don't think about us, a mother alone, an unmarried brother who thinks he's crippled and has no job. Stop holding your breath, Lawrence, mama was kidding. *(back to Tom)* Don't let anything interfere with your selfish pleasure. Go see your pornographic trash that's worse than anything Mr. D.H. Lawrence ever envisioned. Just go, go, go—to the movies!

TOM: Alright, I will! And the more you shout about my selfishness and my taste in movies the quicker I'll go, and I won't just go to the movies!

AMANDA: Go then! Go to the moon—you selfish dreamer!

(Tom exits.)

AMANDA: *(continued)* Oh, Lawrence, honey, what's to become of us?

LAWRENCE: *(holds up a newspaper)* Tom forgot his newspaper, mama.

AMANDA: He forgot a lot more than that, Lawrence honey. He forgot his mama and brother.

(Amanda and Lawrence stay in place. Tom enters down right and stands apart from them in a spot. He speaks to the audience.)

TOM: I didn't go to the moon, I went to the movies. In Amsterdam. A long, lonely trip working my way on a freighter. They had good movies in Amsterdam. They weren't in English, but I didn't really care. But no matter where I went, something pursued me. It always come upon me unawares, it always caught me by surprise. Sometimes it would be a swizzle stick in someone's vodka glass, or sometimes it would just be a jar of pigs feet. But then all of a sudden my brother touches my shoulder, and my mother puts her hands around my neck, and everywhere I look I am reminded of my brother Lawrence. And of his collection of glass. And of my mother. I begin to think that their story would maybe make a good novel, or even a play. A mother's hopes, a brother's dreams. Pathos, humor, even tragedy. But then I lose interest, I really haven't the energy. So I'll leave them both, dimly lit, in my memory. For nowadays the world is lit by lightning; and when we get those colored lights going, it feels like I'm on LSD. Or maybe it's the trick of memory; or the memory of a trick. Play with your cocktail stirrers, Lawrence. And so, good-bye.

AMANDA: *(calling over in Tom's direction)* Tom, I hear you out on the porch talking. Who are you talking to?

TOM: No one, mother. I'm just on my way to the movies.

AMANDA: Well, try not to be too late, you have to work early at the warehouse tomorrow. And please don't bring home any visitors from the movies. I'm not up to it any after that awful girl. Besides, if some sailor misses his boat, that's no reason you have to put him up in your room. You're too big-hearted, son.

TOM: Yes, mother. See you later. *(exits)*

LAWRENCE: Look at the light through the glass, mama. *(looks through a swizzle stick)* Isn't it amazin'?

AMANDA: Yes, I guess it is, Lawrence. Oh, but both my children are weird. What have I done, O Lord, to deserve them?

LAWRENCE: Just lucky, mama.

AMANDA: Don't make jokes, Lawrence. Your asthma. Your eczema. My life.

LAWRENCE: Don't be sad, mama. We have each other for company and amusement.

AMANDA: That's right. It's always darkest before the dawn. Or right before a typhoon sweeps up and kills everybody.

LAWRENCE: Oh poor mama, let me try to cheer you with my collection. Is that a good idea?

AMANDA: It's just great, Lawrence. Thank you.

LAWRENCE: I call this one daffodil, because it's yellow, and daffodils are yellow.

AMANDA: Uh huh.

LAWRENCE: *(holds up another one)* And I call this one curtain rod because it reminds me of a curtain rod.

AMANDA: Uh huh.

LAWRENCE: And I call this one ocean, because it's blue, and [the ocean is...]

AMANDA: I THOUGHT YOU CALLED THE BLUE ONE *BLUE*, YOU IDIOT CHILD! DO I HAVE TO LISTEN TO THIS PATHETIC PRATTLING THE REST OF MY LIFE??? CAN'T YOU AT LEAST BE CONSISTENT???

LAWRENCE: *(pause; hurt)* No, I guess, I can't.

AMANDA: Well, try, can't you?

(Silence.)

AMANDA: *(continued)* I'm sorry, Lawrence. I'm a little short-tempered today.

LAWRENCE: That's alright.

(Silence.)

AMANDA: *(trying to make up)* Do you have any other swizzle sticks with names, Lawrence?

LAWRENCE: Yes, I do. *(holds one up)* I call this one "mama." *(throws it behind the couch onto the floor)*

AMANDA: Well, that's lovely, Lawrence, thank you.

LAWRENCE: I guess *I* can be a little short-tempered too.

AMANDA: Yes, well, whatever. I think we won't kill each other this evening, alright?

LAWRENCE: Alright.

AMANDA: I'll just distract myself from my rage and despair, and read about other people's rage and despair in the newspaper, shall I? *(picks up Tom's newspaper)* Your brother has the worst reading and viewing taste of any living creature. This is just a piece of filth. *(reads)* Man has Sex with Chicken, Then Makes Casserole. *(closes the paper)* Disgusting. Oh, Lawrence honey, look—it's the *Evening Star*. *(she holds the paper out in front of them)* Let's make a wish on it, honey, shall we?

LAWRENCE: Alright, mama.

(Amanda holds up the newspaper, and she and Lawrence close their eyes and make a wish.)

AMANDA: What did you wish for, darlin'?

LAWRENCE: More swizzle sticks.

AMANDA: You're so predictable, Lawrence. It's part of your charm, I guess.

LAWRENCE: What did you wish for, mama?

AMANDA: The same thing, honey. Maybe just a little happiness, too, but mostly just some more swizzle sticks.

(Sad music. Amanda and Lawrence look up at the Evening Star. Fade to black.)

END

New York Actor

by John Guare

NEW YORK ACTOR was directed by Jerry Zaks and stage managed by Randy Lawson with the following cast:

Craig . . . . Bradley Whitford
Nat . . . . Greg Germann
Barry . . . . Patrick Gammer
Eileen . . . . Ann McDonough
The Critic. . . . . Baxter Harris
The Critic's Wife. . . . . Jenny O'Hara
Sammy. . . . . Joseph Siravo
The Waiter . . . . Randy Lawson
The Out of Towners . . . . Kevin Confoy
                                                              Helen Eigenberg

NEW YORK ACTOR FROM BABOONS ADORING THE SUN AND OTHER PLAYS by John Guare ©1993 by John Guare. All rights reserved. Reprinted by permission of Vintage Books, a Division of Random House, Inc. Caution: Professionals and amateurs are hereby warned that NEW YORK ACTOR is subject to a royalty. It is fully protected under the copyright laws of the United States of America, and of all countries covered by the International Copyright Union (including the Dominion of Canada and the rest of the British Commonwealth), and of all countries covered by the Pan-American Copyright Convention and the Universal Copyright Convention, and of all countries with which the United States has reciprocal copyright relations. All rights, including professional, amateur, motion picture, recitation, lecturing, public reading, radio broadcasting, television, video or sound taping, all other forms of mechanical or electronic reproduction, such as information storage and retrieval systems and photocopying, and the rights of translation into foreign languages, are strictly reserved. Particular emphasis is laid upon the question of readings, permission for which must be secured from the author's agent in writing.

All inquiries concerning rights should be addressed to the playwright's representative: International Creative Management, Inc., 40 West 57th Street, New York, NY 10019, Attn: Sam Cohn.

JOHN GUARE wrote THE HOUSE OF BLUE LEAVES, RICH AND FAMOUS, MARCO POLO SINGS A SOLO, LANDSCAPE OF THE BODY, BOSOMS AND NEGLECT, LYDIE BREEZE, GARDENIA, SIX DEGREES OF SEPARATION and FOUR BABOONS ADORING THE SUN. He also wrote the book and lyrics for the Tony-winning musical TWO GENTLEMEN OF VERONA, and the screenplays for ATLANTIC CITY and SIX DEGREES OF SEPARATION. He is the co-editor of the Lincoln Center New Theatre Review and is a council member of the Dramatists Guild. He was elected to the American Academy of Arts and Letters in 1989.

CHARACTERS

Craig

Nat

Barry

Eileen

The Critic

The Critic's Wife

Sammy

The Waiter

The Out of Towners

TIME

The Present

LOCATION

A theatre bar in the West 40s in Manhattan,
Joe Allen's, to be precise

New York Actor

In the darkness we hear the voice of George M. Cohan singing "Give My Regards to Broadway."

The lights come up on a theater bar in the West 40s in Manhattan, Joe Allen's to be precise. One brick wall is lined with brightly colored theater posters.

Under the posters are two tables. At one table Craig, Nat, Barry and Eileen sit, engaged in deep conversation which we do not hear because the noise from the pre-theater crowd is so deafening.

NAT: So he say "I know what the line is. The question is who the fuck says it!"

(All four of them roar with laughter. The song cuts off. The crowd noises stop. We're in the scene:)

BARRY: It's typical. The nightmare that's the daily bread on Broadway.

CRAIG: Nightmare is right! To see these posters. I know I'm back in New York. *(Craig raises his glass to the wall in question.)* To you, "Rachel Lily Rosenbloom."

NAT: Cheers, "Mata Hari."

BARRY: Hail, "Fig Leaves Are Falling."

EILEEN: Hey, "Dude!"

CRAIG: "Here's Where I Belong!"

NAT: "Come Summer!"

BARRY: "Hot September!"

EILEEN: I still remember you, "Carrie!"

CRAIG: "Breakfast at Tiffany's."

NAT: Arriverderci "Via Galactica!"

CRAIG: "I'm Solomon!"

BARRY: And what would we do without you: The ever popular

ALL: "Moose Murders!" Thank you thank you thank you!

EILEEN: The disaster wall. Hail to you, shows that ran for one performance.

BARRY: Yes! Flaunt your failure so it can't hurt you!

CRAIG: The horror these posters represent. The dreams curdled. The surprise is not that something closed. The miracle is that something even opened in the first place. That all these people got together at one time to do good work. Nobody sets out to get on that wall.

EILEEN: I don't know about that. You never played Portland.

CRAIG: Maine?

BARRY: Oregon.

EILEEN: We're all looking for the great part, right? I thought I finally had it. A musical version of "Come Back Little Sheba."

BARRY: That play

NAT: William Inge

BARRY: made Shirley Booth a star

EILEEN: after years of her being nothing.

NAT: Sheba's a dog, right?

EILEEN: Oh, you read the reviews. The authors—two 24-year-old psychotics

BARRY: The Menendez brothers—

EILEEN: thought song writing was making brilliantly clever rhymes— sheba amoeba hey bob ariba. Their life dream was to find the word to rhyme with orange and the word to rhyme with silver—

BARRY: Two words no word rhymes within the entire English language.

CRAIG: Really? *(Thinks.)* Wilbur? Pilfer?

EILEEN: Wilbur and pilfer do not rhyme with silver no matter how the authors want you to bend your mouth. And as for orange—

CRAIG: What happened to the show?

EILEEN: "Sheba?" We open at the Winter Garden in three weeks. Waiter!

CRAIG: Really!

EILEEN: No. "Little Sheba" died with no chance of a comeback. Not even a poster. That's what I regret most. Three months in Portland and not even a poster. I've decided something. I'm going to teach. Waiter!

BARRY: Some shows they should let the audience in for free and then charge them to get out. Make a fortune. Oh! there's my wife.

CRAIG: Call her over.

BARRY: *(Covering his face.)* No!

NAT: Who's that woman she's with?

BARRY: That casting director Betty Newman.

(They peer over their menus.)

NAT: Shapiro and Newman, one of them's human—Hi!

BARRY: No, don't interrupt them.

NAT: What's that Betty's wearing?

BARRY: A neck brace. She threw her back out.

EILEEN: Why didn't she throw out the rest. The way she uses her power, it's a new low.

NAT: No, no I have a new low. At the Newhouse. The Baitz play.

CRAIG: Kathy?

BARRY: *Robbie.*

EILEEN AND BARRY: Kathy??

NAT: Second act. I'm on stage. I hear a phone ring. I look around. I hear a voice in the audience say *(Loud whisper.)* "Hello. Can't talk. I'm in a theater. At a play. A *play!*" People go shhh. The voice says "How is it? Unnnh." I mean to get reviews during the play.

CRAIG: Oh Christ it's good to be back in New York!

(Barry looks up at a TV screen.)

BARRY: Here it is! Here we are!

EILEEN: Yes! Quiet! Omigod!

(They all look up. Eileen and Barry recite along with their TV voices.)

EILEEN'S VOICE: Why would our old cereal want us to get cancer?

BARRY AND EILEEN: *(Together.)* Nu-Trix Bran wants us to live a long, long time.

(They watch in silence for five seconds and then the commercial is over. Everyone applauds.)

CRAIG: You were great!

NAT: You'll save lives!

EILEEN: You looked like a bank president.

BARRY: Very Katherine Hepburn you.

EILEEN: I hope we work together again.

NAT: This is going to go national.

CRAIG: You'll make a lot of money.

BARRY: Residuals.

EILEEN: Don't you have a commercial coming up?

NAT: Athlete's foot powder. The third toe. It can't all be "The Oresteia."

EILEEN: Did you see the Peter Brook?

NAT: Out in Brooklyn? So so. I trekked out there for three nights in a row hoping to find God—

EILEEN: Really? I saw it all in one nine-hour stretch. I think it's shallow to break it up.

CRAIG: Did you see God?

NAT: No, but I did see my agent— *(to Craig)* But here's to *you.* To be on Broadway.

BARRY: Your series finally over.

EILEEN: I liked "Lawyer from Another Planet."

CRAIG: Indentured slavery. Five years of torture.

EILEEN: I refuse to go to California.

NAT: But the series gave you recognizability.

BARRY: Plus cash. And those residuals.

CRAIG: Wait! Wait! Everybody thinks I'm rolling. I didn't come on till the second year.

(An ominous, white faced Waiter enters, puts down menus and very slowly sets the other table. Eileen gets up.)

EILEEN: I'm leaving this restaurant.

BARRY: Sit down.

EILEEN: Why do we have to get this waiter! He was the understudy in that terrific Wilson play.

NAT: Robert?

BARRY: August?

EILEEN: Lanford and he had to go on the night all the papers were there and he froze. The chance of a lifetime and he forgot everything. He just stood there with all of Arctica and Antarctica forming on him. The critics went wild attacking him—a feeding frenzy—the play died. Thanks to him. He's a synonym for failure. Don't look at him!

BARRY: He's not the Angel of Death.

EILEEN: You are wrong. He's worse. Here he is back like some ingenue pretending nothing ever happened. Well, the worst happened and he wasn't prepared. I would rather have the Angel of Death tell me the specials of the day then have this Kiss of Death reminding me of what he lost! K.O.D. Why can't he wait tables on Wall Street. He has no right to work in a theater bar. He's a walking disaster wall.

BARRY: The waiter had stage fright. It's like being seasick. The one thing sailors will never do is make fun of someone being seasick because it could happen to them. So have sympathy for one of our brethren who—

EILEEN: He had his break and he blew it. Destiny smiles and he spit at his fate. He should be a star. He had the part that could have done it. He has no right to work in a theater bar.

(The waiter returns to take orders. She looks up at him.)
No, nothing for me—

CRAIG: Another round. Thank you.

(The waiter leaves slowly.)

NAT: That's all we want. The one part that will do it. Like you "The Lawyer from Another Planet."

CRAIG: Whoa! People think I was the lawyer. I was the lawyer's best friend who didn't know he was from the other planet— "Gee, Ace, when that jury came in with the guilty verdict your ears grew two feet and a blue light shot out of your eyes. You mean I'm just seeing things again?" For five years all of America knew he was from another planet. Everybody except me. But that's an LA actor. Only fit to work inside a box.

NAT: I'm very sorry. I never watch TV. I thought you—

CRAIG: I wouldn't assume any of you watch TV. I never did till I said Uncle one day and went out there with one simple plan. To become a name so I could come back here and call the shots.

EILEEN: And you have

BARRY: and you'll bring a whole new audience to the theater.

CRAIG: Absolutely. I played my cards. It's paid off.

NAT: Was it fun being on a series?

CRAIG: We *were* like a family. Our own repertory company. For a while.

EILEEN: But "The Locksmith." To be in the play of the year. You're my hero! Everyone on tenterhooks!

BARRY: You open in a month?

NAT: I've got *my* tickets. I'm a Tony voter.

BARRY: No disaster wall for you.

EILEEN: Not after two years in London.

NAT: They'll give you respect.

BARRY: But no residuals.

CRAIG: Katinka and I let our place go in LA. Half an acre in Studio City. Took an apartment here. Talk about "Little Shop of Horror." Put the kids in school. Katinka's working. The kids didn't want to move east but I said "Look! your father is back being the greatest thing anyone can be—a New York actor!"

EILEEN: I couldn't get over how big Francesca got.

BARRY: We were there when Milo was born.

CRAIG: The British director's crazy about us. Says the American cast possesses an energy the English lack. Although I'm not crazy about some of the cast.

BARRY: Who are you? I saw it in London.

CRAIG: The Locksmith.

BARRY: The Locksmith! The guy in London won a prize.

NAT: The Olivier!

BARRY: You got the Locksmith!

CRAIG: They called me. I read. I got it. Simple.

BARRY: I use that for an audition piece. "You can stop me but you can't stop all the others who'll come after me. I'm only a locksmith but I look through the keyhole and I see stars. That's the secret. We're all one—there's only one lock—there's only one key."

CRAIG: I do it differently.

BARRY: Really. I look forward to

EILEEN: Tony nomination for sure!

CRAIG: Shut up. Shut up! That's all I hear at the theater. "Start preparing the Tony speech." Just let me do the work—good Christ!

EILEEN: I'm a Tony voter too. I'll vote for you.

BARRY: You have no right to be promiscuous with your vote. It cheapens the Tony. You haven't seen the others. You have to be objective.

EILEEN: First you vote for your friends. Then you vote against your enemies. Then you vote for who you really liked. The Locksmith has my vote. It's so exciting!

BARRY: They didn't want a name?

CRAIG: They got a name.

BARRY: A TV name.

NAT: You went to London?

CRAIG: They came to LA.

NAT: They skipped New York? Fuck em. Although I'm glad for you.

EILEEN: God, to get the part that defines you. Shirley Booth around for years and then "Come Back Little Sheba."

CRAIG: Geraldine Page "Summer and Smoke."

NAT: Jason "Iceman Cometh."

BARRY: Brando "Streetcar."

EILEEN: Somebody told me the one thing about Laurette Taylor in "Glass Menagerie" is how she got a laugh on every line. She really broke your heart at the end because she never went for the pathos. I'll be a good teacher.

NAT: Streisand "Funny Girl." Channing "Dolly."

BARRY: Judy Holliday "Born Yesterday." Merman "Gypsy." "Sunset" Glenn.

EILEEN: Joel Grey "Cabaret." Zero "Fiddler."

NAT: You the Locksmith.

EILEEN: I'll touch you for luck.

BARRY: My part is still out there. My Hamlet lurking around the corner.

NAT: My locksmith.

EILEEN: My locksmith.

CRAIG: It's like what Lawrence Olivier said "If acting decides to embrace you and take you to its heart, it will hurl you up there among the gods. It will change your wooden clogs over night and replace them with glass slippers." I'm not saying I'm Sir Larry

EILEEN AND BARRY AND NAT: No no no

CRAIG: but I'm thrilled to be back in New York. Out there I was ready to kill myself. That's what scared me. I finally got the courage to do it.

NAT: Kill yourself?

CRAIG: Terminal likability. The LA disease. Any time you read a freeway fatality, know it's an LA actor who crashed his Volvo into an overpass, sick of being likable. That's—that's what happened to me.

EILEEN: No!

CRAIG: I tried to crash my new Volvo into a rail guard on the freeway. I pulled over to the side of the road—

NAT: Where?

CRAIG: Out by Valencia. Asthmatic. Sweating. Freezing. My series was canceled. Going through yet another pilot season. No pilot. My daughter comes to me and says "Daddy I want breast implants." I said "Francesca, you're six years old." This LA child looks up at me and says "I don't give a shit. I want them and I want them now." What kind of values are these? My boy Milo is always in his mother's sewing kit. Playing with needles. We can't tell if he's going to be a junkie or a costume designer. What strangers am I raising? Katinka and I gave 'Cesca a gift certificate for some work on her nose which shut her up but only for a while and now she's here getting her head on—I hope. Katinka and I are frightened. Where was I headed? Lawyer canceled. I went up for another series. This time the friend of the best friend. The beginning of the downward spiral. I aimed my Volvo right into that rail guard.

NAT: Hey, you're safe. You're here.

CRAIG: And then the call came.

EILEEN: I'm so glad you're back. And alive. Bravo.

NAT: You can use that. The asthma. The freezing.

BARRY: I was up for a Volvo commercial. Voice over.

CRAIG: The difference between being an LA actor and a New York actor is in LA you don't ever dare be tuned out of somebody's living room. Never be unpleasant or complicated. But a New York Actor is fearsome. A New York actor changes his soul. A New York actor has a soul to change. Christ, listen to me. I'm alive! Being what God meant me to be!

NAT: That's why I could never make it out there. I'm not likable. I like that about me.

CRAIG: An LA actor has to make Jack the Ripper likable.

BARRY: Charlie Manson a sweetheart.

NAT: Richard Nixon a heartbreaker.

CRAIG: Although I got offered an interesting part wouldn't you know the day before I left. Movie of the Week. Richard Nixon's Hairdresser. True story. Haircuts he gave during crises.

BARRY: Vietnam?

NAT: Watergate?

CRAIG: Inside view. Begins with the last haircut. Nixon on his deathbed being laid out. Snip. Snip. Snip. Flashback. Fade In. Snip. Snip. Snip. Very moving.

BARRY: You don't think of Richard Nixon having haircuts.

NAT: I suppose he must have. Nixon in a beehive.

EILEEN: I like it. Who's doing Pat?

CRAIG: The blonde who spins the wheel on that quiz show. What was even more disgusting was the money they offered.

EILEEN: But you turned it down.

CRAIG: Not only turned it down. I told them off. I went right to the agency and said "Adios, I'm out of here." I let them know I'm the greatest thing there can be

ALL: New York Actor!

CRAIG: A killer! A giant! A teller of truths! Brando! Monty Clift!

EILEEN: George Scott!

BARRY: Jimmy Dean!

NAT: Jason!

BARRY: Anne and Eli!

EILEEN: Rip!

NAT: Geraldine Page!

EILEEN: Kim Stanley!

CRAIG: I forgot Kim Stanley!

BARRY: Colleen

EILEEN: Uta

NAT: Maureen

BARRY: Chris

NAT: Chris?

BARRY, CRAIG, EILEEN: Walken

CRAIG: New York actors! They played Broadway. I'll tell you a secret. I was filling out my bio for the playbill and I became overwhelmed with secret shame.

NAT AND BARRY AND EILEEN: What?

CRAIG: It's driven me crazy all these years. No, I can't tell.

NAT, BARRY AND EILEEN: What?

CRAIG: *(A confession.)* I never played Broadway.

NAT AND BARRY AND EILEEN: What? No Really?!!

NAT: Not even replaced?

CRAIG: Oh Christ, did everybody in the restaurant just turn around? I'd wake up in the middle of the night and say my life is worthless because I never played Broadway.

BARRY: And then along came the Locksmith

EILEEN: Tony nomination for sure—

NAT: No. The Tony.

CRAIG: "I'd like to acknowledge all the people who tried to stand in my way of getting here tonight. My parents who said I was nothing. My first wife who called me a pervert. My drama teacher who advised to switch to accounting—" That's what I'm going to say. No no! only kidding. Another round? My treat. Oh god—I'm on Broadway. Hey—syringe—that rhymes with orange.

EILEEN: Sorry. No rhyme for silver. No rhyme for orange. It's just a fact.

BARRY: There's life beyond Broadway. You ever played Seattle Rep? You ever played Yale Rep? Hartford? The Arena.

CRAIG: Readings at the Taper. I kept my hand in.

EILEEN: Seattle Rep. The Goodman. Trinity Square.

BARRY: Williamstown. New Jersey Shakespeare. A.R.T. Burt Reynolds Theater Jupiter Florida. God bless him. I played there.

NAT: That's our national theater. Broadway's a dream for you but it's not for me. Shakespeare in the Park. I won an Obie.

BARRY: An ensemble Obie. The whole cast got the Obie.

NAT: You ever been suggested for anything resembling an Obie?

(A Man and Woman sit at the next table and pick up menus. Her chair backs up to Craig's.)

EILEEN: *(sotto voce)* See who's at the next table? The new guy at the Times.

NAT: The new guy?

EILEEN: They're going to have a Tuesday lynching party. A reviewer reviews all the other reviews. That's him. That's Tuesday. Tuesday roundup. Don't look!

BARRY: What the world needs now. More reviews. Don't look!

NAT: Well, this guy loves me. You read my reviews on "Tomorrow's Meadow?" A love letter from him.

EILEEN: "Tomorrow's Meadow?" That was six years ago in some Tribeca weekly.

CRAIG: So what! Look where he is today. Today he's the Times. Tell him.

NAT: Tell him what?

CRAIG: Thank him for your review. Someone who appreciates your craft. God, we're all in this together! The Theater! This endangered medium! We're all part of a community. A precious craft like lace weaving! Essential to our souls like water. He wrote about you? Thank him for what he wrote. Appreciate appreciation. Stick up for yourself! You're a New York actor.

(Nat pauses, gets up and stands over the other table smiling. The Critic looks up.)

THE CRITIC: I'll have the black bean soup.

THE CRITIC'S WIFE: No, dear. You have an opening tonight. Try the consommé.

NAT: I'm Nat Boyle.

THE CRITIC: Yes. And the La Scala salad.

NAT: "Tomorrow's Meadow?"

THE CRITIC: Is that a horse?

(The Critic and his wife laugh.)

NAT: A play. I was in it.

THE CRITIC'S WIFE: We have a curtain—

THE CRITIC: Can we order?

NAT: Sir, you wrote this review of me—

THE CRITIC'S WIFE: You cannot hold him responsible—

(Nat takes out a clipping from his wallet.)

NAT: You said I was "almost perfect." I had you blown up and laminated.

THE CRITIC: "Tomorrow's Meadow?"

NAT: I just heard your good news about the Times and wanted to tell you it's great news for the theater community having more reviews and how everyone admires you and what an addition and privilege you are. Your judgments are synonyms for perspicacity and insight into the craft of where we theater artists are striving and it's a great day for the New York theater and I speak for all of us personally looking forward to reading you every Tuesday and if you some Tuesday you find yourself writing a column about Down Memory Lane about performances you've admired over the recent years—Nat Boyle! Meeting you. It's a privilege. And let me order you a waiter! Waiter! Pronto!

(Nat smiles and smiles and returns to his seat and sits down.)

NAT: Oh Christ, was I an ass kisser?

BARRY: Oh no! A blow job doesn't make you an ass kisser.

CRAIG: Bravo! Bravo! You did the right thing. We have to stick up for ourselves—if we don't

(Sammy runs in out of breath and sits down, reeling with joy.)

SAMMY: Congratulate me! I just came from a great audition! I got the part! This new English play! They're replacing the guy who's doing the Locksmith. Some LA actor. The playwright—the director—ran up the aisle and kissed me! I auditioned my heart out! I swear to you I sang! *(Cockney:)* "You can stop me but you can't stop all the others who'll come after me. I'm only a locksmith but I look through the keyhole and I see stars. That's the secret. We're all one—there's only one lock—there's only one key." Waiter! A bottle of champagne! No! The Krug!

(The Critic's Wife looks for something.)

THE CRITIC'S WIFE: It was right here. It was right here.

CRAIG: *(To Sammy)* One moment. One fucking moment.

THE CRITIC'S WIFE: It was right here. It was right here.

(The Critic stands at the table.)

THE CRITIC: Did any of you people see my wife's purse?

CRAIG: Shut up, asshole, I'm talking!

(Barry and Eileen cover their faces with their napkins.)

THE CRITIC'S WIFE: I hung my purse over the chair.

CRAIG: *(To Sammy)* What is this? April fools?

(Barry whispers to Sammy.)

SAMMY: What did you say?

(Barry whispers to Sammy, now audibly.)

BARRY: Locksmith. Him.

SAMMY: What did you say?

CRAIG: LOCKSMITH! ME!

(Craig stares at Sammy.)

THE CRITIC'S WIFE: It was right here. It was right here.

SAMMY: *(To Craig)* Oh fuck. I'm really sorry.

CRAIG: What are you saying—you got the part?

BARRY: How did you get a reading?

SAMMY: It was only sort of definite. Look—don't take it personal.

CRAIG: Who's got a quarter?

SAMMY: Here's a quarter.

CRAIG: I don't want a quarter from you.

(Craig goes off to get change. Sammy follows.)

SAMMY: Be happy for me!

THE CRITIC: *(To Nat)* Could we have it back?

NAT: What are you looking at me for?

THE CRITIC'S WIFE: I had it. And then you leaned over. "Tomorrow's Meadow."

(Eileen and Barry move away, napkins on their faces.)

THE CRITIC: You leaned over my wife.

NAT: To talk to you. To talk you got to lean.

THE CRITIC'S WIFE: I hung my purse over the chair. *(The Critic's Wife is down on all fours looking under the table.)* It had everything in it. Keys. Money.

NAT: Why would I take anything from you?

THE CRITIC: Because you're sick! Now I'm in a foul mood and I have to review a play I don't want to see anyway.

NAT: *(Brightly.)* Oh, what play?

THE CRITIC: Wait! I remember you! Nat Boyle! That's your name!

NAT: *(Desperate.)* No! Not Nat Boyle. Pat Doyle. Doyle! Fred Coyle! Eddie Foyle! That's my name. You need money? Here—take mine? You want eye glasses? A wallet?

(Nat empties his pockets. The Critic's Wife holds Nat by the leg.)

THE CRITIC'S WIFE: Thief! Thief!

(The Critic pulls his wife away.)

THE CRITIC: Sweetheart! Quiet! I don't want my name in the paper!

THE CRITIC'S WIFE: Thief! Thief!

NAT: Oh but you can put my name in the paper! "Almost perfect" yesterday. Thief today!

(Nat punches The Critic. The Critic's Wife punches Nat.)

THE CRITIC'S WIFE: Police! Police! Thief! Thief!

(The Critic's Wife runs out. The Critic follows.)

THE CRITIC: The tickets were in your bag—what theater do we go to? *(The Critic stops and points his finger at Nat.)* Nat Boyle. You. Are. Dead. In. This. Town. *(The Critic leaves.)*

NAT: Not Boyle! Doyle! Doyle! Coyle! Eddie Foyle!

(Nat runs after The Critic and is gone. Craig returns. Sammy follows.)

CRAIG: I don't have any change.

(The Waiter appears suddenly like an apparition.)

WAITER: You wanted change?

CRAIG: Not from you!

(The Waiter goes. Sammy holds up a quarter.)

SAMMY: I'm really sorry.

(Craig takes the quarter and dials at the pay phone.)

CRAIG: Yes this is

Oh hello

You're there

Yes yes

Why didn't you tell me at rehearsal

They're my friends. We're a company.

I can be bigger.

Why didn't you tell me to be bigger?

Is it the accent?

I see. Yes.

I've had a lot on my mind.

The move back east

It's true I haven't been on stage in a

But that's not

I can be bigger

Yes yes

I thought I was taking direction

I thought I was listening

I though the rest of the cast was very
Can I come in and
Of course
No no
The announcement
Mutual consent
Of course
Pressing engagements called me back to LA
Of course
Yes
Yes
I'm sure we'll work together again.
Yes
Yes
(Hangs up.)

SAMMY: You need another quarter?

CRAIG: They can't tell me face to face. What kind of business is this they can't tell me face to face!

SAMMY: Maybe they want me for understudy. Maybe it's for the tour...
(A pair of Out of Towners come into the restaurant, sit at the vacated table and look around, thrilled to be actually here. They are called Bob and Beth.)

BOB: "Rachel Lilly Rosenbloom"!

BETH: "Carrie"!

BOB: "Moose Murders"!

BETH: "Ballad for a Firing Squad"!

BOB: "End of the World"!

BETH: "Here's Where I Belong"!

BOB: This place is everything they said it would be!

BETH: Adorable!
(They pick up their menus.)

BARRY: You want to change tables?

EILEEN: People from New Jersey come to look at the actors. This is no zoo. I hate civilians. I'll bear my soul to them but I'll be damned if I'll let them see me eat.

BARRY: I agree. No wonder they're worried in England with that tunnel coming under the channel. Look what the Lincoln Tunnel did to New York. *(Barry notices the TV commercial is on again.)* Here it is again!

(Bob and Beth see the actors.)

BOB: O my god!

EILEEN: *(To the Out of Towners)* Shhh!

(Eileen and Barry look up at the screen. They recite along with their voices.)

EILEEN: Why would our old cereal want us to get cancer?

BARRY: Nu-Trix bran wants us to live a long long time.

(The commercial is over.)

SAMMY: You were great!

BARRY: You gave me so much.

EILEEN: No no no. You gave *me* so much.

(Barry and Eileen go off, arm in arm, so happy. Craig sits bleakly at the table. Sammy starts to say something to Craig, but then checks his watch.)

SAMMY: Oh. I've got to go meet the cast.

(Sammy goes. The Waiter appears and stands over Craig.)

CRAIG: It's so quiet here. Where is everyone?

WAITER: It's eight o'clock. Everyone's gone off to their shows.

CRAIG: I'm the new Kiss of Death. The K.O.D. What will I tell the kids? "Daddy, why aren't you a star?" Not big enough. I'm an LA actor. I fit inside a box. Out there I tried to kill myself. Maybe that's the answer. Why not! Why not!

(The Out of Towners peer over their menus.)

BOB: Look

BETH: Isn't that

(The Out of Towners are amazed. They star at Craig in awe. Craig looks behind him to see who they're gaping at. Craig then turns back to his drink. Bob and Beth get up and go over to Craig.)

BOB: Excuse me? Do you know who you are?

(Craig looks up at them.)

CRAIG: I am a human poster from a life that closed in rehearsals.

BETH: "Lawyer from Another Planet!"

CRAIG: The best friend of the Lawyer. Everybody in America knew he was from another planet but me...

BOB: Every Tuesday night at 8:30 we were there with you.

BETH: No matter who was on opposite.

BOB: And then you were canceled.

CRAIG: That's right. Just canceled.

BETH: We are your number one fans.

BOB: I can't believe we're seeing you.

BETH: We just got here to New York.

BOB: Everything we wanted to see was sold out.

BETH: You come to New York you don't expect to see people you love

BOB: To actually see them!

BETH: You were so innocent and trusting about that alien. The way everybody knew but you.

BOB: Boy, did I ever identify.

CRAIG: Really?

BETH: What are you doing now?

CRAIG: Well... *(Craig becomes expansive.)* Well, I have a number of irons in the fire...

(Bob and Beth happily sit at Craig's table. Music and crowd noise comes up.)

BOB: Was it fun being on a series?

CRAIG: We were like a family. Our own repertory company.

(The sounds of George M. Cohan singing "Give My Regards to Broadway" drowns them out.)

(Blackout.)

END

Paradise

by Romulus Linney

To Curt Dempster and EST,
the best of friends for this playwright, sincere thanks

PARADISE was directed by Christopher A. Smith and stage managed by Christine M. Terchek with the following cast:

Dudley . . . . David Eigenberg
Jean . . . . Lois Smith
Angelina. . . . . Sheri Matteo
Linda. . . . . Gretchen Walther

PARADISE by Romulus Linney. © 1995 by Romulus Linney. All rights reserved. Reprinted by permission of the playwright. All inquiries should be addressed to the playwright's agent, Mr. Peter Hagen, Writers & Artists Agency, Suite 1000, 19 West 44th Street, New York, NY 10036. No amateur or professional performance or reading of the play may be given without obtaining, in advance, the written permission.

This is the seventh play by **ROMULUS LINNEY** to be presented by the
Ensemble Studio Theatre. He is the author of three novels and many
plays.

AUTHOR'S NOTE

PARADISE is part of a full length play in progress, DIVINE COMEDY
SOUTH. Parts one and two are HELL and PURGATORY.

When the Ensemble Studio Theatre created its yearly Marathon of
One Act Plays, it gave the New York theatre a wonderful new forum
for short works. Earlier, Eugene O'Neill laid bloody hands on the di-
verting, clever trifles American one acts were and made them face re-
ality. Tennessee Williams developed them further, exploring great
emotional depths. It remained for a theatre like EST to create a place
where a large number of one acts could be presented as one event,
spawning similar production at other theatres, and giving to the one-
act play a standing equal to that of the short story.

Now Smith & Kraus is publishing Marathon one acts in their own anthology, and that is welcome and fitting.

The Marathon is a challenge to write the play no one else will produce, the play as important to its author as any other, the play short
on length but long on substance.

—*Romulus Linney*

CHARACTERS

Paul

Jean

Dudley

Angelina

Linda

TIME

The Present

LOCATION

A small house near Miami

PARADISE

Small yard, front porch, and living room of Jean's little house in a town near Miami.

Jean sits on the porch, waiting for someone. She is very prettily dressed, made-up, and wears, in the hot sun, a pair of white gloves. She is 65.

She sits very still, waiting. A transistor radio is playing a disk jockey show.

The music gets softer. Paul, in his forties, appears in a light in front of Jean, facing out, speaking earnestly.

PAUL: I just don't know. Your mother's sister, yes. And it's nice of her to invite you. Appreciate it. But she's just been strange in the past. I know, Linda will be here, but still. There's lots to do here. You could stay here.

(Paul moves away, his light goes out. Transistor radio music up again. Jean sighs, shifts her position, but with an effort, inspecting her white gloves, she sits firmly in place. Enter Dudley, with backpack, bag, and Walkman. He is in his early twenties.)

DUDLEY: Aunt Jean?

JEAN: Dudley?

DUDLEY: Yep, it's me. *(Dudley comes onto the porch. He drops his bag, takes off his Walkman, embraces his aunt.)* Hi.

JEAN: *(Looks him over.)* You look just like your mother, God bless her.

DUDLEY: Is Linda here?

JEAN: Uh, no.

DUDLEY: Still at work?

JEAN: Linda's in Richmond. She won't be back for a week. Sit down.

DUDLEY: Something serious?

JEAN: George Bancroft died last night.

(Pause.)

DUDLEY: Oh. That was her father?

JEAN: Yes.

DUDLEY: Your—

JEAN: My ex.

DUDLEY: I'm sorry.

JEAN: Linda wanted to call you at school, but I said, "Let him come." We were happy when you wanted to visit us.

DUDLEY: Are you sure?

JEAN: Positive.

DUDLEY: Well, thanks.

JEAN: And you won't have to stay home with old Aunt Jean. Movies, places to dance, bars, ocean to swim in, beach to jog on. Your father wrote me you run miles every day.

DUDLEY: I do.

JEAN: You miss your mother, Dudley?

DUDLEY: Yeah.

JEAN: I miss her, too. My younger sister was supposed to stay around longer than I did.

DUDLEY: Yeah.

JEAN: Well, you're young and healthy. Miami's a lot of fun. *(She looks at her hands.)* White gloves. I put them on today. My way, I suppose, of going to his funeral. Well— *(She strips off the gloves.)* I've gone. Now, let's get you settled. *(Lights change. They move into the house. The disk jockey program plays. Lights change. Paul's light. Paul appears.)*

PAUL: What I remember about Jean is, she was so feisty. Your mother was the prettiest. Jean was the one just let anybody have it. Flare up over every little thing. With Linda saying, "Now, Mama, now Mama." Course, there was reason for it. Her little boy. But she was always like that! No, son, this isn't good. You leave those women alone, and stay here with me.

(Paul and his light disappear. Jean comes onto the porch. She is drinking a bottle of Coke. Her eyelids droop slightly. Enter Dudley, in running clothes, sweaty and out of breath. He throws himself down in the yard and starts doing push-ups.)

DUDLEY: One-twenty, twenty-one, twenty-two, twenty-three—

JEAN: How many a day?

DUDLEY: One-fifty. Not all at once. One-twenty-six, twenty-seven, twenty-eight—

JEAN: One hundred and fifty push-ups. Imagine that.

(Jean drinks her Coke.)

DUDLEY: Days I can't run, I do two fifty. Thirty-two, thirty-three—
JEAN: Doesn't it hurt?
DUDLEY: I did pull a muscle once. Thirty-six, thirty-seven—
JEAN: Which one?
DUDLEY: What?
JEAN: I understand you can get drunk exercising.
DUDLEY: You get a high.
JEAN: Is that—blissful?
DUDLEY: Sometimes.
JEAN: Really.
DUDLEY: More fun than anything.

(He turns over on his stomach, and lifts his head and feet at the same time. Jean watches, drinking her Coke. Dudley stands up, shakes his head.)

JEAN: Really?

(In the house, the telephone rings.)

Linda. Said she'd call every day about now, and God knows my darling daughter keeps her word. *(Jean goes to the phone, with a very slight lurch. She straightens herself up before answering.)* Hello? Hello, honey. Yes, yes, yes. He just came back from swimming. Now he's doing pushups. You want to say hello? *(The telephone is wireless. Jean takes it into the yard.)* Darling daughter wants to say hello.

DUDLEY: Thanks. *(He takes the phone.)* Hi, Linda. I'm sorry about your father.

(He does knee bends while talking. Jean goes into the house, walks through the living room, exits.)

My Dad's fine. I'm getting over my mother, thanks. Sure. Of course I will. It's great to see her again. Nice to talk to you. Bye.

(Jean enters with a fresh Coke. Dudley meets her on the porch and gives her the phone.)

JEAN: Hang up already?
DUDLEY: She said tell you to take care, and I should keep an eye on you.
JEAN: Did she?
DUDLEY: When's she coming back?
JEAN: When she's buried him.
DUDLEY: Maybe I'll go shower now.
JEAN: Do that.

(Dudley goes into the house. Sudden bright classical music: a Haydn symphony. Paul's light appears. Enter Paul. Jean lifts a plank on the porch. She takes up a bottle of Jack Daniels. She pours some of it, not a lot, into the Coke, replaces the bottle, and sets the plank down again. Jean smiles, and sips delicately. Music plays softly.)

PAUL: Wesley Fones has a new English setter. Well, it's a Lewellyn, really. Not too many bird dogs of that breed still around. I swear it's a good looking thing, all white and peppered black, with hair flying off it like little flags. Stands a point like granite. Looks good! But, son, those beautiful dogs don't hunt. They just don't. They run around, get in a lather, and look good pointing, but when you step past them, half the time the quail have walked, or weren't there in the first place. Too damn much temperament! Lots of people in this life, my son, are just like that. They are pretty. They look right. But when it comes to the goods, they just ain't got it. Your Aunt Jean, for example.

(Paul and his light disappear. Bright Haydn again. Lights up on Dudley, on the porch in shorts and an open shirt. He is listening to the music which comes from tiny speakers he has hooked to his Walkman. He is also trying to read a book with some difficulty, and trying to take notes. Jean sits watching him, sipping from an outsized coffee cup. She has a sardonic look in her eye.)

JEAN: So tell me about college.

DUDLEY: Huh?

JEAN: School!

DUDLEY: Well. *(Dudley removes his earphones. Haydn is still heard in a shrill way, through the earphones.)* College is hard.

JEAN: Don't you like it?

DUDLEY: I try to. I'm not the smartest guy in the world. There's a lot I just can't understand.

JEAN: What does your father say about that?

DUDLEY: He says never mind. Go through it, graduate, and get to work.

JEAN: What you reading?

DUDLEY: *The Divine Comedy.*

(Jean looks at the book's title.)

JEAN: Dante A-lie-g-herry, I guess. What's it about?

DUDLEY: About him. He goes to hell, purgatory, and paradise.

JEAN: What for?

DUDLEY: I can't tell.

JEAN: Why not?

DUDLEY: It's so complicated! All these little footnotes you have to know about. All kinds of stuff doesn't have anything to do with anything! Waste of time, Daddy says.

JEAN: Why take the course?

DUDLEY: I needed some lit. Good teacher. I signed up for it.

JEAN: Maybe I can help. Why did Dante go to hell?

DUDLEY: To find out what it was like.

JEAN: So what is hell like?

DUDLEY: It's well, a kind of self-destruction.

JEAN: People go there themselves?

DUDLEY: Yeah.

JEAN: Why?

DUDLEY: They want to. They belong in hell.

JEAN: Turn the music off, Dudley. This is interesting. How did he get to hell?

(Dudley turns off his Walkman.)

Through a dark forest, where he got lost when he was thirty-five.

JEAN: Thirty-five?

DUDLEY: The middle of life.

JEAN: Oh.

DUDLEY: Half seventy. Everything is all worked out like that. It'll drive you crazy.

JEAN: So what happens when he's thirty-five?

DUDLEY: He wanders into the awful forest. He meet a Leopard, a Lion and a Wolf.

JEAN: What on earth for?

DUDLEY: Nobody knows. Then a poet appears.

JEAN: Poet?

DUDLEY: He's been sent there by a woman in Paradise. His name is Virgil and her name is Beatrice. Here's where it gets complicated.

JEAN: Don't let it. Secret of life, Dudley, keep it simple. Dante, Virgil, Beatrice.

DUDLEY: What do you mean, secret of life?

JEAN: Every question and every answer, to everything, ought to be in five words or less.

DUDLEY: *(smiles)* OK.

JEAN: Why did Virgil help Dante? That five? Yes!

DUDLEY: Beatrice sent Virgil to him. Five.

JEAN: Good! See?

DUDLEY: OK!

JEAN: Who is Beatrice? Three, even better!

DUDLEY: A woman in paradise. Four.

JEAN: Doing what? Two.

DUDLEY: Loving Dante. Two.

JEAN: Why? One.

DUDLEY: His childhood sweetheart who died. Five.

JEAN: She loved him?

DUDLEY: And he never forgot her.

JEAN: And Dante never married?

DUDLEY: No, he did. Had children.

JEAN: But he loved Beatrice.

DUDLEY: More than anybody.

JEAN: Don't understand.

DUDLEY: Because she saves him.

JEAN: Dante goes to hell so a woman can save him?

DUDLEY: That's—eight, nine—ten words.

JEAN: Never mind!

DUDLEY: I told you it was complicated.

JEAN: Interesting, though.

DUDLEY: Yeah.

JEAN: Children. Death. Hell. Purgatory. And one more word makes five. Paradise.

DUDLEY: Yeah. *(Pause.)* I think I *will* go out tonight.

(Blackout. Haydn plays. Jean pulls up a plank in her porch. To one side, Paul and his light appear.)

PAUL: I know it's been a hard year. All that studying about God knows what. But once it's over, summer will be here. Green again. A man can live again. Hot sun. Good sweat. I tell you what. I'll shut the store a whole month. We can afford it. We'll go fishing, way off somewhere. Virginia? Hungry Mother State Park? North Carolina? Boone? Banner Elk? See Grandfather Mountain?

(Jean takes a fresh bottle of Jack Daniels into the house.)

JEAN: Right to hell. All aboard.

(Jean takes the bottle with her into the house. The Haydn plays, fading into soft rock at the end of Paul's speech.)

PAUL: Or even further, son! Colorado! Why not? I heard the water comes down from the mountains cold and so pure, makes your teeth ache! Trout! Bass! You wake up on top of the world, where it's clean and you're strong and the fire is made and nothing is wrong. That's where we'll go. Where everything is all right. You and me.

(Blackout. Soft rock. Dim light finds Dudley and Angelina on the porch, kissing. Angelina is a beat-up brunette, with mileage on her. She whispers in Dudley's ear then pulls away.)

ANGELINA: Would you like that?

DUDLEY: Maybe.

ANGELINA: Maybe?

DUDLEY: Well, yeah.

ANGELINA: What's the matter? I got a disease?

DUDLEY: No!

ANGELINA: Well, I have.

DUDLEY: Oh, yeah? What?

ANGELINA: I always say the wrong thing.

DUDLEY: Then let's talk about something else.

ANGELINA: How about your Aunt Jean?

(At the mention of her name, Jean appears in the living room. In her hand is a large glass dark with whiskey. She sits on the sofa and listens.)

DUDLEY: She started drinking the minute I got here. Booze all over the house. She thinks I don't see it.

ANGELINA: She's drunk right now?

DUDLEY: Probably.

ANGELINA: All passed out back there somewhere?

DUDLEY: Probably.

ANGELINA: Then let's go to bed.

DUDLEY: I don't want to.

ANGELINA: Really?

DUDLEY: Not yet, I mean.

ANGELINA: Well?

DUDLEY: Not now.

(Angelina sits back down.)

ANGELINA: All right.

DUDLEY: I just don't want to, right now.

ANGELINA: Then why did you bring me home?

DUDLEY: To be with you.

ANGELINA: And do what?

DUDLEY: I just wanted to talk to somebody!

ANGELINA: So, talk.

DUDLEY: You don't want me to.

ANGELINA: Yes, I do. Where do you live?

DUDLEY: I live with my Dad. My mother's dead.

ANGELINA: I thought you went to college.

DUDLEY: In town. Live at home. I'm all messed up, OK?

ANGELINA: That why you came to see your Aunt? She's your Mama's sister?

DUDLEY: Maybe, yeah.

ANGELINA: I can make you forget all about your Mama, Dudley.

DUDLEY: I just want to talk to you.

ANGELINA: What that means is, you saw one thing in a bar and something else when you got it home. You a virgin? That would be all right.

DUDLEY: No.

ANGELINA: You only make it with sluts like me? That would be all right, too.

DUDLEY: No!

(Pause.)

ANGELINA: Are you thinking about your Mama, and her dying and all?

DUDLEY: No. I'm thinking about Dante.

ANGELINA: Who?

DUDLEY: You wouldn't understand.

ANGELINA: Then what will I understand? *(Angelina gets up.)* Goodnight!
(Dudley gets up, too.)

DUDLEY: You didn't have a good time.

ANGELINA: Thanks anyway.

DUDLEY: Want me to walk you home?

ANGELINA: I live three blocks from here.

DUDLEY: Oh.

ANGELINA: All the best.

DUDLEY: All the best.

(Exit Angelina. Dudley sits down again. Jean comes onto the porch. She is in her nightgown.)

JEAN: Know I drink, do you?

DUDLEY: Yes.

JEAN: That puts me in Hell, with Dante?

DUDLEY: With the gluttons.

JEAN: What happens to gluttons in hell?

DUDLEY: They get eaten by a giant three-headed worm-like dog.

JEAN: Yeah. *(Pause.)* That was a pretty girl who just left.

DUDLEY: Yeah, she is.

JEAN: College kids on vacation try to get themselves laid, Dudley.

DUDLEY: I'm an exception.

JEAN: Think *I'd* care?

DUDLEY: No.

JEAN: Don't you like sex, Dudley?

DUDLEY: Not always.

JEAN: I didn't either but I tried. Goodnight.

> *(Jean goes back into the house. Pause. Dudley sits on the porch. He starts to cry. Enter Angelina.)*

ANGELINA: Hi.

DUDLEY: Oh, hi.

ANGELINA: I couldn't just go to bed.

DUDLEY: Me, either.

ANGELINA: How are you?

DUDLEY: Awful.

ANGELINA: I wasn't nice and I'm sorry.

DUDLEY: I'm impossible and you're right and what can I say?

ANGELINA: You're sweet and sad and you make me feel terrible. I was wrong to be mean.

DUDLEY: You were just honest.

ANGELINA: Just let me tell you that, OK?

DUDLEY: OK. Thanks.

ANGELINA: I just wish we could both feel good instead of bad. But goodnight, Dudley. Thank you for taking me home. I don't deserve you.

> *(Dudley suddenly take her in his arms and kisses her.)*

DUDLEY: Did you like that?

ANGELINA: Well, yes.

DUDLEY: Come on.

> *(They go into the house, open the sofa bed, take off their clothes as the lights go down and jump into bed. Music: fun rock, fading under Paul. Paul appears.)*

PAUL: I have always done my best since she died. You are the best part of my life, son. Just like your mother was, and I love you like I loved her. But you are a man, not a woman. And your father, with all his faults, knows the world. It's hard, and it's mean, and it will eat you alive, if you don't beat it at its own game. Not being a tough guy, not a bully. Just strong. Knowing what's right and what's wrong. And when you have to be, rougher than the other son of a bitch who'll come right down your throat if you let him. Or crazy women who get lost, stay that way, and wreck everything. Like your Aunt Jean, who's drinking her life away, just like, sometimes, I'm sorry to say it but it's true, your mother did. No, no, son. I'm not going to let you go to Florida. You stay here, with me.

(Light fades on Paul's determined face. Rock music plays. Lights up on Dudley, sleeping in the sofa bed. Angelina is hidden under a sheet. Pause. Music stops suddenly. Door bangs. In staggers Jean, bathrobe, hair unkempt, bottle in hand. She gets in bed with Dudley, without seeing Angelina.)

JEAN: Oh, my God!

DUDLEY: Huh?

JEAN: My God!

DUDLEY: You're drunk, Aunt Jean.

JEAN: Listen!

DUDLEY: Aw, come on!

JEAN: For one minute! Please!

DUDLEY: For one minute. *(He puts his arms around her.)* What?

JEAN: My little boy.

DUDLEY: Yes, Aunt Jean.

JEAN: He would have looked like you!

DUDLEY: Maybe.

JEAN: Big and strong!

DUDLEY: Maybe.

JEAN: Playing in the yard one minute, under a car the next! Splat! No more little boy! Little girl, she grew up, but no little boy, no Johnny! Splat!

DUDLEY: I'm sorry.

JEAN: Hug me!

DUDLEY: All right.

(Pause. Jean thinks.)

JEAN: How long did you take naps with your mother?

DUDLEY: What?

JEAN: You were too close, Dudley. Your mother had her hands up your pants all day. Talked about nothing but you all night. Her beautiful little wonderful Dudley while my Johnny got squashed flat and you're all grown up now and can't fuck a girl. What's the connection?

DUDLEY: Jack Daniels.

JEAN: Gluttons.

DUDLEY: I guess.

(Angelina emerges from under the sheets.)

ANGELINA: Hi.

JEAN: Oh!

DUDLEY: Aunt Jean, this is Angelina.

JEAN: You scared me to death!

ANGELINA: Sorry.

JEAN: Quite all right. This is a great improvement in your behavior, Dudley. Hello, Angelina.

ANGELINA: I know you but you don't know me. I live three blocks down Raymond Street.

JEAN: I've seen you around.

ANGELINA: What are you drinking?

JEAN: Jack Daniels. Want some?

ANGELINA: Sure.

JEAN: Here!

(She hands Angelina the bottle. Angelina takes a swig, hands it back.)

JEAN: Have another.

ANGELINA: OK. *(She takes another swig.)*

ANGELINA: Dudley?

DUDLEY: I don't drink.

JEAN: Doesn't drink.

ANGELINA: I know.

JEAN: What's he like in bed?

ANGELINA: He's good.

DUDLEY: Hey!

ANGELINA: Well, you are. You don't know it yet, but you are.

JEAN: Who would believe it?

(Angelina takes another swig and hands the bottle back to Jean.)

ANGELINA: Here. Thanks.

(Jean reaches for the bottle, misses, grabs it.)

JEAN: Goodnight.

(Exit Jean, clutching the bottle.)

ANGELINA: She'll be out for awhile.

DUDLEY: Yeah.

ANGELINA: I feel great. You're so sweet.

DUDLEY: Yeah.

ANGELINA: Let's go back to sleep.

DUDLEY: OK.

ANGELINA: Kiss me.

DUDLEY: OK.

(He kisses her. They fall back in each other's arms. Music. Change of light. Silence. Paul appears.)

PAUL: All right. Go ahead, if you have to. You're making a mistake, but go on. Make it. When you get back, we'll see what you've learned, from those women.

(Paul disappears. Angelina and Dudley sleep. Jean, drunk and haggard, staggers in to them, holding out her empty bottle of Jack Daniels.)

JEAN: GET HIM OUT OF THE YARD! GET AWAY FROM THE STREET! I won't drink! I won't be bad! GET HIM OUT OF THE YARD!

(Angelina and Dudley hold her.)

ANGELINA: Hush now.

DUDLEY: It's all right, Aunt Jean.

JEAN: Give me the bottle!! *(Jean tries to drink.)* ALL GONE!!

(Jean quickly gets another bottle of Jack Daniels from under a floorboard, and staggers back to them. Dudley and Angelina hold her in bed.)

DUDLEY: It's all right, Aunt Jean.

ANGELINA: Hush, now.

JEAN: Where am I?

DUDLEY: In bed, Aunt Jean.

ANGELINA: Safe with us.

JEAN: Passed out, huh?

DUDLEY: Right.

JEAN: The dog-face worm will get me, right?

DUDLEY: Right.

ANGELINA: Why?

DUDLEY: That's the punishment for a drunk.

JEAN: In hell. Right.

ANGELINA: He'll get me, too.

JEAN: For drinking?

ANGELINA: For fucking around.

(*Jean smiles at Angelina.*)

JEAN: Do you?

ANGELINA: All the time.

JEAN: Because something hurts?

ANGELINA: Yes.

JEAN: What?

ANGELINA: I wish I knew.

JEAN: Ask Dudley.

DUDLEY: You want to be blown around in a big black storm. That's lovers in hell.

ANGELINA: Can I have another drink?

JEAN: Here. (*Hands her the Jack Daniels.*) You know about big black storms?

ANGELINA: Maybe.

JEAN: Dudley just reads books. He doesn't have a clue.

ANGELINA: He's trying.

JEAN: He's never had anything hurt him at all.

ANGELINA: His mama died.

JEAN: Everybody's mother does that.

DUDLEY: Give me the bottle!

(*Dudley drinks from the bottle. They pass it around. They relax and stare at nothing, say nothing. Enter Linda. She has a small suitcase, is dressed in old-fashioned Southern Lady traveling clothes, complete with white gloves, but everything is dusty and wrinkled.*)

LINDA: Mother, what is this?

JEAN: Linda!

LINDA: What are you people doing?

JEAN: Well—

LINDA: Why are you all in bed with my mother?

ANGELINA: Hi.

LINDA: Who are *you?*

ANGELINA: I live three blocks from here! My name is Angelina.

LINDA: How much have you drunk, Mother?

JEAN: Not much!

LINDA: A fifth a day? A quart a day?

DUDLEY: Quart.

LINDA: And you! You're as drunk as she is!

DUDLEY: Wish I was.

LINDA: God damn it, Mother—

JEAN: You came home too soon? Why?

LINDA: Why? WHY?

JEAN: Yes!

LINDA: Give me the bottle!

ANGELINA: Here!

(Angelina gives Linda the bottle. She takes a huge drink, then swigs as she talks.)

LINDA: Jesus. You prepare all your life for great big things like your father dying, and what happens when he does? (Linda takes off her dress and most of her clothes as she talks. She drops them on the floor and gets in bed with the other three.) First that miserable undertaker had my Daddy laid out in a ten-thousand-dollar burnished copper coffin, with a glass cockpit sort of headpiece, looked like a Star Wars movie. I said, "Something less grandiose, please, my father wasn't Lenin, laid out in Red Square for all the world to see, he was this alcoholic landowner tobacco farmer died of lung cancer finally, after smoking three packs a day for sixty-five years, he doesn't deserve a state funeral." Then that mangy Methodist minister gave a eulogy, you'd have thought Daddy and daughter were the apotheosis of loving family value, instead of a twice-a-year how-can-you-treat-my-mother-and-me-like-this visit that always ended up with him drunk on the floor calling for his little darling and me throwing up in the bathroom, he didn't deserve to be called Father-Of-The-Year. Then those low-down rotten herds and hoards of that pig-faced side of his family, all over me with the stench of perfume, cigars and hypocritical tears, wanting to know how much money he'd left to who and was I going to be reasonable about this farm and would I let that store get renovated for a chiliburger restaurant and did I think my Father was in heaven now or not, well, he sure didn't deserve to be there, God knows, but what could I say? Then with the blister from the new shoes I bought for his death, I say goodbye to everybody and one hour before the bus leaves I hobble back to the cemetery where I never had the time or peace to say goodbye to him and stand there crying for my Daddy like any little girl, get on the bus, come home to my beloved mother I live with because no man will have me, who's on a tearing drunk in bed with a college boy cousin and some slut from three blocks down the street. How do you think I feel?

DUDLEY: You're the lion.

LINDA: I'm the *what?*

DUDLEY: In the forest. Outside hell.

LINDA: Is he all right in the head?

JEAN: No.

ANGELINA: Sometimes he is and sometimes he isn't.

(Dudley figures it out. He stares at Angelina.)

DUDLEY: You're the Leopard.

ANGELINA: I am?

DUDLEY: Beautiful but all spots, and snarling and passionate.

ANGELINA: All right, I'm the Leopard.

DUDLEY: And you're the Wolf. Hungry.

JEAN: Me?

DUDLEY: You're the Lion. Strong.

LINDA: I'm a lion, you lunatic?

DUDLEY: I understand it now.

ANGELINA: In bed with Jack Daniels and three women, what's to understand, Dudley? Squalor in Florida, forget it.

DUDLEY: *(To Linda.)* Your Daddy died. *(To Angelina.)* You pick up creeps like me. *(To Jean.)* Your baby boy went splat years ago.

JEAN: Yes.

ANGELINA: Yes.

LINDA: So what?

DUDLEY: We'll see.

(Dudley picks up the copy of The Divine Comedy.)

LINDA: See *what?*

DUDLEY: Hell?

(Dudley closes his eyes, lets the book fall open and sticks his finger in its early pages, reads.) "Amid this cruel and dismal swarm, were people running, naked and terrified, with no hope of finding a hole to crawl into."

JEAN: Oh, ugh!

ANGELINA: Really.

DUDLEY: Purgatory? *(He closes his eyes, sticks a finger in the middle of the book. Reads:)* "I bent forward, over my clasped hands, looking into the fire, seeing in flames human bodies I once knew, burning."

JEAN: Dudley, give up.

ANGELINA: That can't be the way to study anything.

LINDA: I'm finally getting really drunk. I couldn't before.

DUDLEY: Paradise? *(Dudley sticks his finger in the last part of the book, reads.)* "Through your beauty and your grace alone have I understood the beauty and grace inherent in all the things I have witnessed." *(Pause. Dudley looks at Angelina, Jean and Linda and smiles.)* Give me the bottle. *(He takes a drink.)* I'm happy here.

LINDA: *Happy* here?

DUDLEY: I don't want to live with my father anymore.

JEAN: Oh.

ANGELINA: Don't you want to go to college?

DUDLEY: No.

LINDA: You want to stay *here?*

DUDLEY: Yes.

LINDA: Mama?

JEAN: He can use the cot in the back room.

DUDLEY: Can I drink?

LINDA: Elsewhere than here.

DUDLEY: Agreed!

LINDA: Mother, you will commence to dry yourself out, at once!

JEAN: Agreed!

LINDA: And I will take care of you, until you are clean and neat and dressed like a Southern Lady, complete with white gloves and a decent perfume, and we can go to church on Sunday.

JEAN: I was getting around to it. You got home too soon.

LINDA: Angelica—

ANGELINA: Angelina—

LINDA: Angelina, you can have sex with Dudley a. one hour after my mother and I go to bed for the night or b. when we are at church on Sundays.

ANGELINA & DUDLEY: Agreed!

LINDA: Dudley, you will do chores around the house. And you will get some kind of a job within a month, and pay us what you can for rent.

DUDLEY: Sure!

LINDA: I can talk about my Daddy and you can talk about your Momma.

DUDLEY: All right.

LINDA: And you can read to me from that book.

DUDLEY: OK.

LINDA: What's it called?

JEAN: *The Divine Comedy.*

LINDA: A book about hell can't be a comedy.

DUDLEY: It has a happy ending.

JEAN: What about the wolves and leopards and lions?

DUDLEY: They stayed in the dark forest. Beatrice took Dante to Paradise, where he saw this beautiful white light, which was God. That was the happy ending.

JEAN: Did Dante say anything?

DUDLEY: Sure.

JEAN: What did Dante say at the happy ending when he saw God?

DUDLEY: *(reading)* "By now everything I wanted to do was good, like a wheel rolled forward, by the Love that moves the sun and all the stars."

(Pause.)

LINDA & JEAN: Oh.

(Linda smiles at Jean through her tears. Jean smiles back at Linda. Then All smile at each other. Lights fade. Stars shine.)

END

Wasp

by Steve Martin

WASP was directed by Curt Dempster and stage managed by Heather Robinson with the following cast:

Dad . . . . Jack Gilpin
Mom . . . . Cecilia de Wolf
Sis . . . . Melinda Hamilton
Son . . . . Josh Sobosai
Female Voice . . . . Jenny O'Hara
Male Voice . . . . Richmond Hoxie

WASP by Steve Martin. ©1994 by 40 Share Productions. All rights reserved. Reprinted by permission of International Creative Management, Inc. Caution: Professionals and amateurs are hereby warned that WASP is subject to a royalty. It is fully protected under the copyright laws of the United States of America, and of all countries covered by the International Copyright Union (including the Dominion of Canada and the rest of the British Commonwealth), and of all countries covered by the Pan-American Copyright Convention and the Universal Copyright Convention, and of all countries with which the United States has reciprocal copyright relations. All rights, including professional, amateur, motion picture, recitation, lecturing, public reading, radio broadcasting, television, video or sound taping, all other forms of mechanical or electronic reproduction, such as information storage and retrieval systems and photocopying, and the rights of translation into foreign languages, are strictly reserved. Particular emphasis is laid upon the question of readings, permission for which must be secured from the author's agent in writing.

All inquiries concerning rights should be addressed to the playwright's representative: International Creative Management, Inc., 40 West 57th Street, New York, NY 10019, Attn: Sam Cohn.

Steve Martin has written the screenplays for ROXANNE (Writers Guild Award, Best Screenplay), L.A. STORY, and the upcoming TWIST OF FATE. He also co-wrote the screenplays for THE JERK, DEAD MEN DON'T WEAR PLAID, THE MAN WITH TWO BRAINS and THREE AMIGOS. He won an Emmy writing for the SMOTHERS BROTHERS COMEDY HOUR. Mr. Martin has also published a collection of short stories entitled CRUEL SHOES. His first play, PICASSO AT THE LAPIN AGILE, is currently running in Boston at the American Repertory Theatre.

AUTHOR'S NOTE

WASP is the result of taking various words appearing in the dictionary and arranging them so they have meaning.

—*Steve Martin*

CHARACTERS

Dad
Mom
Sis
Son
Female Voice
Male Voice

LOCATION

An American Home

WASP

A kitchen in a fifties' house. A dining table is center stage, with four chairs around it. Mom sets the table in silence. Around the table are Dad, Son and Sis. Mom sits.

DAD: Oh God in heaven which is seventeen miles above the earth, bless this food grown on this earth that is four thousand three hundred twenty-five years old. Amen.

(They pantomime eating. We hear loud, amplified prerecorded chewing sounds. A long time goes by.)

SON: Jim, where's heaven?

DAD: Son, it's seventeen miles above the earth. You enter through clouds. Behind the clouds there are thirteen golden steps leading to a vestibule. Inside the vestibule is St. Peter. Next to the vestibule are gates 27 feet high. They are solid gold but with an off-center hinge for easy opening.

SON: Then heaven's closer than the moon?

DAD: What do you mean?

SON: Well, according to my science teacher, the moon is 250,000 miles away.

(There is a moment of silence while they contemplate this. Mom bursts into tears. Dad stares at him and starts to chew. Sounds of loud chewing for a long time.)

SON: Jim, if Adam and Eve were the first people on earth and they had two sons, where did everybody else come from?

DAD: Huh?

(Mom stares at Son.)

SON: Well, if there were only two sons, then who did they marry and where did everybody else come from?

(Another moment of silence. Mom bursts into tears.)

DAD: Do you like your science teacher?

SON: Yeah.

DAD: Well, that's too bad because he's going to have his tongue pierced in hell by a hot poker.

(The phone rings. Sis looks up in anticipation, grips the table.)

SIS: Oh my god it's Jeremy!

(Mom goes to wall phone and answers.)

MOM: Oh hi June!

(Sis dies when she realizes it's not for her.)

...uh huh...yeah...really?...REALLY? Good news! Thanks! Bye. *(Hangs up, then to herself.)* Oh great! Great! *(She looks at everyone in anticipation. No one asks her anything. She sits back down.)*

(Sounds of loud chewing.)

SIS: Guess what I learned in home economics.

(More munching.)

MOM: I went to a flower show today and I just thought it was beautiful; they have the most beautiful things there...I went with Miriam and she had been before but there was a new exhibit so...

(Dad starts talking loud and over Mom.)

DAD: *(Loud and over Mom.)* Boy oh boy when I was in college I remember we used to wear these skinny little pants and shirts with big collars, boy we must have looked silly. *(To son.)*

MOM: ...she wanted to go again and she knows someone there and she got tickets for me so I got in free. Normally it costs 3 dollars to go in so I used the money I saved and picked up a nice arrangement.

(Mom dialogue peters out.)

(The phone rings. Sis looks at the phone in anticipation.)

SIS: *(Frantic.)* It's Jeremy, it's got to be!

(Mom answers it.)

MOM: Hello? Oh. Jim, it's for you. It's Mister Carlyle.

(She collapses again.)

DAD: I'll take it in the living room.

(Dad exits. Big relax from the family.)

DAD: *(Offstage, loud and muffled.)* I don't give a damn what they're talking about if they can't meet us halfway then we've got to reconsider the whole arrangement. There's no sense in doing what we talked about unless we're willing to do it without a contract and I don't want to see the situation turn around unless we want it to turn around...

(Mom, Sis and Son begin to quake, rattling dishes and cutlery. Mom starts to clear dishes, shaking her way with cups and saucers to the sink. Phone call is over.)

SON: *(Relieved, trying to make conversation.)* Where's the dog?

SIS: Yeah, what happened to Coco? I haven't seen her in about two days. And it's not like she comes back at night, the food's always left in the dish.

MOM: She just wouldn't stay off the furniture so I put her to sleep.

(Sis stares horrified into space. Dad returns, sits.)

DAD: Where's grandmom? We haven't heard from her in about a week.

(All the kids look horrified at Mom. Mom looks guilty, shifts uncomfortably.)

MOM: *(then)* In Europe they eat the salad after the main course and that's what we're doing tonight.

DAD: *(incredulous)* Salad *after* the main course?

SON: Weird.

MOM: Here it is....

(Mom brings out huge cherry jello ring with fruit bits on it. Dad looks into the cherry ring and points to a piece of fruit.)

DAD: What's that on top?

MOM: Mango.

(Son stifles a vomit.)

SIS: Eyew. I don't think I want any salad. May I be excused? I have to go to choir molestation.

MOM: Okay you run off.

DAD: I'll have a little piece.

(He takes a piece, carefully cutting around and avoiding the mango. Mom starts to cut a piece for Son.)

SON: I don't think I want any either, Mom.

(Dad glares at him.)

SON: Okay just a little piece. *(Bows his head and utters to himself.)* No Mango, no mango, no mango....

(Mom carefully cuts him a piece. Son's eyes widen in terror as she gives him the piece with the mango in it. He thinks about it for a second and starts rubbing his forehead rapidly back and forth with his hand. He continues to do this during next dialogue. Mom takes out a letter and sets it nervously on the table.)

DAD: What's that?

MOM: *(Nervous.)* It's a letter from the Chamber of Commerce.

SON: *(Finishes rubbing his forehead.)* Mom, can I be excused? I feel like I have a temperature.

(Mom feels his forehead with the back of her hand.)

MOM: My oh my you sure do. You better go straight to bed.
(He disappears quickly, not having to eat his mango.)
MOM: *(As he goes.)* Do you want to take your salad to your room?
(Son indicates he has a stomachache too.)
DAD: What's it about?
MOM: Well, you know our lawn jockey?
DAD: Yeah.
MOM: They want us to paint its face white.
DAD: Why on earth would they want us to do that?
MOM: They feel it's offensive to some of the negroes in the community.
DAD: That's like saying there never was such a thing as a negro lawn jockey. It's really a celebration of the great profession of lawn jockeying.
MOM: They think it shows prejudice.
DAD: Well, that's ridiculous. Some of my best friends are negro. Jerry at work is a negro and we work side by side without the slightest problem.
MOM: That's true, he is a negro. Well, he's a Navajo.
DAD: But times have changed. I'll make a compromise with them. I'll paint the nineteen on the north side of the driveway white but I'm leaving the 19 on the other side of the driveway alone and I'm not touching the six on the porch.
MOM: That sounds fair. Jim, I have something to discuss with you. Maybe you can help. Lately, I've been having feelings of...distance. My heart will start racing and I feel like I'm going to die. I don't like to leave the house because when I get to the supermarket I always start to feel terrified...
(Sis, dressed for choir, enters with the evening paper.)
SIS: Evening paper's here. (She exits.)
DAD: Thanks, Judy...uh Sandy.
(She turns away, it says "Kathy" on the back of her choir robe. Dad takes the paper, opens it spread eagle, covering his face and starts to read silently.)
MOM: ...my mouth gets dry...my palms get moist, and I feel like...like I'm going to die *(Mom continues as though nothing is different)*. And when I don't feel that way, I spend most of the day in fear that the feeling is going to come over me. Sometimes I hear things. I don't think I can live like this.
DAD: *(From behind paper.)* Honey, it's sounds to me like you're having

symptoms of fear without knowing what it is you're afraid of. I'm not going to pretend to know how to cure something like that, but I want you to know that I will be beside you while we together figure out how to conquer this thing. I appreciate how difficult your job around this house is. You are deeply loved. I admire you as a person as well as a wife. I'm interested in what you say and if there's anytime you need me, I will stop everything to help you.

MOM: Oh my God Jim.

(She is moved. He leans over to kiss her, and although he still holds the newspaper in front of his face, he kisses her through it. It's a tender smooch and he's so moved he closes his arms around her head, still holding the newspaper. Her head is completely encircled in it. They break.)

DAD: *(Still holding newspaper.)* You still get me excited. *(Brings down paper.)* Now why don't you pour us a drink and I'll meet you upstairs?

MOM: Oh! Oh yes....

(Dad exits. She goes to the cupboard, removes a cocktail shaker, throws in some ingredients, shakes it. She takes out two glasses, one a tiny shot glass, the other glass tankard size. She pours the drink in the tiny glass, then in the large one. She picks up the two drinks, starts to exit, then walks center.)

MOM: *(To the air.)* Voices?

FEMALE VOICE: Yes?

MOM: Hello.

FEMALE VOICE: Hello Diane.

MOM: Would you visit me if things were different?

FEMALE VOICE: There would be no need.

MOM: Does heaven exist?

FEMALE VOICE: No.

MOM: Does hell exist?

FEMALE VOICE: No.

MOM: Well that's something anyway. Do things work out in the end?

FEMALE VOICE: No.

MOM: Am I still pretty?

FEMALE VOICE: *(Pause while she thinks.)* Happiness will make you beautiful.

MOM: You've made me feel better. *(Starts to go, then)* Voices...?

FEMALE VOICE: Yes?

MOM: Is there a heartland?

FEMALE VOICE: Yes.

MOM: Could I go there?

FEMALE VOICE: You're in it.

MOM: Oh. Does the human heart exist?

FEMALE VOICE: Listen, you can hear them breaking.

MOM: What is melancholy?

FEMALE VOICE: Wouldn't you love to dance with him in the moonlight?

MOM: *(She starts to go, then turns back.)* Voices, when he says he loves me, what does he mean?
(Silence. Lights slowly fade.)

SCENE II
Lepton

(Lights up. Son's room. We hear Mom's sexual cries coming through the wall. She finishes. Immediately, Dad comes into the room, wearing a robe.)

DAD: *(Holding a doorknob sign that says private.)* Private? It's not really private is it?

SON: No.

DAD: Well let's not have the yablons. Der fashion rests particularly well. I hop da balloon fer forest waters. Aged well-brood water babies. In der yablons.

SON: Huh?

DAD: Oh year, you're too young to understand now, but one day you'll have response not too fer-well keption.

SON: Jim, do you think I could get a bicycle?

DAD: Sure you could get a bicycle. How would you pay for it?

SON: Well. I don't know. I was hoping...

DAD: You see son, a bicycle is a luxury item. You know what a luxury item is?

SON: No.

DAD: A luxury item is a thing that you have that annoys other people that you have it. Like our very green lawn. That's a luxury item. Oh, it could be less green I suppose, but that's not what it's about. I work on that lawn, maybe more than I should, and pour a little bit o'money into it, but it's a luxury item for me, out there to annoy the others. And let's be fair, they have their luxury items that annoy me. On the corner, that mail box made out of a ship's chain. Now there's no way I wouldn't like that out in front of our house but I went for the lawn. What I'm getting at, is that you have to work for a luxury item. So if you want that bicycle you're going to have to work for it. Now, I've got a little lot downtown that we've had for several years, and if you wanted to go down there on weekends and after school and say, put up a building on it, I think we could get you that bicycle.

SON: Gosh.

DAD: Yes, I know, you're pretty excited. It's not easy putting up a building son, but these are the ancient traditions, handed down from the peoples of the epocian Golwanna who lived on the plains of Golgotha. Based upon the precepts of Hammurabi. Written in cuneiform on the gates of Babylon. Deduced from the cryptograms of the Questioner of the Sphinx, and gleaned from the incunabulaw of Ratdolt. Delivered unto me by the fleet-footed Mercury when the retrograde Mars backed into Gemini, interpreted from the lyrics of "What a Swell Party." Appeared on my living room wall in blood writ there by God himself and incised in the Holy Trowel of the Masons. Son, we don't get to talk that much, in fact, as far as I can remember, we've never talked. But I was wondering several years ago, and unfortunately never really got around to asking you until now, I was wondering what you plan to do with your life.

SON: Well...

DAD: Before you answer, let me just say that I didn't know what I wanted to do with my life until I was twenty-eight. Which is late when you want to be a gymnast, which I gave up when I found out it was considered more an art than a sport. But now, your mother and I have seventeen grand in the bank, at today's prices that's like being a millionaire. See, if you've got a dollar and you spend twenty-nine cents on a loaf of bread, you've got seventy-one cents left. But if you're got seventeen grand and you spend twenty-nine cents on a loaf of bread, you've still got seventeen grand. There's a math lesson for you.

SON: All I know is, it's going to be a great life.

DAD: Well son, I have no idea what you're talking about but I want to suggest that you finish school first and go on to college and get a Ph.D. in Phrenology. But let me just say, that no matter what in life you choose to do, I will be there to shame you, unless of course you pass the seventeen thousand mark. Then you will be awarded my college sigma delta phuk-a-lucka pin. Goodbye, and I hope to see you around the house.

(He shakes the Son's hand, exits.)

SON: Okay dad, I mean Jim.

(Son stays in the room, takes out a purple pendant which he puts around his neck. He then takes out a small homemade radio with antenna, dials it; we hear glitches and gwarks, then the sound of a solar wind.)

SON: Premier....Premier...come in Premier.

(A cheesy spaceman walks out on the stage.)

PREMIER: Yes?

SON: How are things on Lepton?

PREMIER: 385 degrees Fahrenheit. It rained molten steel. Now that's cold.

SON: Tell me again, okay?

PREMIER: Again?

SON: I need it now.

PREMIER: How long has it been since my first visit?

SON: Ten years.

PREMIER: Ah yes. You were four and you were granted the Vision.

SON: Yes.

PREMIER: So much is credited to the gene pool these days. But the gene pool is nothing compared to the Vision. It's really what I enjoy doing most. Placing the Vision where it's least expected. Anyway, you need to hear it?

SON: Yes.

PREMIER: All right. Her skin will be rose on white. She will come to you, her breath on your mouth. She will speak words voicelessly which you will understand because of the movement of her lips on yours. Her hand will be on the small of your back and her fingers will be blades. Your blood will pool around you. You will receive a transfusion of a clear liquid that has been exactly measured. That liquid will be sadness. And then, whatever her name may be, Carol, Susan, Virginia, then, she will die and you will mourn her. Her death will be final in all respects but this: she will be alive, and with someone else. But time and again you will walk in, always at the same age as you are now, with your arms open, your heart as big as the moon, not anticipating the total eclipse. They call you a WASP, *but it's women who have the stingers.* However, you will have a gift. A gift so wonderful that it will take you through the days and nights until the end of your life.

SON: I'm getting a gift? What is it?

PREMIER: The desire to work.

(Fade out. [Possible: "no bike?"])

SCENE III
Choir

(Lights up. Choir practice. Sis, wearing her choir robe, stands on a riser. A conductor faces upstage, conducting the rest of the invisible choir.)

SIS: *(Singing)* I saw three ships a-sailing in
On Christmas day
On Christmas day.
I saw three ships a-sailing in
On Christmas day in the
Morning
And all the bells on earth
Shall ring
On Christmas day
On Christmas day
And all the bells on earth
Shall ring
On Christmas day in the
Morning.
(Pause...she waits with the count.)

SIS: ...On Christmas day
On Christmas day
(Waits another count.)

SIS: On Christmas day in the morning
(Pause. She waits, then starts to sing on her own. The conductor can't hear this and he keeps on conducting "Three Ships.")

SIS: She was only sixteen...
Only sixteen
I loved her so.
(The conductor points at her.)

SIS: On Christmas day in the morning
(Pause.)
But she was too young to fall in love

And I was too young to know.

She was only sixteen...

All pink and white and fluffy like a marshmallow. So many desirable qualities. She could have been on a poster in black sunglasses and blond hair. Her pretty ears admired by the choirmaster. All this at sixteen, the weight of the years not yet showing. Entering the stage in a beaded dress that weighed so much she could hardly stand up straight. But she did, this tiny girl from the Southland, her pupils made small from the flashbulbs. On Christmas Day on Christmas Day...I love to sing; I wish I could be a castratti. Boys get all the fun.

CHOIRMASTER: Kathryn...

SIS: Yes?

CHOIRMASTER: You're not paying attention.

SIS: Sorry...On Christmas Day... I guess pretty pink ears don't count for much. How can I possibly pay attention? How can I possibly focus on this little tune when I am so much more fascinating? Those who pass within the area of my magnetism know what I'm talking about. My power extends not just to the length of my arms but all around me like a sphere when I pass, in the hallways, lockers, to those who hear my voice. I am a flame and I bring myself to the unsuspecting moths. Unnaturally and strangely the power ceases when I'm home. There, my sphere of influence stays within here *(she indicates her head),* all within. It's all silent in the presence of my mother and father and brother. What they don't realize is that one idea from *this* little mind changes the course of rivers. Not to mention families.

CHOIRMASTER: Kathryn!

SIS: Sorry. *(Pause.)* I know from where my salvation will come. I will give birth to the baby Jesus. The baby Jesus brought to you by Kathryn, the near virgin. I will have to buy swaddling clothes. The sweet baby Jesus, the magician. He will wave his hand and the dishes will wash themselves and he will wave his other hand and the water on the dishes will bead up and rise to the heavens in a reverse dish-drying rain. *I* will put them away. And I will sweetly cradle him. People will come to him for miracles and I will look proudly on. He will grow and become my husband, the true virgin and the near-virgin. Both of us perfectly unspoiled, perfectly true. He couldn't work the miracles without me. I would run the mini-mart and be the inspiration, the wife of Jesus. And at the end of our lives, he would become the baby Jesus again and I would put him in the swaddling clothes and carry him upward, entering heaven in a beaded dress that weighed so much she could hardly stand up straight. But she did, this tiny girl from the Southland, her pupils made small from the flashbulbs. On Christmas Day, On Christmas Day. I saw three ships a-sailing in on Christmas Day in the morning.

CHOIRMASTER: Kathryn, see me after class.

SIS: Finally.

(Lights down.)

SCENE IV

Ye Faithful

(Lights up. Christmas morning around a tree. Several presents lie under it; a shiny bicycle stands next to it with a small ribbon around the handlebars. Son enters.)

SON: Yeah!

(Dad enters in his robe.)

DAD: Aren't you going to open it?

(Son unwraps the ribbon.)

SON: Great bicycle! Thanks Jim!

DAD: Well, that was a nice little seven-story building you put up, Son.

SON: Did you really think so?

DAD: Well you're no Frank Lloyd Wright.

(Sis enters.)

SIS: Christmas already? Wasn't it just Christmas?

(She goes over and casually starts tearing open presents. Mom enters, carrying an elaborate Christmas goose on a tray.)

MOM: Good Morning!

EVERYBODY: Not really hungry...I'm full, I had some cereal, etc.

MOM: *(Cheery.)* Fine!

DAD: How would all you kids like to take a trip to Israel? *(They stare at him.)* Well, all that history, going back four thousand three hundred twenty-five years. All the big names: Moses, David, Solomon, Rebecca, Daren the magnificent, Sasafrass. See the manger, the palm fronds, go on the rides, see the tablets with the ten commandments...

SON: Wow!

DAD: Not the originals of course, those are put away. Since it's Christmas, what if we went through those commandments? Who can name them? Huh?

SON: Thou shalt not kill? Thou shalt not lie...

DAD: Right. Numero uno and numero duo. Don't kill, don't lie. Good advice around the home.

MOM: Don't worship false gods?

DAD: Exactly. Now who can tell me what that means?

SON: Uh..

MOM: Don't know.

(Sis shrugs her shoulders.)

DAD: Well, you know, false gods. Don't worship 'em. What's another? *(They all think.)*

SON: How about, thou shalt not commit adultery? *(Dad goes into a coughing fit.)*

DAD: Next.

SIS: Don't change horses in the middle of the stream.

DAD: Good one, peanut. If you start out as one thing, don't end up another thing. People don't like it.

SON: Everything's comin' up roses?

DAD: Good, that's six.

MOM: Honor thy father and thy mother. *(The children cough violently.)*

DAD: Good. Well there you go. Ten commandments.

SIS: How come it's ten?

DAD: Ten is just right. Fourteen you go enough already. Eight's not enough, make things too easy. But ten, you can't beat ten. That's why He's God. We got ten fingers, ten toes, and through His wisdom we don't have ten heads. All thought out beforehand. Well, this has been a real fun morning. Oh by the way, unhappy childhood, happy life. Bye. *(He exits.)*

(Mom, Sis and Son wait a beat to see if he's gone. They all begin to speak in upper-class English accents.)

SON: Is he gone?

(The children gather round Mom and kneel.)

SON: Mummy, this has been the most wonderful Christmas ever.

MOM: Well now off you go to write your thank you notes. When you're done, you bring them down here and we'll take each note and set it next to each present you received and we can make sure you've mentioned each gift in the right way.

Sis: I've already written my thank you notes. I did them last week.

Mom: How could you have written a thank you note before you knew what the gift was?

Sis: I didn't mention the gift.

Mom: Well, we'll have to do them all over again, won't we?

Sis: Yes, Mummy.

(Dad enters. The kids break away from Mom and they all revert to American accents.)

Dad: Where are my keys...

Son: Over there Jim.

Dad: *(To Son)* Christmas or no Christmas, I want that lawn mowed today.

Son: *(American accent)* I don't wanna!

Mom: *(American accent, faking anger.)* You do as you're told!

Son: *(Faking.)* Oh Mom!

Dad: Christ! Where are my keys?

Sis: *(American accent)* In the drawer Dad.

Dad: *(Picking them up.)* How could they get there?

Mom: The butler must have put them there.

(Dad starts to exit.)

Dad: What butler?

Mom: I mean, I must have put them there. Did you remember your clubs?....

(But he's gone. The children kneel by Mom again.)

Sis: *(English accent)* I have never understood golf.

Mom: *(English accent)* Nor I.

Son: *(English accent)* Nor I.

Mom: *(English accent)* Scottish game 'tisn't it?

Son; *(English accent)* Oh yes, Scottish.

Sis: *(English accent) Very* Scottish!

(They all chuckle.)

Mom: Oh Roger!

(An English butler enters carrying a tea tray.)

Roger: Yes'um?

Mom: Oh Good. Tea. Has he gone?

(Roger looks off stage.)

Roger: Just driving off now, Ma'am.

Mom: We're so naughty!

Sis: You know what I'd like, a big bowl of Wheat-a-bix!

MOM: On Christmas you can have anything you want. Roger, would you be so kind, one bowl of Wheat-a-bix?

SON: Oh I'll have a bowl too!

MOM: Well, me too.

ROGER: Three bowls of Wheat-a-bix. Clotted cream?

MOM: Of course, Clotted cream and oh just bring a big bowl of bacon fat.

ROGER: Mango?

SON: Mango? Oh Mummy pretty please!

MOM: Oh you do love your mango. We'll take it in the garden. *(Afterthought.)* By the Folly.

ROGER: Yes'um.

MOM: Go along then.

(The children and Roger exit. Mom is left alone on stage. Mom still speaks with her accent.)

MOM: *(English accent)* Voices?

FEMALE VOICE: Yes?

MOM: *(English accent)* Thank you for these moments.

FEMALE VOICE: Would you like to be Italian?

MOM: Oh no, I'm afraid I would burst. Unless...

FEMALE VOICE: Unless what?

MOM: *(English accent)* Unless, late at night, when I'm with him, you know, sort of, in bed, well, you know. Maybe just for five minutes.

FEMALE VOICE: You'd like to be Italian for five minutes?

MOM: I was thinking him.

FEMALE VOICE: I see.

MOM: Well, I'll be in the garden by the folly.

(She starts to go.)

FEMALE VOICE: One moment. I have an answer to your question.

MOM: *(English accent)* Which one?

FEMALE VOICE: When he says he loves me, what does he mean?

MOM: *(Normal voice.)* Please.

FEMALE VOICE: He means if only, if only. If only he could call to you from across a river bank.

MOM: Like Running Bear.

FEMALE VOICE: Yes, as well as Little White Dove. He would dive into the river, swim to you and drown. He knows this. He cannot come close. He would drown. He knows this. The water has no value like it does to you, it is only trouble. He does not know the meaning of the water like you do. Standing on the bank, calling to his Little White Dove, with her so small in his vision he loves her fully. Swimming toward her, his words skipping across to her like flat rocks, he drowns, afraid of what she wants, not knowing what he should be, realizing his love was in the words that she shouted while on the bank, and not in the small whispers he carries to hand to her.

MOM: Is it ever possible for them not to drown?

FEMALE VOICE: Oh yes.

MOM: What makes the difference?

FEMALE VOICE: When the attraction is chemical.

MOM: Chemical?

FEMALE VOICE: Oh yes. The taste of the skin to the tongue. The touch of the hand to the neck. Can the chemistry of the breath across the lips inhibit the chemistry of bitterness. Oh this is too hard long distance, let me come down to earth. *(The female voice appears from offstage, she wears a conservative Chanel suit and holds a handbag. It doesn't strike Mom as unusual that the Voice walks into her living room.)* Chemistry. The scientific combination of the voice and the shade of the hair. The shape of the face on the retina. The way the prepositions strike the eardrum: do his vowels produce pleasure.

MOM: I see. Would you like something?

FEMALE VOICE: Oh no thank you. I can only stay a few minutes.

MOM: Coffee?

FEMALE VOICE: Well maybe some coffee.

MOM: Cake?

FEMALE VOICE: No thanks. I'm trying to lose a few pounds. Maybe a small piece. Here let me help. *(She helps set the table.)*

MOM: You were saying about pleasure?

FEMALE VOICE: Oh yeah. Uh, where was I? Oh, what I'm trying to say is, sex is the kicker. It's there to cloud our judgment. Otherwise *nobody* would pair off. Once I slept with a guy just to get him to quit trying to sleep with me. I knew he just wanted to go to bed with anything that moved, so I laid there like a lump.

MOM: Did it work?

FEMALE VOICE: Not really. I guess I was better than nothing. Although I tried not to be.

MOM: I could never do that.

FEMALE VOICE: You're forty. I'm four thousand three hundred twenty-five.

MOM: Any kids?

FEMALE VOICE: I have a girl eleven hundred and a boy eight hundred thirty-five. The eight hundred thirty-five year old is a terror.

MOM: So, how did you get to be omniscient?

FEMALE VOICE: I went to class.

MOM: They have a class? What do you study?

FEMALE VOICE: Every teeny weeny little thing. We memorize it. Every little rock; every blade of grass. Everything about people, about men, about cats, every type of gravy, every possibility, every potentiality, ducks. It's one class where et cetera really means et cetera.

MOM: That must be hard.

FEMALE VOICE: It is one son of a bitch. You know what one of the questions on the final was?

MOM: What?

FEMALE VOICE: Name everything.

MOM: Wow.

FEMALE VOICE: When I read that question, my mind went blank. Which is a terrible thing when you're asked to name everything.

MOM: What happened?

FEMALE VOICE: Oh you know, you get through it; I got a eighty-four. Eighty and above is omniscient. Well, I better be going...PMS in Bogata...

MOM: *(Stops here, concerned.)* So you know everything.

FEMALE VOICE: Somewhat.

MOM: SO...what would it be like if I left him?

FEMALE VOICE: You won't believe this but that was one of the questions on the final. Let's see...you will live in a small cottage. It will be surrounded by a white fence. In the backyard will be many colored flowers. Inside will be small lace doilies like your mother's. You will stand outside on the green lawn, your face up toward the sun, your hands will be outstretched, palms open, and you will speak these words: "what have I done, what have I done, what have I done."

(Slow blackout.)

SCENE V

The Logic of the Lie

(The dinner table again, the family of four sitting around. Dad's in the middle of a golf story of which the family feigns enjoyment.)

DAD: ...Phil tees off, lands midway down the fairway but off to the right. With the three wood, I'm about ten yards shy of him but straight down the middle. I can see the flag damn straight up with a trap off to the right. *(Aside.)* Voices? *(Back to scene.)* Phil's gotta fly over the trap.

(Mom and family emit sounds of delighted interest.)

What happens? Phil eight irons it and flies the trap; he's on the green, I full swing my nine and land right in the trap!

SON: *(Laughs.)* Oh man!

SIS: Wow.

MOM: *(Laughing.)* Man, you don't need a nine iron, you need a hoe!

DAD: So now...*(aside)* Voices? *(Back to scene.)* ...Phil on the back of the green putts and rolls right past the hole and it keeps going to the edge of the fringe.

SIS: *(Laughing.)* Did he use a eight iron for that too?

(The whole family over-laughs.)

DAD: I pop it out of the trap and...*(starts to laugh)*...the damn thing... *(more laughs)*...rolls right up about ten inches from the hole!

(More laughter.)

DAD: Phil three putts and I drop it without hardly looking.

(Really big response from family.)

MOM: Oh...ha ha ha.

(She has to drink water and fan herself. The phone rings. Mom answers it.)

SIS: Oh my god it's Jeremy!

MOM: Hello? Just a minute. *(To Sis)* It's Jeremy.

SIS: Tell him I'm not in.

MOM: She's not in right now. *(Hangs up.)* I thought you wanted to talk to him.

SIS: *(Practically sinister.)* He'll call back.

(The table goes to silence as Dad is lost in thought. He hears the sound of the solar wind. Suddenly he stands up, but the rest of the family can't see him.)

DAD: Voice? *(No answer.)* Voice? *(No answer.)* Voices? Voice? Typical, nothing. Left here on my own, with only the images of Washington,

Jefferson and Lincoln. Hello? Hello? I'm living the lie, I know it. Nothing but the rules of the road, the ethics of the lumberjack, the silence of the forest broken only by the sound of the axe getting the job done, the axe never complaining. Truth handed down through the pages of *Redbook*, and the *Saturday Evening Post*. Becoming leader and hero, onward and stronger to a better life. I know my feelings cannot tolerate illumination under the hard light, but when seen by the flickering light of the campfire surrounded by the covered wagons heading west, I am a God that walks on earth. Must be strong, must be strong and in my silence I am never wrong. The greater the silence the greater the strength. And therein is the logic of the lie.

MOM: Butter? *(She passes the butter to Son.)*

DAD: *(Looks back at Mom.)* Her. Once, with one hand I held her wrists behind her back and kissed her. Once, I entered her like Caesar into Rome. Once, I drank her blood. I would repeat her name in my head; it swam across my vision to exhaustion. I saw it flying toward me and flapping with wings. I exploded it with the letters flying off in all directions. I inverted it; I anagramed it. Every word she spoke destroyed or created me. She was the tornado and I was the barn. I remember her in a yellow chair, leaning forward, her underwear ankled, delivering to me the angel's kiss. Now I stand at the foot of her bed and watch her sleep, and silently ask the question, "who are you?" but the question only echoes back upon myself. Oh, I know what she goes through. She aches with desire. She reaches out for nothing and nothing comes back. She is bound by walls of feeling. They surround me too; but I must reach though the walls and *provide*. There is no providing on a lingering summer's walk; there is no providing in a caress. I have been to the place she wants me to go. *(Bitterly.)* I have seen how the king of feelings, the great god Romance seats us in his giant hand and thrusts us upward and slowly turns us under the sky. But it is given to us only for minutes, and we spend the rest of our lives paying for those few moments. Love moves through three stages: attraction, desire, need. The third stage is the place I cannot go.

SON: Jim, can I be excused?

DAD: Finish your meal. *(Back to his soliloquy.)* If I can't be excused, why should he? The denial of my affection will make him strong like me. I would love to feel the emotions I have heard so much about, but I may as well try to reassemble a dandelion. *(He snaps out of it and speaks to the family, back to his vigorous delivery.)* Ninth hole, dog-leg left, can't see the pin. *(The family reacts with oohs and ahs. He turns, walks back to the table.)* I decided to go over the trees but I hit a bad shot and it goes straight down the middle of the fairway. I don't say a word! Phil *(he starts chuckling)* ...just slow turns and stares at me with this look...! *(The family laughs.)*...

(The sound of munching resumes as they fall silent. Slow fade out.)

END

The 'Far-Flung'

by Julie McKee

For my mother

THE 'FAR-FLUNG' was directed by Ethan Silverman and stage managed by Tamlyn Freund with the following cast:

Mrs. Gilbert . . . . Dolores Sutton
Mrs. MacWhirter . . . . June Ballinger
Mrs. Corban . . . . Joan Copeland
Mrs. Younghusband . . . . Allison Janney
Mr. Freddy Allnut . . . . Keith Reddin

THE 'FAR-FLUNG' by Julie McKee. © 1994 by Julie McKee. All rights reserved. Reprinted by permission of the playwright. All inquiries should be addressed to 333 West 57th Street, New York, NY 10019. No amateur or professional performance or reading of the play may be given without obtaining, in advance, the written permission.

JULIE MCKEE is a pakeha New Zealander, residing in the US since 1978. Other plays include: A FAREWELL TO MUM, EST Marathon '93, RON'S GARDEN, The Ensemble Studio Theatre's New Voices '91; New Zealand International Festival of the Arts, 1992; and winner of Synchronicity Space's first Annual Director's Project Festival 1994 where it will receive a further production in 1995. DIG'N ARCH, Yale Cabaret; FREE ASCENT, Yale School of Drama; GET IT WHILE YOU CAN, Yale Summer Cabaret. She is currently working on a new play THE AD-VENTURES OF AMY BOCK. Julie is a recipient of the Eugene O'Neil Scholarship awarded by The Yale School of Drama where she is a student. She is also an actress, a member of the Dramatist's Guild and The Ensemble Studio Theatre.

AUTHOR'S NOTE

I wrote THE 'FAR FLUNG' for a class exercise. I had to use a photograph which included at least three people and was of some importance to me. The photograph I chose was of a group of women dressed as ladies-in-waiting to Queen Victoria for a church pageant such as the one described in this play. One of the women was my mother. She is now 80 years old and remembers with glee that she and her girlfriend Phil Hayworth paraded up and down the aisle giggling to the tune of 'Land of Hope and Glory.' On the back of the photo was a rubber stamp advertisement for the photographer listing his specialties which included brides, pets and livestock. I remember this photo being in the family photo album when I was a little girl. I believe this photo may have been my first theatrical experience.

—Julie McKee

CHARACTERS

Mrs. Corban — 60s. Married to the Canon.
Bossy, over-bearing, formidable and ruthless.

Mrs. Gilbert — 60s. Parishioner. .
Will go where angels fear to tread. Ambitious.

Mrs. MacWhirter — 40s. A new parishioner.
A very superior person.

Bobby Younghusband — Also known as "Happy Day
Washerwoman." Of indeterminate age.
Probably 40s. Androgynous.

Mr. Freddy Allnut — 40s. Assistant director of the Papakura
Little Theatre and part-time photographer. Fastidious.

TIME

Early 50s

LOCATION

New Zealand. Provincial town of Papakura.

* *denotes simultaneous dialogue*

THE 'FAR-FLUNG'

SCENE 1

In the blackout "Land of Hope and Glory" is being played not quite perfectly, on the organ. As the lights come up, a church bell chimes twice. The set is the interior of St. Luke's Anglican Sunday School Hall. Mrs. Corban is standing on the proscenium facing Mrs. Gilbert, and Mrs. MacWhirter. They are both seated.

MRS. CORBAN: Ladies, ladies. Attention please. Shall we begin? Anyone missing? Who is missing?

MRS. GILBERT: Bobby Younghusband

MRS. CORBAN: Oh dear. Well...What time is it?

MRS. GILBERT: Eleven o'clock.

MRS. CORBAN: Well we should start. I think we should start don't you? Let's start. Now...What I'm...I should say what we're going to do is organize a pageant. That is Canon Corban and myself. Actually Canon Corban. It's his pageant and he's asked me to organize it. So here we are. Right, a pageant. And I've asked you both, and Bobby Younghusband of course, to assist. In return you can be in the pageant if you so choose.

MRS. GILBERT: Mrs. Corban?

MRS. CORBAN: Yes, Mrs. Gilbert.

MRS. GILBERT: Don't you think we should wait for Bobby Youngblood?

MRS. CORBAN: YOUNGHUSBAND!

MRS. GILBERT: Oh good, Bobby's here.

MRS. CORBAN: No, no, Bobby's not here. Bobby's late. Which is why we're not waiting.

MRS. GILBERT: Oh I see.

MRS. MACWHIRTER: Should we not...

MRS. CORBAN: No. I have so much to get through and...

MRS. GILBERT: I think we should wait, after all if there's so much to do, then we're going to need Bobby, aren't we?

MRS. CORBAN: No. I think that...if Bobby Younghusband is of the lateish sort, then we're not going to be able to rely on 'Bobby' are we? No. Alright then. Mrs. MacWhirter?

MRS. MACWHIRTER: Present.

MRS. CORBAN: I don't think we've been formally introduced. I'm Mrs. Corban, the Canon's wife.

MRS. MACWHIRTER: How do you do.

MRS. CORBAN: Welcome to the parish. Do you know what a pageant is?

MRS. MACWHIRTER: Yes, it's a...

MRS. CORBAN: It's a procession with costumes and music.

MRS. MACWHIRTER: Isn't it a...

MRS. CORBAN: No. It's a procession with costumes and music. Now this pageant I have in mind is to celebrate our young Queen Elizabeth's upcoming visit to New Zealand and to celebrate the Glory of God.

MRS. GILBERT: What's one got to do with the other?

MRS. CORBAN: The Queen is the head of our church, and that's exactly what one has to do with the other! So, this is what I have in mind and please, please I want your thoughts. I cannot do without your thoughts, so please, please feel free. I cannot do this alone. It is a tremendous responsibility. Now let me show you how...You see the pageant will start at the front door...no, not this front door, the other front door, the front door of the church...and parade down the aisle where we will form a tableau to the tune of "Land of Hope and Glory"...

MRS. GILBERT: Who's we?

MRS. CORBAN: I'm coming to that, I'm coming to that. Now. Every nation in the British Empire, during the reign of Queen Victoria will be represented.

MRS. MACWHIRTER: Every nation?

MRS. CORBAN: Yes.

MRS. MACWHIRTER: That's a lot of nations.

MRS. CORBAN: Yes.

MRS. GILBERT: How're we going to do that?

MRS. CORBAN: We will manage.

MRS. GILBERT: I mean you've got your Indians, your Fijians, your Nigerians, your Bermudans, your Canadians, your Rhodesians, your Irish, your...

MRS. CORBAN: Yes, yes, I know, I know...

MRS. GILBERT: Your Burmese, your Australians,

MRS. MACWHIRTER: Your Canadians.

MRS. GILBERT: Yes and your Malayans.

MRS. MACWHIRTER: Don't forget your Hong Kong.

MRS. GILBERT: Your New Guinea.

MRS. CORBAN: Yes, yes, yes. I know all that!

MRS. GILBERT: Well, whose going to dress up as a New Guinean?

MRS. MACWHIRTER: Not me.

MRS. GILBERT: Not me either. After all, they're mostly naked, aren't they?

MRS. MACWHIRTER: I'll say.

MRS. CORBAN: We don't have to have a New Guinean represented.

MRS. GILBERT: But you just said...

MRS. CORBAN: I know what I just said.

MRS. GILBERT: No, no, no, no, no. I'm not going to be anyone naked. My husband isn't going to like it.

MRS. MACWHIRTER: Here, here.

MRS. CORBAN: No one said you had to be naked, Mrs. Gilbert.

MRS. GILBERT: Though I wouldn't mind, but it's him, you see.

MRS. CORBAN: Mrs. Gilbert!

MRS. GILBERT: What?

MRS. CORBAN: You can choose to be anyone you like. That's the point of participating at this level, you get first choice of who you want to be.

MRS. GILBERT: I choose to be the Queen.

MRS. CORBAN: Oh?

MRS. GILBERT: Yes, I want to be the Queen.

MRS. CORBAN: Oh I see. Well ah, ah, ah, that's...

MRS. MACWHIRTER: The Queen is going to be in it, isn't she?

MRS. CORBAN: Oh yes. Most definitely. She has to be, after all, she was the head of the largest empire in the history of the world. So we want this pageant to be one of spectacle, of style, of superiority, of courage and of sacrifice. After all, everybody loves a parade, loves a maharajah, loves a duke, etcetera, etcetera, etcetera and so on and so forth. She will be coming in last with her ladies-in-waiting and everyone will stand around her over here, the rest of the empire will be lined up along the walls.

MRS. MACWHIRTER: I'd like to be her lady-in-waiting.

MRS. CORBAN: Yes, alright.

MRS. GILBERT: And I'm going to be the Queen.

MRS. CORBAN: Well, you see...

MRS. GILBERT: I can just see me now.

MRS. CORBAN: Well, no because...

MRS. GILBERT: If I can't be Queen, I'm not going to be in it.

MRS. CORBAN: Oh. Oh. Um... Actually Canon Corban has asked me to be the Queen.

MRS. GILBERT: Oh.

MRS. MACWHIRTER: Oh.

MRS. CORBAN: So you see, you can be anyone else you want.

MRS. GILBERT: I don't want to be anyone ELSE, I want to be the QUEEN!

MRS. CORBAN: Now, now calm down. We can't let our pride get in our way, now can we, after all we are in the house of God.

MRS. GILBERT: I knew it. I knew it!

MRS. MACWHIRTER: Are we going to have any jungle drums?

MRS. CORBAN: No, no, no. Millie the organist will provide the musical arrangements.

MRS. MACWHIRTER: What are we going to wear?

MRS. CORBAN: We have access to the Papakura (*Papa-koo-rah*) Little Theatre's costume shop.

MRS. MACWHIRTER: Oh.

MRS. GILBERT: I say.

MRS. CORBAN: Yes, the director of the theatre is a member of the parish and he has kindly offered to assist us in anyway he can.

MRS. MACWHIRTER: Super.

MRS. GILBERT: Super. Has he got any Indian outfits?

MRS. CORBAN: I don't know.

MRS. GILBERT: Because if I can't be the Queen, I want to be an Indian.

MRS. CORBAN: Well, actually...

MRS. GILBERT: I like those what-cha-ma-call-its, all made out of silk and that.

MRS. CORBAN: Actually, Mrs. Bond is going to come as an Indian.

MRS. GILBERT: Her?

MRS. MACWHIRTER: But you said...

MRS. CORBAN: *(Overlap...)* She has been to India so she has her own sari and I'm pretty sure she's not going to lend it to you. Also she's a bit on the dark side, so she'll look very becoming in it, I'm sure.

MRS. GILBERT: Well, who am I going to be then?

MRS. CORBAN: There's plenty to choose from.

MRS. GILBERT: Most of them are naked.

MRS. MACWHIRTER: Why don't you be a lady-in-waiting like me?

MRS. GILBERT: No. I want to be an exotic! Why can't I come as a Geisha Girl?

MRS. CORBAN: Because the Japanese are not members of the Commonwealth.

MRS. GILBERT: Well, how about a Chinese?

MRS. MACWHIRTER: Are they in the Commonwealth?

MRS. CORBAN: Hong Kong.

MRS. MACWHIRTER: Ah!

MRS. CORBAN: Mrs. Pahewa *(Pah-he-wa)* is coming as a Hong Kong Chinese.

MRS. GILBERT: Mrs. Pahewa?

MRS. CORBAN: She's Chinese, Mrs. Gilbert.

MRS. GILBERT: Part Chinese, Mrs. Corban.

MRS. CORBAN: Part's enough.

MRS. GILBERT: Most of her is Maori. *(Mao-ree)*

MRS. MACWHIRTER: She has those eyes though.

(Mrs. Gilbert has sunk to her knees.)

MRS. GILBERT: Dear Lord. I don't often ask anything of you, but in this instance I would really like to...

MRS. CORBAN: *(Overlap...)* Mrs. Gilbert!

MRS. GILBERT: What?

MRS. CORBAN: Get up off your knees. I won't be blackmailed.

MRS. GILBERT: I was just talking to...

MRS. CORBAN: *(Overlap...)* Well, don't.

MRS. MACWHIRTER: I say, no need for rudeness.

MRS. CORBAN: Yes, yes, you're right. I'm sorry, I'm so sorry. But Mrs. Gilbert, this is not the time or the place.

MRS. GILBERT: It certainly is the place.

MRS. CORBAN: Yes, yes, but not the time.

MRS. GILBERT: This is God's house and don't you forget it.

MRS. CORBAN: Of course I won't forget it. How could I forget it. I'M MARRIED TO HIM!

MRS. MACWHIRTER: I say.

MRS. CORBAN: SAY ALL YOU WANT! I just want a little cooperation, that's all. I'M FED UP! And where's Bobby Youngblood...!!

MRS. GILBERT/MRS. MACWHIRTER: YOUNGHUSBAND!

MRS. CORBAN: Don't interrupt!

MRS. MACWHIRTER: I say.

MRS. CORBAN: SHUT UP! JUST SHUT UP SHUT UP SHUT UP BOTH OF

YOU! I am in charge here. Please remember that. And remember too that this is a collaboration and improvisation is not allowed! *(Pause...)* So sorry. Where were we? Now then...last Sunday, the Canon made an announcement calling for volunteers to participate. Tonight we will have costume fittings and next week a final rehearsal. And your job is to help me with the...

Mrs. MacWhirter: *(Overlap...)* What do we do when we get up there?

Mrs. Corban: Nothing. We just form a tableau and stay here. The Canon will say a few words and then we'll all parade out again, led by me, I mean Queen Victoria, to the tune of "Land of Hope and Glory" once more.

Mrs. MacWhirter: Lovely, that's lovely.

Mrs. Corban: Then we will all go over to the Sunday School hall where we will be joined by the congregation for refreshments. Do you both know "Land of Hope and Glory"?

Mrs. Gilbert: Yes.

Mrs. MacWhirter: Yes.

Mrs. Gilbert: *(Singing... The second line is to a completely different hymn and tune.)* Land of hope and glory, Marching off to war...

Mrs. Corban: NO NO NO NO NO! NO! WHAT ARE YOU DOING? WHAT ARE YOU DOING?

Mrs. MacWhirter: Look it up in your hymn book,, Mrs. Gilbert.

Mrs. Corban: Yes, do! Thank you, Mrs. MacMahahum, and when you have done that, Mrs. Gilbert, I will return anon. Are you with me, Mrs. Gilbert?

Mrs. Gilbert: Oh yes. I am so sorry.

(Mrs. Corban exits to another room.)

Mrs. Gilbert: Are we going to have a rehearsal, do you think?

Mrs. MacWhirter: I should think so.

Mrs. Gilbert: So we'll all have a get-together with Millie and go over it then, is that right?

Mrs. MacWhirter: Yes.

Mrs. Gilbert: A rehearsal?

Mrs. MacWhirter: Yes, a rehearsal, exactly.

Mrs. Gilbert: I do love the theatre, don't you? I always wanted to play Camille. I see myself as a tragedienne, you see. Wouldn't think it to look at me though, would you? No, I suppose not. I always wanted to be St. Joan, you know that sort of a part. Heroic, going up in flames. But I had to give it up when I got married. My husband, you see.

MRS. MacWHIRTER: When's the Canon going to show up, do you think?

MRS. GILBERT: In the dark recesses of his limited mind, I know there must be a fondness for the theatre, but I've never been able to drag it out of him. He's an atheist by nature. A gardener, grows vegetables which is why he doesn't bother much with religion. Says it's all there in your vegetable. Take your tomato, for instance. You plant the seed, you water it, it grows, you eat it, you...and so on and so forth. Nature, you see. Very fond of nature. He wants to be buried in our backyard, underneath the tomatoes, but trouble is, after I'm gone, some bugger's going to come along and buy the house, and what happens then, ay? He doesn't believe in graveyards. He reckons I'd never come to visit him in one of them, because they're so far away and he's right, I wouldn't. How would I get there, ay? Ever think of that?

MRS. MacWHIRTER: I'm really looking forward to meeting him. I hear he has a lovely speaking voice and a lovely head of hair. And those eyes, so blue, so piercing.

MRS. GILBERT: Who?

MRS. MacWHIRTER: The Canon.

MRS. GILBERT: Oh, the Canon. Where's Mrs. Corban got to? Yoo hoo!

MRS. MacWHIRTER: I imagine she's in there having a little respite, Mrs. Gilbert, nothing a little communion wine couldn't fix, I shouldn't think.

MRS. GILBERT: What?

MRS. MacWHIRTER: She's much older than the Canon, isn't she?

MRS. GILBERT: Yes.

MRS. MacWHIRTER: Well, there you are.

MRS. GILBERT: There you are, what?

MRS. MacWHIRTER: Don't be so naive, Mrs. Gilbert.

MRS. GILBERT: I wouldn't mind a little communion wine myself right at this moment.

MRS. MacWHIRTER: Mrs. Gilbert.

MRS. GILBERT: Par for the course, Mrs. MacWhirter.

MRS. MacWHIRTER: But the Canon's given it his blessing.

MRS. GILBERT: What?

MRS. MacWHIRTER: The wine.

MRS. GILBERT: Oh.

MRS. MacWHIRTER: Everyone knows.

MRS. GILBERT: Everyone knows what?

MRS. MACWHIRTER: She drinks!

MRS. GILBERT: She drinks?

MRS. MACWHIRTER: I mean, look at the picture. How old's she? How old's he? Stands to reason in my opinion. I mean the Canon's a "rescuer of souls," and those EYES, so BLUE, piercing, disturbing...I hear. Course I don't know, never met the man...and I've also heard that...

(Mrs. Corban enters with a couple of chairs slightly disheveled. Mrs. Gilbert tracks her sniffing...)

MRS. CORBAN: Gather round, gather round. I want to set the scene you see, get the overall effect. Gosh, there's still so much more to cover. But, as I have to keep reminding myself, this is a collaborative effort and you are both here to assist. For example, Mrs. Gilbert, I want you to organize the Sunday School Hall into dressing rooms, galvanize the volunteers into refreshments, call the parishioners who don't show up for tonight's meeting, set the rehearsals and costume fitting...

(Mrs. Gilbert gets a whiff and recoils.)

Mrs. Gilbert, what are you doing?

MRS. GILBERT: Nothing.

MRS. CORBAN: Well, don't!

(Mrs. Corban exits.)

MRS. GILBERT: *(Lying)* Not a trace, Mrs. MacWhirter.

MRS. MACWHIRTER: You wait and see, Mrs. Gilbert, that's all I have to say and what's more, I heard...

MRS. GILBERT: What?

MRS. MACWHIRTER: Oh no, I shouldn't.

MRS. GILBERT: No, you shouldn't. Anyway I don't like to gossip, never have, never will, I'm completely immune to it. Of course, if people insist, because people do...often...insist...well, then mum's the word.

MRS. MACWHIRTER: The Canon's got a playmate.

MRS. GILBERT: A what?

MRS. MACWHIRTER: A playmate.

MRS. GILBERT: *(Devastated, aghast...)* The Canon? The Canon? No. No. He would never do a thing like that. I don't believe it and I don't want to know. Who?

MRS. MACWHIRTER: Can't say, Mrs. Gilbert, can't say. But I have it on the best authority. That's why I came over to this parish. Nothing's going on over in the other parish.

(The door opens and sunlight pours in. A ghostly figure is seen in silhouette. Bobby Younghusband enters dirty, dazed, wearing goggles, hat and a leather jacket. Underneath the jacket, she wears her "Happy Day Washerwoman" uniform of trousers, shirt and tie.)

MRS. GILBERT: Bobby!

MRS. MACWHIRTER: That's her?

MRS. GILBERT: Hello, Bobby, we've been waiting for you. This is Mrs. MacWhirter. She's from the other Parish. She's come over to sort us all out, haven't you, Mrs. MacWhirter.

BOBBY YOUNGHUSBAND: I think I've seen God!

MRS. GILBERT/MRS. MACWHIRTER: You have not. / Oh.

BOBBY YOUNGHUSBAND: I think I've had one of them mystical experiences!

MRS. GILBERT/MRS. MACWHIRTER: One of those moments of ecstasy? / Oh.

BOBBY YOUNGHUSBAND: You know what I'm talking about?

MRS. GILBERT: No.

MRS. MACWHIRTER: No.

BOBBY YOUNGHUSBAND: Never again can I think evil or have an enmity towards any man or woman. Praise God.

MRS. GILBERT: Praise God. Praise God, Mrs. MacWhirter.

MRS. MACWHIRTER: Praise God.

BOBBY YOUNGHUSBAND: This morning I was hurtling along at my normal speed and I had this puncture see, and I was flung head first into a ditch. I could have been...

MRS. GILBERT: Killed! She could have been killed!

BOBBY YOUNGHUSBAND: ...I flew though the air...

MRS. GILBERT: With the greatest of ease...

(Bobby Younghusband faints...)

MRS. GILBERT: Bobby!

MRS. MACWHIRTER: Mrs. Corban, Mrs. Corban!

(Mrs. Corban enters tipsy with two more chairs.)

MRS. CORBAN: Bobby, what are you doing down there? Better never than late. Get up, get up. We want to scene the set you see.

MRS. GILBERT: She's had another accident.

(Bobby Younghusband comes to.)

BOBBY YOUNGHUSBAND: Yes, officer, I'm the Happy Day Washerwoman, I had to wave down a truck, leave my motorcycle and washing machine on the side of the road. Can't miss it, the washing machine's

screwed to the sidecar. Hope no one steals it, no one can lift it.
(Bobby Younghusband succumbs.)

MRS. MACWHIRTER: I say.

MRS. GILBERT: Oh my...

MRS. CORBAN: Heavens.

(Bobby Younghusband opens her eyes.)

BOBBY YOUNGHUSBAND: Saturday too, my busiest day. Don't know anyone who wants their washing done, do you? I'm mobile, I come
to you. Just park the washing machine that's screwed to the sidecar next to the outlet and we're away. Need any references, just
ask around. I'm the Happy Day Washerwoman, ha ha ha ha ha ha
ha ha ha.

MRS. GILBERT: It's the shock.

MRS. MACWHIRTER: I think we should slap her.

MRS. CORBAN: You alright, Bobby?

MRS. MACWHIRTER: Slap her!

(Bobby Younghusband stands up.)

BOBBY YOUNGHUSBAND: I have to confess!

MRS. MACWHIRTER: Oh yes!

*(Mrs. Corban takes a swipe at Bobby Younghusband, misses and
hits Mrs. Gilbert instead.)*

MRS. GILBERT: Oh my.

BOBBY YOUNGHUSBAND: I have a confession!

MRS. CORBAN: NO! I am so sorry.

MRS. GILBERT: Goodness.

BOBBY YOUNGHUSBAND: I have something to say.

MRS. CORBAN: I am so very sorry.

MRS. GILBERT: Quite alright.

BOBBY YOUNGHUSBAND: But I have something to say!

MRS. CORBAN: No, you do not!

BOBBY YOUNGHUSBAND: But I...

Mrs. Corban: *(Overlap...)* We don't want to hear it! And we have a lot
of business to attend to and you were late. You were very very
very very late.

BOBBY YOUNGHUSBAND: *(Overlap...)* Yes, I know, but...

MRS. CORBAN: *(Overlap...)* Now, I can see that you're had a bit of a "to
do," but you're here now, you're all in one piece, praise the Lord...

BOBBY YOUNGHUSBAND: *(Overlap...)* Praise the Lord...

MRS. CORBAN: *(Overlap...)* ...but now we have to carry on!

BOBBY YOUNGHUSBAND: *(Overlap...)* But I have to...

MRS. CORBAN: *(Overlap...)* So make yourself useful! These chairs I'm placing here are to signify...

(The door opens and the sun falls in the aisle. A ghostly silhouette of a Man appears.)

BOBBY YOUNGHUSBAND: Ah!

MRS. MACWHIRTER: *(Hopefully...)* The Canon?

(Freddy Allnut enters.)

FREDDY: Anyone here by the name of Mrs. Corban?

MRS. CORBAN: She am I.

FREDDY: Good morning. I'm Freddy Allnut from the Papakura Little Theatre. The director sent me over to say hello, give you a hand and take some measurements while I'm here. Save time later you see...

MRS. CORBAN: No, sorry, sorry...!

FREDDY: I mean I've got the whole blimmen empire to measure and I want to get a good head start.

MRS. CORBAN: No, sorry, sorry, Mr...?

FREDDY: Freddy, Freddy, thank you.

MRS. CORBAN: Ah ah...Mr...Freddy. No not now, later, later, you see, we're still at the planning stages and...

FREDDY: Aren't you a nice lot of old lovelies, ay?

MRS. CORBAN: Excuse me?

FREDDY: What kind of a show are you putting on?

MRS. GILBERT: A spectacle, we hope.

(He takes out his measuring tape.)

FREDDY: Won't take a minute. Now all you have to do is to put your arms out like so.

(Mrs. Gilbert is the first to do it.)

That's right.

MRS. GILBERT: Oh I say. Ha ha ha ha. Doesn't that feel nice?

MRS. CORBAN: Now, really.

MRS. GILBERT: Mrs. Gilbert.

FREDDY: Mrs. Gilbert. I'm also a photographer if you would like to record the event. Here's my card. I also do children, bridal, commercial, social, sports teams, gardens, pets and livestock.

MRS. GILBERT: Lovely.

MRS. MACWHIRTER: Lovely.

MRS. CORBAN: Mr. Allnut, would you please resist and decease!

BOBBY YOUNGHUSBAND: *(Sobs throughout the scene...)* I must get back on the road!

MRS. CORBAN: Bobby, would you please cheer up and do as you're told and everything will be alright. Now sit.

MRS. GILBERT: *(Overlap...)* What kind of costumes have you got?

FREDDY: All kinds.

MRS. CORBAN: *(Overlap...)* And you, Mrs. MacWhirter, over here.

MRS. GILBERT: *(Overlap...)* Have you got any with tassels?

MRS. CORBAN: Mrs. Gilbert!

MRS. GILBERT: I want to be an exotic.

MRS. CORBAN: Mrs. Gilbert, Mr. Allnut!

FREDDY: Won't be long.

(Mrs. Gilbert continues to giggle while being measured...)

MRS. CORBAN: *(Overlap...)* I want to see how it looks, please...

MRS. MACWHIRTER: *(Overlap...)* Don't you think it would look nicer if we...

MRS. CORBAN: No!

MRS. MACWHIRTER: Why so many chairs?

MRS. CORBAN: Because there are going to be five of us up here for the tableau.

MRS. GILBERT: Have you got everything you need?

FREDDY: Next.

MRS. CORBAN: I want you all to stand side by side.

MRS. MACWHIRTER: I thought we were sitting.

MRS. CORBAN: And I want to put you into groups of two.

MRS. GILBERT: Your turn, Bobby.

BOBBY YOUNGHUSBAND: What? What?

MRS. GILBERT: Might cheer you up a bit.

FREDDY: Well, Bobby, what were you thinking of coming as?

MRS. GILBERT: *(Overlap...)* Should I stand here?

MRS. CORBAN: No!

   *MRS. MACWHIRTER: Are you going to stand there?

   *BOBBY YOUNGHUSBAND: I don't want to come as anything.

   *MRS. CORBAN: You, over there!

   *FREDDY: Any ideas anyone?

   *MRS. GILBERT: For heavens sake!

   *BOBBY YOUNGHUSBAND: I won't be measured, I won't be measured!

   *MRS. MACWHIRTER: Up down, up down!

MRS. CORBAN: *(Overlap...)* STOP! ATTEND TO ME, ATTEND TO ME!

BOBBY YOUNGHUSBAND: I HAVE TO CONFESS!

MRS. CORBAN: NO!

MRS. MACWHIRTER: Yes!

MRS. CORBAN: *(Overlap...)* NO NO! YOU MUSTN'T! PLEASE!

BOBBY YOUNGHUSBAND: *(Overlap...)* I've seen God. I've seen God today! He's NOT GOT BLUE EYES. Piercing, disturbing BLUE EYES. He's not got any eyes at all! HE'S LOVE. HE'S LOVE.

MRS. CORBAN: *(Overlap...)* For God's sake, just SHUT UP! Just...

BOBBY YOUNGHUSBAND: *(In joyful tears.)* HE'S LOVE!

MRS. CORBAN: He's not! You silly stupid...

MRS. MACWHIRTER: She's the playmate!

MRS. GILBERT: The playmate.

MRS. CORBAN: NO! NO!, she's lost her mind!

MRS. MACWHIRTER: She's having a breakdown!

MRS. CORBAN: SHE'S MAD!

FREDDY: What's happening?

BOBBY YOUNGHUSBAND: *(Overlap...)* He's love.

MRS. CORBAN: *(Overlap...)* BE QUIET ALL OF YOU...Oh my God, I think I'm going to be sick.

MRS. MACWHIRTER: Look out, she's going to be sick!

MRS. GILBERT: Give her a chair. Sit! Sit!

MRS. CORBAN: Excuse me, so sorry.

MRS. GILBERT: Head down! Head down!

(Mrs. Corban, defeated at last, sits with her head between her legs.)

MRS. MACWHIRTER: Well...

MRS. GILBERT: Well...

FREDDY: Well...

MRS. MACWHIRTER: Told you so.

MRS. GILBERT: Told me what?

MRS. MACWHIRTER: Don't be so naive, Mrs. Gilbert.

MRS. GILBERT: If there's one thing I'm not, Mrs. MacWhirter, it's naive.

BOBBY YOUNGHUSBAND: *(With well-springs of emotion...)* It was lovely too, really, really lovely, not at all what you'd expect. I was at peace. I was at one. It was ecstasy. The heavens opened up and I felt it, I transcended, I flew through the air.

FREDDY: What's happening now?

MRS. GILBERT: A respite, Mr. Allnut, just a respite.

(Silence)

FREDDY: Anyone here interested in photography: It's my hobby, my *raison-de-tree*... My favorite subject is the pig. But it's a so very difficult subject you see, because although they're very cooperative, they're just not very photogenic. It's an art you see, to make a pig look beautiful or interesting or intelligent, because pigs are, as you know, rather intelligent creatures, but dirty, very dirty, but rather nice on the whole and better behaved than dogs I find, with their bums up and their noses down... Ha ha ha. *(Pause...)* Mrs. MacWhirter, I need to do you next. Would you be my assistant, Mrs. Gilbert, and write these down for me?

MRS. GILBERT: Your assistant? Me? No. Really? I say. Are you sure?

MRS. MACWHIRTER: I'll do it...

MRS. CORBAN: Ah ah...

(Mrs. Gilbert grabs the notebook and pencil.)

MRS. GILBERT: *(Fiercely...)* Arms up, arms up, Mrs. MacWhirter, that's it, that's it!

(Everyone has their arms up as lights fade to black.)

BOBBY YOUNGHUSBAND: 'Whilst we are at home in the body, we are absent from the Lord.'

(Blackout)

ALL: Corinthians!

(A peal of church bells, one chime)

SCENE 2

(Same day, early evening. A tight spot up on Mrs. Gilbert standing on the proscenium. Freddy is seated beside her. She speaks to unseen Parish members.)

MRS. GILBERT: Hello everyone, Mrs. Corban is decomposed, so I am taking over for the time being. Mr. Allnut, so glad you could come to help things along. Everyone know dear Daphne Pahewa? Mrs. Bond? Good. Everyone knows everyone, lovely.I just have to ask everyone to please send flowers, for what will surely be, Bobby Younghusband's brief sojourn in the hospital. Thank you. Thank you so much. Also thanks to everyone who brought a plate tonight. Mm. Yum, Yum. By the way, for those of you who were fortunate enough to meet Mrs. MacWhirter, she has decided to go back to her own parish where she belongs. Now does everyone know what a pageant is? Of course, you do. You're not stupid. It's a procession with costumes and music and every nation during the reign of Queen Victoria will be represented. Well, no, not quite, no New Guineans, I'm afraid. And now I am absolutely thrilled to announce that I am going to be, at Mr. Allnut's suggestion, Queen

Victoria herself, unless of course Mrs. Corban composes herself in time, though highly unlikely. I will be having private meetings with the Canon "himself," on a regular basis, to report on the progress of this pageant. Therefore, I shall need you, Mrs. Pahewa, to make sure the church is spotless, lavatory sparkling. Mrs. Bond, I want you to make sure the lawns are mowed, and the hedges clipped. Mr. Allnut, who is the assistant director whatever that is, of the Papakura Little Theatre, assures me, that although pathos and tragedy are allowed, disorder and decomposure are not. So we had all better be good girls. Oh ladies, we are going to have a marvelous time, just marvelous and we are going to make Mrs. MacWhirter's parish just green, green with envy. Mr. Allnut, please do pass your little cards around. Mr. Allnut is a photographer, you know, brides, children, chickens, livestock, sheep, pigs, etcetera, and so on and so forth...

(As the lights fade, a rousing chorus of "Land of Hope and Glory" is heard.)

END

Lunch with Ginger

by Marsha Norman

LUNCH WITH GINGER was directed by George de la Peña and stage managed by Charlotte Volage with the following cast:

Ginger . . . . Mary Beth Hurt
Friend #1 . . . . Polly Adams
Friend #2 . . . . Katherine Leask
Friend #3 . . . . Socorro Santiago

LUNCH WITH GINGER: A SCENE FROM TRUDY BLUE by Marsha Norman. ©1994 by Marsha Norman. All rights reserved. Reprinted by permission of the playwright. All inquiries should be addressed to the playwright's agent, Ms. Charmaine Ferenczi, The Tantleff Office, 375 Greenwich Street, Suite 700, New York, NY 10013. No amateur or professional performance or reading of the play may be given without obtaining, in advance, the written permission.

Marsha Norman received the 1991 Tony Award for the musical THE SECRET GARDEN. She is also the Pulitzer Prize–winning author of 'NIGHT, MOTHER. For that play, she also received the Hull-Warriner Award and the Susan Smith Blackburn Prize. Her first play, GETTING OUT, received the Gassner Medallion and the Newsday Oppenheimer Award. Other plays include THIRD AND OAK, THE LAUNDROMAT, THE POOL HALL, SARAH AND ABRAHAM, and LOVING DANIEL BOONE. She has also published a novel, THE FORTUNE, and has written for film and television.

AUTHOR'S NOTE

I wrote LUNCH WITH GINGER as a ten-minute play for the EST Marathon. Then I incorporated it into the full-length TRUDY BLUE for the Humana Festival at the Actors Theatre of Louisville. Quite simply then, this play exists because people asked me for it. There is some kind of message here, probably the same one that's in the play, which is, it is good if you ask someone for what you want, but it works better if you ask someone who can actually give it to you.

—*Marsha Norman*

CHARACTERS

Ginger
Friend #1
Friend #2
Friend #3

LUNCH WITH GINGER

A woman sits at a table for two in a popular lunch spot. She is attractive and cheery, but mysterious somehow. There is more to her than you would think.

What we are seeing is a series of lunches, in which her conversation remains continuous, but the three friends she is lunching with rotate from time to time. This change in companions occurs while Ginger looks at the menu, unfolds her napkin, talks to the waiter, or for some other reason, simply looks away. And while she notices that she's talking to different people when she looks up, she seems to accept that this is how things are.

The waiter does not have to actually be there.

The first friend approaches.

FRIEND #1: Ginger, hi. Sorry I'm late. The traffic is terrible.

GINGER: It's O.K. I just got here. You look terrific.

FRIEND #1: So do you. Are those new glasses?

GINGER: They are. Do you like them? Don doesn't think they look like me, but—

FRIEND #1: What a great little place. How did you know about it?

GINGER: I'm going to an ear doctor in this neighborhood.

FRIEND #1: *(looking at the menu)* Nothing serious, I hope.

GINGER: Well. We still don't quite know what it is. My left ear keeps plugging up, like I have water in it from swimming or something. It doesn't actually hurt, it just makes me feel a little further away. Not that I need to feel any further away. If I get any further away, sooner or later, someone will realize I'm actually gone.
(Lights go out on Friend #1 and come up on Friend #2.)

FRIEND #2: This day. Lord. Oh well. What's good?

GINGER: I like the omelets. You know, eggs in time of stress.

FRIEND #2: *(reaching in her bag)* Oh here. I brought you the new Anna Quindlen. How's *your* book coming?

GINGER: Good. God knows who's going to read it, but hey.

FRIEND #2: What are you talking about? Everybody who reads will read it. How close are you?

GINGER: I just have to do the last chapter. But I seem to be stuck on—

FRIEND #2: *(seeing the waiter)* Know what you want?

GINGER: *(looking up as if at the waiter)* Swiss and bacon, I think. And a small salad. And some juice. Can you make a mix of orange and pineapple?

(Lights go out on Friend #2, and come up on Friend #3.)

FRIEND #3: Everything O.K. at home?

GINGER: The kids are good. Don's good. Except he thinks he's too fat. *(She has to laugh.)* I had this weird thought the other day about how different the world would have been if Darwin had called it, "The Survival of the Fattest."

FRIEND #3: You're so funny.

GINGER: But then I thought, maybe that's why diets don't work.

FRIEND #3: None of them work.

GINGER: Well, what if the reason they don't work is that diets are about individuals, you know, what individuals want. Whereas what the *species* wants is for people to have enough fat on them to survive. And the more fat you have, the better your chances are of survival. So even though *you* want to be thin, your body takes its direction from the species and the species says eat. You know?

FRIEND #3: *(not following this entirely)* The bread looks great. Want some?

GINGER: Thanks. I mean, what if the species is really in charge of everything. What if the stuff we *think* we need, love and children and a place to live, are really things the species needs, to keep itself going. Only the way the species *gets* these things is to trick us, with hormones mainly, into thinking *we* need them.

FRIEND #1: Well, I know what I need. A new coat. I've looked all over town, and I can't find what I want.

(Ginger knows she's said too much, and tries to take a lighter approach.)

GINGER: Well, the species would certainly like for you to be warm. What are you looking for?

FRIEND #1: Oh, you know, black, soft, something I can wear everywhere.

GINGER: Like something a species would put on a big black Labrador.

FRIEND #1: Exactly. Or a lot of little rabbits. You're so funny.

GINGER: You'll find it. Did you try Bergdorf's?

FRIEND #1: I'm waiting for the sale. You should try this dill butter. Or maybe it's chive. I can't tell. What's your book about? Anybody I know?

GINGER: No, no. It's about some people who can't figure out why they have the lives they have. Not that they don't like their lives, just that the thrill that made them choose this particular man, or this particular kind of work, they don't feel that thrill anymore. All they feel is the guilt that they're not taking good enough care of them.

FRIEND #1: Oh good. The food is here. Yours looks wonderful.

GINGER: Want to trade?

FRIEND #1: No, no.

GINGER: I mean, maybe the reason people don't change more than they do, is the species likes for you to stay put. Or maybe, after it gets what it wants from you, the species just cuts you loose, and without those chemical jolts from the species, you really don't want anything any more.

FRIEND #1: *(to the waiter)* Could I have some ketchup please?

GINGER: I'm sorry. I should know not to talk about something before I'm finished with it. It's just...well, did you ever look at your family and think, "Who are these people?"

FRIEND #1: But you love your family.

GINGER: I do. I know. My work too. I don't know what it is.

FRIEND #1: Do you believe this Michael Jackson thing?

GINGER: I know. Its crazy. But I also have the feeling the species doesn't want us to know it controls us like this, because we think of ourselves as free, you know. We think we have dreams and needs and all, but maybe we just have bodies. But it's some kind of big secret. I mean, nobody will talk about this with me. Nobody.

FRIEND #2: How's your ear doing?

GINGER: About the same. Thanks for asking, though. I'm seeing this new doctor Mary told me about tomorrow. Are you reading anything?

FRIEND #2: Just *Anna Karenina.* Again.

GINGER: Well. We all know what that means.

(A moment.)

FRIEND #2: You?

GINGER: The new Marquez is good. The last story is unbelievable. About three pages in, I got this incredible sense of dread about what was going to happen. Worse than any horror story I ever read. And all I wanted to do was turn to the last page to see if I was right. My hand actually went up to turn to the end, and I literally had to put my hand under the covers to keep reading the page I was on. You have to get it.

FRIEND #3: And what happened? You can tell me. You know I won't read it.

GINGER: Oh nothing. Just this amazing girl died, and this boy she was so in love with didn't know about it till after she was buried.

FRIEND #3: How are the kids?

GINGER: They're good.

FRIEND #3: Want any dessert?

GINGER: Does anybody ever ask you a personal question?

FRIEND #3: What do you mean, personal?

GINGER: Something they're not supposed to ask. Something you'd tell them if they asked, but they don't ask.

FRIEND #3: I don't think so.

GINGER: Why not?

FRIEND #3: Is there something you want to talk about?

GINGER: But why is that? Does the species not want us to get personal, so we won't realize how bad we feel and won't go around tearing things up?

FRIEND #3: You don't think people know how they feel?

GINGER: I don't. I think after a certain point, people put these huge sections of their lives on auto, you know. Like there's this big switch-board and people go through and... *(mimes flipping switches)* this is my family, and this is where I live, and this is what I eat, and these are the people I have lunch with, and these are the books I read, and this is my radio station and here's what I think about this and this and this. And they don't think about it anymore. So they never try anything else.

FRIEND #1: But if you know you like something, why should you try something else?

GINGER: Because if you don't, then all you are is comfortable. Is that what we're doing here, trying to get comfortable? Do you think it's even possible? O.K. Say you actually *got* comfortable. *Then* what would you do? Go to sleep? Die? What?

FRIEND #1: Would you like to come to the gym with me someday?

GINGER: You don't feel silly exercising with all those young people?

FRIEND #1: I think they're cute, actually.

GINGER: Anyone in particular?

FRIEND #1: I wish. It's really been a long time since I've been attracted to anybody. It used to happen all the time.

GINGER: I know.

FRIEND #3: Like in college.

GINGER: It's not us, I can tell you that.

FRIEND #2: Oh good.

GINGER: It's the species. It doesn't need us to find mates anymore, so it just doesn't turn us on to anybody. Or them to us.

FRIEND #1: I can't believe how cold it is out there. I don't know what I would've done if I hadn't found my coat. I love my new coat. So what are you up to?

GINGER: I'm taking a painting class.

FRIEND #1: I didn't know you were interested in painting.

GINGER: Maybe I'm not. Maybe the species needs me to find something to keep me occupied so I'll stay out of the way till I die. You know, so it can save all the jobs for the people who are having babies.

FRIEND #1: *(laughs)* How's Don?

GINGER: He's good. He's set up this woodworking shop in the country.

FRIEND #2: Is he any good at it?

GINGER: No. He says it soothes him.

FRIEND #2: How's your ear?

GINGER: It's O.K. I can hear enough.

FRIEND #2: You seem a little down.

GINGER: Put your money away. It's my turn.

FRIEND #2: Are you sure?

GINGER: Are you reading anything?

FRIEND #2: I read your book.

GINGER: And?

FRIEND #1: I'm glad she stayed where she was. I got real afraid about what would happen if she went off somewhere.

GINGER: Yeah.

FRIEND #1: I mean, I didn't blame her for thinking about it. I guess we'd all like to start over.

GINGER: Would you really? What do you think you'd do?

FRIEND #1: I don't know. Pretty much the same thing, I guess. Wouldn't you?

GINGER: I don't know.

END

Blood Guilty

by Antoine Ó Flatharta

BLOOD GUILTY was directed by Kevin Confoy and stage managed by Mark Roberts with the following cast:

Tom. . . . . Paul Ronan
John. . . . . Dylan Chalfy
Dan . . . . Chris O'Neill
Pat . . . . Edward Hyland

BLOOD GUILTY by Antoine Ó Flatharta. © 1994 by Antoine Ó Flatharta. All rights reserved. Reprinted by permission of International Creative Management, Inc. Caution: Professionals and amateurs are hereby warned that BLOOD GUILTY is subject to a royalty. It is fully protected under the copyright laws of the United States of America, and of all countries covered by the International Copyright Union (including the Dominion of Canada and the rest of the British Commonwealth), and of all countries covered by the Pan-American Copyright Convention and the Universal Copyright Convention, and of all countries with which the United States has reciprocal copyright relations. All rights, including professional, amateur, motion picture, recitation, lecturing, public reading, radio broadcasting, television, video or sound taping, all other forms of mechanical or electronic reproduction, such as information storage and retrieval systems and photocopying, and the rights of translation into foreign languages, are strictly reserved. Particular emphasis is laid upon the question of readings, permission for which must be secured from the author's agent in writing.

All inquiries concerning rights should be addressed to the playwright's representative: International Creative Management, Inc., 40 West 57th Street, New York, NY 10019, Attn: Bridget Aschenberg.

ANTOINE Ó FLATHARTA, originally from the West of Ireland, lives and works in Dublin. He writes plays in Irish and English and his first play, GAEILGEOIRI, was produced by the Abbey Theatre in 1981. Other plays produced by that theatre since then include: IMEACHTAI NA SAOIRSE (1983), AG EALAIN IN EIRINN (1986) BLOOD GUILTY (1989) and SILVERLANDS (1992). He wrote two plays, THE NATIVE GROUND and DREAMWALKER, while writer-in-residence with Team Theatre Company in 1989–90. There have also been productions of his plays at the Projects Arts Centre, The Taibhdhreach, the Passion Machine, the Dublin Theatre Festival, and The Old Red Lion Theatre in London. His play GRACE IN AMERICA received its American pre-mière at the Cleveland Playhouse in November 1993 and had recently been produced at Traverse Theatre in Scotland. Television and radio work for RTE and the BBC includes RAIC (1984), LAND LOVERS (1986), GRASTA I MEIRICEA (1990), ROS NA RUN (1993), and BOSTON ROSE (1994). An RTE radio version of BLOOD GUILTY won a special commendation at the 1994 Prix Italia awards, His most recent stage work was a new production of SILVERLANDS which was di-rected by Garry Hynes at the Druid Theatre in Galway as part of the 1994 Galway Arts Festival.

Towards the end of the 1980s, a spate of robberies and murders oc-
curred throughout rural Ireland. The victims were mostly old people
living in isolated areas. The perpetrators were mostly young men. It
was the first time such events had happened on a widespread scale.
Photographs of battered and confused old people began appearing in
the daily newspapers. They were often accompanied by "state of the
nation" articles that speculated on the changing times. There was a lot
of anger and frustration in the air.

I wrote the play in a month, during a dark Irish November. It began
as a reaction to the events described above and out of a need to mark
them in some way. It became a story about four people trapped in
time and place and the deep human need for escape. For the first production of it, I used a quotation from the English dramatist Edward
Bond to preface the program. It was:

> "We remain human only by changing
> Each generation must create its own humanity."

I can still think of no better introduction to what the play is about.

—*Antoine Ó Flatharta*
Dublin, November 1994

CHARACTERS

Tom
John
Dan
Pat

TIME

The late 1980s

LOCATION

Rural Ireland

BLOOD GUILTY

Before the light goes up we hear the sound of a French radio station broadcasting a news programs on long wave.

The light comes up. The set could be the "Abbey kitchen" of the 1950s were it not for the fact that there are some plastic bags, milk cartons, etc. around to show we are in the late 80s.

Dan, a blind man in his late 60s, sits in a chair upstage. By his side is a transistor radio broadcasting a news program in French.

Pat, his brother who is in his 70s, sits nearby reading a Sunday newspaper. He speaks to Dan without looking up from his paper.

PAT: Turn it down or turn it over.

(Dan pays no attention. Finally, Pat looks up from his paper.)

PAT: Turn it down or turn it over I said.

(Again, Dan pays him no attention but continues to listen to the radio with his eyes closed. Pat suddenly gets up and turns off the radio. He goes back to his chair and sits down. As soon as he does, Dan switches the radio back on. Pat throws down his paper.)

PAT: No! No! No! You'll drive me mad. Why are you doin' it to me? Why?

DAN: It's my only company. I found it.

PAT: You found it? What kind of talk is that?

DAN: It's coming from miles away.

PAT: And you don't know a word of it! Why won't you listen to something you can understand then you mad old goat? That's a foreign station you're listening to.

DAN: I know.

PAT: You don't know a word of what they're sayin'. It's gettin' madder you are. Gettin' madder by the bloody day. I could have you put away any time I want. The doctor said I only have to sign the form. Remember that.

(Dan pays him no attention but continues to listen to the foreign station. Pat looks at him and shakes his head. He gets up and turns off the radio again.)

PAT: Anything could be happening. They could be exploding the atom bomb and we wouldn't know a thing about it.

DAN: It would be on the foreign station.

PAT: *(Getting angry.)* It would! It would, but what good would that be to use! We wouldn't know what they're sayin'!

DAN: We'd know.

PAT: How would we know? We don't have a word of the language...why am I wastin' my breath on you. Do you know what I was readin in that paper? I was readin about a man over in England who took a shotgun and went out and shot everyone he met. Even his mother. Then he shot himself. I think I know what was in that man's mind. *(Pause)* I'm banning the foreign station. Are you listenin to me? If I see you going near that knob again I'm signing the form.

(Dan closes his eyes and doesn't reply. Pat looks at him. It's clear he is already sorry and starting to feel guilty. It's also clear that it's an endless cat and mouse the two brothers have been playing for many years. Lately, the arguments have become more frequent and direct. Pat sits down and takes up the paper again. He looks at the story he is reading.)

PAT: It's a terrible story...he just lost his mind...do you want me to read it to you?

(Dan doesn't reply.)

PAT: You can put the radio on if you leave off the foreign station. That's just wastin the batteries. And drivin me into the ground with it...will I put a right station on for you? *(Pat gets up and turns on the radio, he tunes it till he finds an Irish talk station.)* Now. Listen to that and don't be like a madman.

(Pat goes back to reading his paper. As soon as he has settled down, Dan takes the radio and retunes it to the French station. Pat gets up and angrily confronts his brother.)

PAT: Why are you doin this to me? Answer me that question? Answer me that question will you? If it wasn't for you I wouldn't be here. I could be anywhere...over in Montana...anywhere. "A year from today I'll be over in Montana." That's what I used to say when I was younger.

(Dan increases the radio volume. Pat angrily switches it off.)

PAT: I could murder you. Often, I could murder you. I could bury you alive and not care twopence.

(Dan puts out his hand to turn on the radio. Pat catches his arm, it seems he is about to strike him. He stops.)

PAT: I'll have to put you away. I'll have to, because if I don't, if I don't...some night I'll take the tongs and split your head open. I'll bury you out in the garden and no one will be the wiser.

(Dan puts out his hand again and turns the radio on. Again, we hear the French station. Pat stands in front of him. Finally he speaks.)

PAT: We're driving each other mad. Tomorrow morning, tomorrow morning I'm signing that form. I'm calling the doctor and signing that form. I should have done it years ago. Years ago. *(Pat goes over to a side table and picks up a pair of binoculars lying there. He holds it.)* Not a sinner for miles. God's curse on whatever it was brought us onto this earth. *(He puts down the binoculars.)* I could be over in America. Could be as good as the next one. *(He looks over at Dan.)* Families are the curse of God.

(Pat stands there looking at his brother, the French station still on. Finally he walks to the door, takes his jacket and goes out. As soon as Pat leaves, Dan increases the radio volume. He relaxes in his chair. He could be sleeping, but he isn't. He is listening to the foreign station. The image should be held for a time, the stillness, the strangeness. The mood is broken by a loud knock at the door. Dan leans forward in his chair and turns down the radio volume. The knock is repeated. Dan slowly gets to his feet and makes his way to the door. He opens it. John and Tom are standing there. Tom is holding the blankets.)

DAN: Yes?

JOHN: Would you be interested in buying some blankets?

DAN: Blankets?

TOM: Yeah. Pure wool. Best quality. We only have a few left, everyone's buyin them...it's going to be a cold Winter...you won't find a better bargain...you're welcome to have a look at them.

JOHN: Look, it's freezing out here, mind if we come in.

(They enter.)

JOHN: Is there someone else in the house with you?

DAN: No.

(They move around, showing their disgust at what is to them squalid conditions.)

JOHN: *(To Tom)* Put them down.

(Tom puts the blankets down on the floor. The French station is still playing.)

TOM: *(To Dan)* Are you a foreigner?

JOHN: Don't be an eejit.

TOM: *(To Dan)* You're learning a language.

DAN: I'm a blind man. I can't see what you're selling.

JOHN: Well, we'll give you our word. Our word is our bond. They're top quality blankets, real wool.

TOM: We wouldn't con a blind man.

JOHN: Come on over here, sit down and I'll show you.

(John takes Dan's arm, starts to show him to a chair [the wrong one]. Dan stiffens. This is the first time anyone has touched him in many years.)

JOHN: Okay, okay. Sit where you like.

(Dan goes and sits in his chair.)

TOM: Want to hear how we got them? They were smuggled across the border. A shop was bombed, you see...

DAN: What kind of shop?

JOHN: A, a blanket shop.

DAN: They bombed a blanket shop?

JOHN: Yeah. Animals, aren't they? Anyway, they fell into our hands and we're selling them for half nothing.

DAN: Did this bomb kill people?

JOHN: What?

TOM: No..no...no one was killed..they gave a warning.

DAN: Is there blood on the blankets?

JOHN: Jesus!

TOM: Look, we didn't get them from the North. That's only a story we tell people to make them think they're getting a bargain...

JOHN: Which they are.

TOM: We buy them wholesale. Up in Dublin. Wool mixture. Better than wool, last longer. Fire resistant too.

(John takes the plastic wrapping off one of the blankets. He hands it to Dan.)

JOHN: Feel the quality. See how heavy it is.

(Dan switches off the radio. John takes another blanket and pushes it into Dan's hands.)

JOHN: Weighs a ton. They'd keep out the frost.

TOM: *(Quietly to John)* We should go, John.

JOHN: Shut up.

DAN: You're brothers, aren't you?

TOM: How'd you know that?

(Dan smiles.)

JOHN: From our voice, you fool. *(To Dan)* Are you buyin?

TOM: It's a lovely blanket mister. Full a colours. An big stripes. Orange, blue, yellow, green.

(Dan is now holding a blanket in his hands. It is multicoloured like an Indian rug. He shifts it from hand to hand.)

JOHN: A tenner. It's for nothing.

DAN: I only have twenties.

TOM: We'll give you three for twenty.

JOHN: He's goin t'ruin me business one a these days.

TOM: Do you mind me asking you, how can you tell the difference between the notes?

JOHN: Are you sure there isn't anyone else living here with you?

DAN: Not a soul.

(John sees the binoculars.)

JOHN: What's a blind man doin with a pair of binoculars I wonder?

TOM: Million years old. But I'd say they're good ones.

JOHN: *(To Tom)* Put them down.

TOM: And women's shoes. Shoes! Pair of women's shoes over here, John! *(To Dan)* You go in for a bit a dressin up do ya?

JOHN: What was the last time ya cleaned this place?

TOM: Yeah, things breed in dust like this ya know. *(Tom is now over by the table.)* Shouldn't leave the sliced loaf out like that for the flies. *(Picks up cheese carton.)* Galtee cheese. You like peas, too, don't you? Mountain a tins outside your door. Why don't you grow your own things? Livin out this far...

JOHN: We could rob you.

TOM: Don't mind him.

JOHN: We could murder you and no one would know.

(Tom looks at John. It is as if he has heard this line before. He looks away.)

DAN: How would you murder me?

JOHN: I could stab you.

TOM: Buy the blankets Please buy the blankets, mister.

DAN: You could bury me alive.

(John looks at him. Tom starts to gather up the blankets.)

TOM: Leave him. Can't you see he's crazy.

JOHN: Give us all the money you have in the house and we won't lay a finger on you. Plus we'll leave you a free blanket. Couldn't be fairer.

(Tom is looking at John, aware of how quickly the mood has changed and how easily they have slid into this.)

DAN: Who are you?

TOM: We'll go, John.

JOHN: We've come a long way to visit you in your shit-coloured bog hole. You could be a bit more welcoming.

TOM: *(To John)* Come on, let's go.

JOHN: A lot of old people have been murdered in lonely places like this this Winter. Know that?

DAN: Was it you that murdered them?

JOHN: Yeah. Some of them.

(Tom puts the blankets down. He sits on the edge of the table and lights a cigarette. There is suddenly a change of atmosphere. A real sense of danger in the air. It is as if by placing down the blankets and deciding to stay a tragedy has been set in motion. We don't know, and in a way it doesn't matter, if John is telling the truth. The young men may or may not be murderers. Things are now happening moment to moment.)

JOHN: We only want the money. Every penny you have in the house. You can live.

DAN: And I get a free blanket.

TOM: You can have the lot. I'm not carrying them any further.

JOHN: Shut up you.

TOM: Sick a this crack.

JOHN: So what d'ya say Mr. Blind Man with the binoculars?

(Dan sits down in his chair by the radio. He turns on the radio [French station] and throws a blanket towards John.)

DAN: I say you can keep your blankets. More weight in an old sack.

(The blanket hits John in the face. A speck of dust gets into his eye.)

JOHN: *(Rubbing his eye.)* You old fucker.

TOM: Some look in his eyes when he did that John! Like Freddy back from the grave!

JOHN: *(To Tom)* Have a look around.

(Tom sighs and gets up.)

TOM: I mean it. I'm leaving them here. I've carried them far enough.

JOHN: Shut up and look. So me blankets aren't heavy enough for you bogman.

(Tom starts to rummage around in old jar, jugs and cardboard boxes. He finds nothing except lots of old government forms and notices, old almanacs, old calendars and old yellowing rate payment slips. He empties the stuff out on the floor.)

TOM: Why are you keeping all the old calendars?

JOHN: Suppose we should have heavy duty blankets just for you. Bogman's special.

TOM: *(Looks at calendar.)* 1950. Jesus. There's stuff here going back to day one. *(He takes an old yellowing postcard. Reads it.)* "The vet will be in your area at 11 a.m. next Friday...August 11th 1961." *(He looks over at Dan.)* Did he come?

DAN: He did.

JOHN: Stop messin you and look for the money.

(Tom finds a stack of old magazines.)

TOM: "Old Hoor's Almanac," oh sorry, "Old Moore's Almanac 1964." Must have kept every scrap a paper that ever came into the house.

JOHN: Are ya goin to tell us where the famous twentys are Freddy?

(John goes and stands in front of Dan. He is holding a blanket. Tom now finds an old booklet. It is the booklet ["Bás Beatha"] sent out by the government in the mid-60s to tell people what to do if a nuclear war breaks out.)

TOM: Look at this... "what to do if a nuclear war is declared. Always have the radio by your side...always have a spare set of batteries in the house...."

JOHN: Shut the fuck up and find the money!

(Tom looks at the booklet, shakes is head and throws it on the floor on top of the other pile of stuff.)

TOM: You have a strange collection here old man.

JOHN: *(In front of Dan)* Tell us where the money is.

TOM: The old fool could be skint.

JOHN: He has money. Haven't you?

DAN: Yes.

JOHN: Where is it?

(John moves in towards Dan and places the blanket over his head. He holds it down.)

JOHN: Where is it?

(Tom is still searching. The radio, French program, is still on. After

a few seconds John takes the blanket away from Dan's face. The old man gasps for breath. Tom looks over and starts to search with more vigour.)

JOHN: I'm giving you one more chance. Next time I put this blanket over your head, you're dead.

(Tom finds an old faded photograph. A man and a woman, standing stiff and frozen, dressed up to the nines in a turn-of-the-century photographic studio.)

TOM: I found his father and mother.

JOHN: Keep your fuckin mind on what you're doing!

TOM: *(Reads back of photo.)* "Hall's Studio. Boston. 1902."

(John looks over at Tom.)

JOHN: For fuck's sake....

TOM: The shoes! The shoes must have been....

JOHN: I told ya to keep lookin!

(Tom puts down the photo and continues to search. John moves closer to Dan)

JOHN: Maybe ya want me to do it Freddy. D'ya know what I'm goin t'tell ya? I think we should be paid money by the government to do jobs like this. We could finish ya off in style. Pictures of yer bog hole on the nine o'clock news. *(He holds the blanket over his head.)* Imagine that, Freddy. For three minutes tomorrow night everyone in the country will be thinkin about ya! *(Tightens blanket.)* Where are yer twenties bogman?

TOM: Look at the way he's wigglin.

JOHN: Knows he's goin to be a famous man.

TOM: Say he was a strong bastard in his time.

JOHN: Brutal murder of blind bogman. Then again maybe they'll never find yer body. Someone'll dig ya outa the bog a thousand years from now.

(He holds down the blanket over the old man's head. Suddenly, someone is heard coming to the door. Tom stops searching. John drags Dan from the chair, blanket still over his head. He falls on the floor. Tom goes and stands behind the door.)

JOHN: Who is it? I thought you said you lived alone you old fucker.

TOM: Maybe it's the social worker or someone...

(The door opens and Pat enters.)

PAT: You're the murderers, aren't you?

JOHN: Yeah. We are.

TOM: We only want the money.

PAT: There's no money here.

(John moves forward.)

JOHN: He said there is.

(Pat looks at Dan who is trying to get up from the floor. He goes over to him and helps him into a chair.)

PAT: Have ya killed him.

JOHN: Not yet.

TOM: We're busy people you know, can't do everything.

PAT: *(To Dan)* Did you let them in?

DAN: They're brothers too.

PAT: You let them in. You opened the door and let murderers into the house. After everything I told you. After all the stories.

JOHN: Stop talkin!

(Pat continues to give out to Dan.)

PAT: Told you about the pictures in the Sunday paper. I told you about that man.

(John empties out the contents of an old jug, coins, medals, papers.)

JOHN: We'll take this fuckin bog hole apart!

PAT: Not a mile from here and half his head gone. *(He looks at John and Tom.)* Savages.

TOM: Just give us the money.

PAT: Told you about that woman.

(John goes over to Pat and attempts to push him into a chair.)

JOHN: Sit down you fucker.

PAT: Blood on her face, her sister dead.

TOM: Just say where it is.

(As Pat is speaking he is eyeing a knife that is on a nearby table. As he moves to get the knife, John jumps and grabs it. He stands in front of Pat holding the knife.)

JOHN: No way Jose. You'd like to stick it in my back wouldn't you?

PAT: That sort of death would be too easy for you. I seen pictures of what you done.

TOM: Just give us the money and we'll go.

PAT: You came here to kill us. I knew you'd find us.

(Pat is now standing in front of John, staring straight into his eyes.)

PAT: Kill me and I'll be on your back till the day you die. I'll stick to you like a barnacle. I'll be inside your dirty head like a fat rat. And it won't only be me. It'll be everyone who was murdered round here since Cain killed Abel.

TOM: He's a madman, John.

JOHN: People talk like that when they want to live.

PAT: Did you ever kill a pig? I killed pigs. Killing you now, killing you would be like killing a pig.

TOM: Look at his fuckin eyes.

JOHN: Come on mister, make my day.

PAT: A few screams, then the eyes would see no more and that would be the end of it. Bacon.

JOHN: Stop answerin back you fucker.

PAT: Make puddin outa the blood.

TOM: Jesus it's like "Cannibal County," remember the video.

JOHN: Keep lookin you and shut up!

PAT: Kill me, kill me and you'll know what it's like to kill. I'll not go easy.

TOM: *(To John)* Let's go....

JOHN: No. *(John is staring back at Pat, he is taken aback by the old man's outburst. Finally, he speaks.)* Think that scares me? Think that crap scares me? Think that crap will save your life?
   (John quickly pulls the knife and grazes the old man's hand.)

JOHN: See. I don't feel anything inside my dirty head. Bet you feel something though.
   (Dan finally gets to his feet. He goes to his chair and sits down. Tom begins to search again for the money.)

TOM: Just tell us where the money is...tell us and nothing will happen.
   (Pat is holding the side of his wounded hand in his palm. He looks at the blood. He takes a dirty old handkerchief from his pocket and wraps it around his wound. Tom looks over.)

TOM: Cover it with something clean for fuck's sake. You'll get an infection from that old rag.

PAT: I got an infection the day you were born.

JOHN: Jesus if I had to live here. I'd hang myself if I had to live like you.

PAT: There's a tree outside the window. Will I get you a rope?

JOHN: Don't answer me back you old fucker. Your life is in my hands.
   (Tom stops searching.)

TOM: I give up.

JOHN: Keep lookin!

TOM: Freddy was goin to tell us when Rambo came in.

(John takes the blanket and goes over to Dan. He places it over his head once more.)

JOHN: Tell us where it is or he's dead.

PAT: I'd prefer to be buried alive than hand you anything of mine.

(John loosens his grip on the blanket. Suddenly Dan lets out a piercing scream that shocks everyone in the room. John lets the knife fall to the ground. Pat grabs it. He quickly makes a run for John. John steps aside, Tom who is standing behind him gets stabbed in the side.)

TOM: Jesus Christ....

(John makes a dive for Pat, but the old man holds the knife in front of his face and he quickly backs off. Tom is now on the floor holding his bleeding side.)

TOM: We didn't come here to murder.

(John goes over to his brother.)

JOHN: Are you alright?

TOM: What do you think.

JOHN: Why didn't you step aside...you're fuckin useless.

(Pat is now standing upstage, holding the bloodied knife in his hand.)

PAT: It isn't a half-starved child who doesn't know who he is or where he is that is going to kill us off.

DAN: Do you have the knife now?

PAT: I do.

TOM: Christ, we have to get out of here John. Look at the blood...just look at all the blood.

(John takes a blanket and puts it around Tom.)

DAN: Tell me what's happening.

JOHN: He stabbed my brother.

TOM: We didn't come here to murder.

PAT: Do you deny it then?

TOM: We were just tired.

PAT: Deny it!

TOM: Just tired.

PAT: Murderers.

(Dan quickly turns on the radio. Again, the French station. Pat viciously turns it off again.)

PAT: *(To Dan)* I said I don't want that! Never parade your madness in front of my naked eyes again! Go to bed! Go to bed you. Only for me you'd be dead under a blanket now. *(Pat takes a blanket and looks at it. He reads the label.)* Made in Taiwan. Warm wash 30. Made in Taiwan.

TOM: I think I'm dying.

JOHN: You are not.

PAT: You are. Too true you're dying.

TOM: Give me a drink of water.

(John gets up to get water. Pat comes over and stops him.)

PAT: No water. Did you give them water?

(John takes a small plastic statue that is on the floor nearby. He unscrews the top and holds it to Tom's lips. Tom drinks, then he spits it out.)

TOM: It's salty!

JOHN: Drink it.

(Tom looks up into his brother's eyes)

TOM: I'm dyin', John. I really think I'm dying'. I'm feeling awful weak and everything...like people say you feel when you're dying...

PAT: Never forget that woman's face.

(John looks over towards Pat.)

JOHN: Let us go and you'll never see us again. I promise.

PAT: Her eye clean taken out of her head.

JOHN: You can even call the guards, we'll drive away fast.

PAT: You did them, you did the murders didn't you? Tell me you did them and I'll let you go.

JOHN: Yeah. We did them. Let us go.

PAT: You can't go, your brother is dying. He can't walk. I'll let you go.

(John looks at Tom.)

JOHN: Try and get to your feet.

(Tom shakes his head. John tries to lift him to his feet.)

TOM: I can't. *(Showing him the blanket now soaked in blood.)* Look.

PAT: *(To John)* Are you going?

(Tom looks at his brother again.)

TOM: Don't leave me here.

JOHN: I can't carry you.

TOM: Don't go, John.

PAT: I'm giving you your life.

JOHN: *(To Tom)* I might be able, I might be able to do something if I went...I might be able to get help.

TOM: No. Look at the blood...look at the blood. Don't go.

JOHN: Why didn't you fuckin duck or something!

TOM: I'm dying, John.

JOHN: Don't keep talkin like you're in a fuckin video. *(John quickly gets to his feet and goes to the door.)*

TOM: No! No! Stay with me, John.

JOHN: *(At the door.)* I'll get help.

TOM: No! No! Stay! Stay!

(John has his hand on the door handle. He opens it.)

TOM: John.

(John quickly turns around and comes back in. He slams the door. He bangs his fists against the wall.)

JOHN: Fuck it! Fuck it! Fuck it! *(He takes the picture of the old men's parents and throws it against the wall shattering the glass. He turns and looks at his brother, tears in his eyes.)*

(Pat is watching all this. He still sees John as a murderer, but he now also sees him as something else. A member of a family carrying the guilt and obligations of blood ties.)

DAN: Are they gone?

(John looks at Pat.)

JOHN: You knew. You knew I couldn't do it.

PAT: No. I didn't know. I didn't know.

(John goes over to his brother and puts his arms around him. Tom is slipping into a coma. He closes his eyes as John takes his hand. Pat is standing in the middle of the floor, years of government forms at his feet. Dan is sitting in his chair looking straight ahead.)

PAT: That's the curse. That's the curse. It's your own flesh and blood. The fondness. You stay because of the fondness. Not a thing you can do about it. Even if you went as far as China.

(John stands up and looks at Pat.)

JOHN: My brother is dying. Don't even know where I am. I'm going to kill you.

PAT: What did you kill all them people for? Tell me! Tell me! Tell me! You don't know who you're killing. I can't understand it.

JOHN: You stabbed my brother. You didn't know him.

PAT: He was your brother. *(Holding up his bandaged hand.)* And you drew my blood. And the blood of my neighbours. You couldn't have done worse, you couldn't have done worse in this county of dead lines. Did you go to school? Did you?

JOHN: School.

PAT: Did you?

JOHN: Yeah.

PAT: Did they teach you about the great famine?

JOHN: Fuckin mad bogman.

PAT: Did they teach you about the famine?

JOHN: Yeah. Yeah.

PAT: Well you know then. That makes it worse.

(Pat looks at the knife in his hand, then looks away. He stares at John, then he quickly goes over to him and holds the knife to his throat.)

PAT: Should kill you now.

JOHN: I promise we'll never come this way again.

PAT: Kill you for all the bad things that was done to us.

JOHN: I'm only young.

(Pat isn't listening to John. He is staring deep into his eyes.)

JOHN: Let me go.

PAT: It was like someone somewhere, far away, made up his mind we were to die out.

(John stands, shell-shocked by what has happened to his brother and the fury of the old man. Still holding the knife, Pat gets down on his knees and starts to gather up the old forms, almanacs, etc. He takes an old yellowing form and looks up at John.)

PAT: Do you know what this is? The rates, a rate bill. *(Reads)* "Paid with thanks. May 1958." *(He gathers up some more forms. Still on his knees, he holds up a fistful of forms in John's face.)* Paid with thanks. Every year, every single year. Owing no one nothing. That was the way in all the tins and cardboard boxes you scattered to the wind. *(He throws the forms to the ground and looks up at John. Pat looks over at Tom.)* What age was he? Twenty years ago.

JOHN: Eighteen. He wasn't born.

(Pat takes away the knife.)

PAT: He wasn't born. Lyin there like a beast in the field.

(As Pat looks down at Tom he is trying to make some sense of the fact that he has possibly murdered someone who wasn't even born when his own body started to break down. Thinking these thoughts, he is off guard. John seizes the opportunity. He gets behind Pat and, after a brief struggle, he gets the knife. Pat is lying on the ground, near Tom. All around him is a mess of old forms, calendars and almanacs. John kicks the mess to one side and stands over Pat.)

DAN: What's happening?

PAT: I was taking pity on him.

JOHN: Least we live in the fuckin times we're livin in. Get up and get yer money.

(Pat gets up.)

PAT: *(Laughs)* It's more than money now. Look at that knife you're holding, that's your brother's blood! How can you ask for money? *(Pat looks at the blood-stained blade.)* That's his blood! Your brother's blood!

JOHN: Get it and I might let you have a quick death.

PAT: If I could put some nature into you...That's his blood, eighteen years of it...that's his blood.

(John is staring at Pat.)

JOHN: Shut the fuck up! Crap talk comin outa ya all night. *(John looks over at Dan who is still sitting in his chair.)* Fuckin mad house. Why did we have to come to this fuckin mad house! *(John goes and picks up a milk bottle, brings it over to Tom.)* I had a dream once, when I was goin to school. About two old men in a room, one of them blind. And I was outside, walkin the land. *(John looks around him. He is feeling displaced. He almost forgets that he is holding the knife. He stares at Dan.)* We spent the whole of the fuckin Winter going from door to door. House to house. The stuff was crap and everyone knew it. You can't fool people. They know it all, from TV programs. Shows about rip-offs. They look at your face and all they see is a balaclava from the TV.

(He attempts to give Tom a drink from the milk bottle.)

JOHN: Tom.

(Pat looks over at Dan.)

PAT: Dan.

(Pat goes over to Dan. Pat goes in closer to his brother.)

PAT: Dan.

DAN: That's the first time you said my name in twenty years. They were only selling blankets.

PAT: You haven't seen the wildness that's abroad out there.

DAN: What wildness?

PAT: Lorries that are bigger than a house. Drums blasting from shop doorways...and the young...the young dressed like they're in some war.

DAN: They're brothers.

PAT: Killers.

DAN: You said you'd bury me alive.

PAT: That was talk! That was talk! That was, family...family talk.

DAN: You said /

PAT: That was family /

DAN: You were going to lock /

PAT: Family talk /

DAN: Me in the mental /

PAT: I said! I said! I only said it, I never did it, did I?

DAN: Every day, every time I want to listen to the foreign station you say you'll lock me in the mental.

PAT: That's only talk!

DAN: I believe it.

PAT: Only talk!

DAN: I'm a frightened man for a many a year. Frightened of you, Pat and the power you have over me.

PAT: I'd never have done it, Dan. You know I'd never have done it, don't you? (*Pat sees the picture of his parents that John hit against the wall. He picks it up and shakes away the pieces of broken glass from the frame.*)

DAN: It wasn't because of me you stayed.

PAT: No. It wasn't. There was the land, the family...I had reason.

DAN: I'm not mental. It was a terrible sin for you to hold that over my head. That was cruelty.

PAT: But it was only....

DAN: I hear the key turn. They're locking me up. Taking away my radio. I hear it every time you talk. Every time you turn off the foreign station.

PAT: The foreign station! There's a mad child holding a knife over us and you talk about the foreign station!

DAN: You know that station is my salvation. All the other wireless talk is like you in the evenings. Talk about trouble and days for lockin doors. When I listen to the foreign station I know there's a world out there.

(*John has been watching the last bit of this conversation. Pat looks at Tom.*)

PAT: That boy is on the way out.

JOHN: Tell me where we are.

PAT: What? What are ya askin me?

JOHN: Tell me where we are so I can get outta here.

PAT: And leave your brother half dead on the floor.

JOHN: You can look after him.

DAN: God help him so.

PAT: Your heart is gone to stone.

JOHN: Tell me where we are.

PAT: I look into your eyes and I see nothing. No past, no people, no land.

(John gets up and moves in closer towards Pat.)

JOHN: Big talk. From a man who's lived on tinned peas for the past hundred years.

PAT: There was more than tinned peas in this house!

JOHN: When will ya get it into yer thick culchie skull that once is worth fuck all!

PAT: There was cattle and sheep, pigs. Stock on the land.

JOHN: Don't be listin your dead stock to me. Give me the money.

PAT: I'll give you nothing. *(Picks up an old rate bill.)* The cows and bullocks I took to market had more feeling and history in their eyes than you ever will. Your face is a calamity from the Sunday newspaper.

JOHN: Where are we?

PAT: What begat you? What begat you?

(On the floor, Tom stirs and groans.)

JOHN: If he died in this house.

PAT: He'll not be the first to die in this house.

JOHN: Killed by old man's talk.

PAT: My father and mother were waked in this house. My grandfather was laid out on that table. But you aren't from any country I know.

(Pat is looking straight into John's eyes now.)

PAT: Go over to your brother. He's on the way out.

(John goes over to Tom again.)

JOHN: Tom, Tom...think you can walk now?

(Pat laughs quietly.)

PAT: Where were you reared?

JOHN: Tom?

(John puts more blankets over Tom's shoulders.)

PAT: If them that built this house saw this night. A child's blood comin, wrapped in a blanket the colour a the rainbow.

JOHN: Bogman, for the love a Christ, no more talk.

PAT: You'll have to hear it. I was born in this room *(Looks over at Dan.)*

He was too. Winters, Summers, things that came and went. Stories about wars that were on far away. Letters from America, forms from the government. Tales of terrible things going on out-side...wars in China. What did we know about wars? We only heard the stories, the stories of terrors far away. Soldiers killed in the Congo. Hacked to death. Terrible things done to missionaries. President Kennedy shot in America. *(Pat takes the radio in his hands.)* They were terrible stores. Terrible, terrible happenings. But in the end, in the end you could sleep at night. And in the morning this place would still be here, sun shining or rain falling, cows in the field. And whatever story we heard yesterday, about the terrors outside...we'd forget it in time. It was the same when the North started. Bombings, "only next door we used to say." But we could still sleep at night. And after a while, after a while it was as far away as the Congo. We laughed at Paisley and that crowd. It was hard to feel anything for all that. It was only when we heard stories of bad things happening to one man or woman...Kennedy's blood on Jacqueline's dress. That was terrible. But it was so far away. It was all wireless talk. *(He places the radio in Dan's lap.)* Wireless stories.

(John breaks the spell that Pat has cast over him. He takes a rate bill and sets it alight. He drops it into a bucket.)

JOHN: It's all goin to go up in flames.

(Pat is still staring at him. John takes another old form and sets it on fire. Pat suddenly picks up a bundle of old forms and notices. He holds them to his chest. John keeps setting forms alight and throwing them into the bucket. Pat takes an old yellowing calendar and looks at it.)

PAT: Tides. Holy days and Bank holidays. What did we keep them for anyway? Every year. Was it my mother who started keeping them? Or was it me? *(He takes a rate bill.)* Rates. Rates...poor law...paid in full. *(He sees the old booklet "Bás Beatha." He takes it and looks at it.)*

PAT: "Bás Beatha." This came in the post in 1966. Telling us how to stay alive when the bomb was dropped. We were supposed to keep it in a safe place. Always have it handy so that we'd know what to do when the war started. *(Looking through the booklet.)* "Have the radio by your side...put sandbags against the door." Sit in a safe corner under the table when the big war comes. Bloody government.

They never told us about the real terrors to come. *(Takes some old forms.)* Brucellosis testing. TB. The vet will call...general election...referendum...dog license. For a dog's been dead for 40 years...there's nothing here that matters...nothing that matters. Why did we keep them?

(John takes the bundle. Pat goes over and stands behind Dan.)

PAT: They said, they promised us it was always going to be the same...they told us to keep the old ways...and we did. We did! We did keep them, we did keep them, did like we were told. *(Pause)* And what harm, what harm blanketseller but we had it in us...we had it in us to be heaven and earth.

(Pat goes over and takes a bundle of forms. He throws them into the blazing bucket. They burn. John still stands holding the bundle of calendars and almanacs Pat thrust into his hand. He looks at John. It is no longer a stare. John bends down slowly and throws the bundle into the bucket. Tom starts sobbing again. John goes over and sits by his side. He takes a blanket and puts it around his own shoulders. Pat stands by the blaze coming from the bucket, occasionally throwing in another form or calendar. They all look like refugees from some war. After a time, Dan switches on the radio. The French announcer is introducing a piece of music. The lights fade as the music from Europe plays and the forms and calendars of a lifetime burn.)

END

Dear Kenneth Blake

by Jacquelyn Reingold

For Brian

DEAR KENNETH BLAKE was directed by Brian Mertes and stage managed by
Mike Bucco with the following cast (in order of appearance):

Tina . . . . Jodi Long
Kenneth . . . . Matthew Cowles

DEAR KENNETH BLAKE by Jacquelyn Reingold. © 1994 by Jacquelyn Reingold. All rights reserved.
Reprinted by permission of the playwright. Caution: Professionals and amateurs are hereby warned
that DEAR KENNETH BLAKE is subject to a royalty. It is fully protected under the copyright laws of the
United States of America, and of all countries covered by the International Copyright Union (including the Dominion of Canada and the rest of the British Commonwealth), and of all countries covered by the Pan-American Copyright Convention and the Universal Copyright Convention, and of all
countries with which the United States has reciprocal copyright relations. All rights, including professional, amateur, motion picture, recitation, lecturing, public reading, radio broadcasting, television,
video or sound taping, all other forms of mechanical or electronic reproduction, such as information
storage and retrieval systems and photocopying, and the rights of translation into foreign languages,
are strictly reserved. Particular emphasis is laid upon the question of readings, permission for which
must be secured from the author's agent in writing.

All inquiries concerning rights should be addressed to the playwright's representative:
The William Morris Agency, Inc., 1350 Avenue of the Americas, New York, NY 10019, Attn: Erica
Silverman.

JACQUELYN REINGOLD received the Kennedy Center's 1994 Fund for New American Plays Roger L. Stevens Award and the 1993 Greenwall Foundation's Oscar Ruebhausen Commission for her play GIRL GONE which was produced by the Manhattan Class Company in 1994. Other plays include DEAR KENNETH BLAKE (Ensemble Studio Theatre Marathon '94), TUNNEL OF LOVE (EST Marathon '93 and Naked Angels), ROLLERS ON RHODE ISLAND (MCC and Shake-a-Leg), A.M.L. (MCC Class-1 Acts), LOST AND FOUND (Circle Rep Lab), FREEZE TAG (Working Theatre). Her work has been published by Dramatists Play Service, Samuel French, in WOMEN WRITING, THE ANTHOLOGY and in THE QUARTERLY. Jacquelyn has had the good fortune to work with the 52nd Street Project. She is a member of New Dramatists, EST, MCC, and Circle Rep's Playwrights Project.

AUTHOR'S NOTE

I wrote DEAR KENNETH BLAKE for The Mortality Project, Manhattan Class Company's annual collaborative experimental event that no longer exists. That workshop was directed by Arnold Mungioli, and acted by Larry Bryggman and Jodi Long. The play was then work-shopped at Ensemble Studio Theatre in the Octoberfest, directed by Brian Mertes, and acted by Matthew Cowles and Dawn Saito. My heart-felt thanks to Arnold, Brian, Larry, Jodi, Dawn, and Matthew for their inspired and inspiring work.

—Jacquelyn Reingold

CHARACTERS

Tina — 30s, from Cambodia. She has great dignity and strength.
She has a sense of humor, and knows how to be blunt.
She wears a blouse and a skirt.

Kenneth — 40s. Gruff. Blunt. Used to solitude.
He has great dignity and strength.
He wears work clothes and work boots, no socks.

TIME

The present. Late spring.

LOCATION

The apartment where Tina works and
the farm where Kenneth works.

Dear Kenneth Blake

SCENE I

Two separate areas. Tina is in the apartment where she works. She sits behind a window box that rests on a small bench, a watering can beside her. Kenneth is on the farm where he works. He stands behind a makeshift barbed wire fence he is building. He talks to an unseen person.

TINA: Dear Kenneth Blake, I saw you this afternoon on the television talk show, and I want to say I wish you best of luck in your new home. You seem like a nice man.

KENNETH: If this is the best I can do then this is the best I can do, but I tell you I'm not sleeping with that bunch of beggars and drug addicts!

TINA: *(She starts to make small holes in the soil.)* I hope you stop drinking and smoking, and learn to breathe fresh air and have a new start.

KENNETH: *(He starts cutting "barbs" out of a wire hanger.)* Telling me when to sleep and how to comb my hair and wash my asshole, and when to snore, and who the hell are they, huh? Bunch of panhandlers trying to steal my cigarettes?

TINA: You say you are looking to meet a wife in the country and maybe a pretty one with blonde hair.

KENNETH: Well, I never begged for nothin' in my whole life, you hear?

TINA: Maybe we can write letters and be friends.

KENNETH: And I'll tell you another thing, I'm not a slave, and the only time anyone ever wants something from me around here is when they want something from me!

TINA: Dear Kenneth Blake, I hope you are doing well. I did not hear from you, and I wonder if you got my last letter.

KENNETH: You expect me to get up at the crack of dawn after sleeping with this bunch of losers and work all day, and pay me next to nothin'—

TINA: Maybe you did not. I hope you are learning to plant, and getting along with the other people that have no homes and are also learning to plant. Have you met any nice friends?

KENNETH: —to grow these organic damn vegetables, like they're a religion 'cause they have no damn chemicals on them—

TINA: *(She puts seeds into the soil.)* Dear Kenneth Blake,

KENNETH: —and you charge a fortune of money by selling 'em to a bunch of long hairs and yuppies who pay quintuple price for 'em 'cause they don't want any toxins in their food—

TINA: My letters don't get returned, so I hope you are reading them, and are too busy to write.

KENNETH: —while they go out into the street and breathe in more toxins than could fit on all the organic tomatoes they could eat in twenty years. And you do all this 'cause you say you have a pact with Mother Earth.

TINA: In the house where I work they have a terrace with plants and flowers, and I think about you. I watched you on that show while I ironed, and was sad you had to live in a train tunnel for so many years, and then they made you leave. When I was a girl we had a house, and they made us leave. I am glad they have a good program to teach you to be a farmer.

KENNETH: And now you tell me I can't keep my pet rabbit in the damn "communal sleeping room" 'cause those stinky bums don't like the smell?! 'Cause I won't give the rabbit a shower!?

TINA: How does your rabbit like it there?

KENNETH: Well, I ain't gonna just dump her! Where I goes, she goes!

TINA: P.S. When I saw your face I think you have a look in your eyes I understand.

KENNETH: I would leave here if I could, but I can't 'cause you don't pay enough money. Even Mr. Greenjeans made enough money!

TINA: Dear Kenneth Blake, Do you like being on a farm? Do you work too hard maybe?

KENNETH: I got nowhere to go and no way to get there.

TINA: Do your eyes look different now that you live in the country? Is it hard to get along with people after being alone for so long? Is it different to have a home after not having one?

KENNETH: Working like a dog for a do-good-for-the-homeless organic hippie—

TINA: Do you wish you had a family? Have you found a wife?

KENNETH: —think you take a bunch of drug addict drunks and put 'em on a farm—

TINA: *(She waters the soil.)* Is it lonely to be in a far away place?

KENNETH: —and they'll turn into a do-good organic hippie like you.

TINA: I think about your face, and I wonder if you wonder about me. Maybe we will never meet, but at least there is someone who knows how I feel.

KENNETH: I may not be able to leave here, but me and my rabbit will not sleep with those smelly animal-hating bums! You say you got a pact with Mother Earth, well, she gave birth to my rabbit, and she don't mind the smell!

TINA: Dear Kenneth Blake, You have a look in your eyes I know.
(Pause, as they both change their focus.)

KENNETH: Dear Tina, Uh. Thanks for your letters. Things here stink. I don't know how to keep doing this, and I don't know what else to do. They got me planting these guru tomatoes all day. My feet are so tired they're gonna drop off. Keep writing, if you like. It's nice to get to know you. They want me to give up my rabbit, and I won't. Maybe someday we could meet.

TINA: Kenneth, Kenneth, Kenneth, we can.
(Scene transition. Lights dim. Music.)

SCENE II

(Lights up. Kenneth is working on the barbed wire fence. Tina enters, carrying a tote bag. She carefully looks to see if it is him. He doesn't see her.)

TINA: Kenneth.

KENNETH: *(He doesn't look up.)* Yeah?

TINA: Tina Sen.

KENNETH: *(gruff)* Your what?

TINA: Tina Sen.

KENNETH: *(He looks at her, he stands.)* Oh.

TINA: You remember?

KENNETH: Uh.

TINA: I come to see with you.

KENNETH: What?

TINA: I come to see you.

KENNETH: Oh. Well, uh. I'm, uh, not much to look at and—

TINA: You said maybe we could meet, and I thought maybe we could.

I brought you some shoes for your feet and some food for the rabbit.

KENNETH: You work for a charity, is that it? Some kind of pen pal United Way? Well, I don't take no charity.

TINA: No. From me. A present from me.

KENNETH: Huh?

TINA: A gift. Like, uh, birthday.

KENNETH: Oh. Well, you got the wrong guy, I ain't got no birthday. *(He crosses away from her to his tool box.)*
(She takes a new pair of shoes out of her bag, puts them on the ground.)

TINA: See?

KENNETH: Look, uh, I, uh, don't know what to say.

TINA: You can say thank you.

KENNETH: Yeah, right. Thank you.

TINA: And you can say, "please let's talk," or you say, "I don't wish to see you," and I can go.

KENNETH: Now, now, how-how did you get here?

TINA: I walked.

KENNETH: You walked all the way from New York?

TINA: No. I take the bus.

KENNETH: And from the bus stop you—

TINA: —Walked.

KENNETH: How long it take you?

TINA: Ten hours.

KENNETH: Jesus. I. Look, um, I'm a little, I mean, what made you come here, I, uh, don't imagine you were just in the neighborhood, I mean you didn't just come to get some fresh organic air.

TINA: No.

KENNETH: No.

TINA: Kenneth.

KENNETH: Listen, I'm uh. I'm doing something here. And it's important. I mean. I wrote you that—but. I didn't. You shouldn't. See. I'm...busy. *(He crosses to the window box.)*

TINA: I give myself to you, and I wonder if you give yourself to me.

KENNETH: What?

TINA: There is no one to choose for me, and I saw you and you say you wanted a wife, and I want to be your wife, but I don't have blonde hair.

KENNETH: What?

TINA: If you want me. Do you think you might want me?

KENNETH: Well, I mean—

TINA: I would be a good wife.

KENNETH: Well, we just, we just don't do it like that, I mean, you don't just take a bus and, that's not how we do it, maybe that's how you do it from—where are you from?

TINA: Cambodia.

KENNETH: Well, that's very far from here, and this isn't. I mean, we take our time here.

TINA: How old are you?

KENNETH: Forty-five.

TINA: That's time enough, don't you think?

KENNETH: Well, well, I uh—what about your mother and your—

TINA: Dead.

KENNETH: *(He picks up window box, crosses back to fence, puts it down.)* Well, I'm sorry, but that still—

TINA: At home it would be different. I would never be so bold. I would always be modest, but this is America, and they say on the talk show if a horse gallops by your house you must jump on or it will gallop by without you.

KENNETH: What?

TINA: Maybe we can go inside to your house and talk more.

KENNETH: This is my house.

TINA: *(She looks around.)* This?

KENNETH: This is where I sleep.

TINA: Outside?

KENNETH: It's a lot better than with those creeps, and I can keep Bugs with me. Suits me fine. I don't need much. Plenty of fresh air out here.

TINA: Oh.

KENNETH: You wouldn't believe some of the things that go on around here. You just wouldn't believe it.

TINA: I would believe.

KENNETH: Well, I guess that's it. Maybe you were looking for a nice home in the country, I mean, maybe that's what this was. Well, I ain't got that, and I ain't got a white picket fence or a dog named Spot, and there ain't no galloping horses around here, just me and a rabbit, and a barbed wire fence to keep out the creeps, so I'm not your ticket to a better life. I guess you can get the next bus.

TINA: *(She leans over the fence to him.)* It's private here?

KENNETH: Believe me, no one comes out to where I am. Popular, I ain't, and I guess you can see why.

(She puts her scarf on the ground, and sits.)

KENNETH: What are you doing?

TINA: I think that you sit down now, and we sit here together in your house...Your feet hurt?

KENNETH: Does a rabbit shit on a farm?...Yeah.

TINA: Then you sit here, and maybe we eat something for lunch and—

KENNETH: Boy oh boy, I don't, I mean, I don't, what you just, who said you could—

TINA: If your feet hurt, it's good to sit and take off your shoes.

KENNETH: Well—

TINA: I see you don't want to. You think what is this crazy—a crazy lady—why would I do that? I am afraid of this crazy lady I do not even know. But what can be bad, huh? What is there for you to lose? You don't have to want to get married. I am just asking you to come here, and we say words to each other, and we see which words come out.

(He is looking away.)

I see you look around. Sometimes you can look around so much you don't see what's next to you.

(He almost looks at her.)

I see you almost look at me. You can look at me. I understand hurting feet.

KENNETH: Oh yeah?

TINA: Yeah. You ask why I came here, well, I learn that life is short, and in this country you have to go for it, or it's gone. But first you have to sit, and you have to take off your shoes, and then we see.

KENNETH: Lady, if I sit next to you and take off these shoes, you'll want to get away so fast you won't need a bus to get to New York. I mean, they stink. I mean, we're talking about stink.

TINA: I decide that.

KENNETH: My feet, well, see my feet are like a hot foot, you know what that is? It's like on a cartoon, you ever see that? They put a match on your feet and it burns, and I got one on each toe that won't go out and, well, it's kinda like rotting burning foot flesh. Not too nice. So, I don't think so. *(He crosses to the tool box.)*

TINA: *(She takes handfuls of dirt from the window box, and puts them on the ground.)* Maybe if you put them in the ground, it's cooler.

KENNETH: No amount of organic dirt is gonna help me.

TINA: Maybe not, but you do it anyway.

KENNETH: Oh?

TINA: Maybe if we think things aren't going to work sometimes we do it anyway. Maybe we are just afraid. Maybe we think it cannot be different. You say Cambodia is far from here, but they write about it in The New York Times. And do you know what they write about now? They had elections this year. And this country is trying to make peace there. How do they think they can do that— now? How can they think they can do that?

(He looks at her.)

I lose my family, my home, my country. I come here and see a man on TV, and he has the eyes of my father when they took him away. I watch him, and I feel a love for this man, this man I don't know, this man I am afraid will think I'm crazy if I tell him. I write him many letters, he writes me one back, I take a bus and I find him, and I see he does have those eyes, and I see—I can see—he has a soul like my family, and he doesn't smile when he looks at me, and he does not want the gifts I bring him, and he says he has no home, and I am afraid, and I do it anyway. I ask him to take off his shoes, and when he says "no" I am again afraid, and I think it will not work, but I know, I know what I see, even if he doesn't, even if he will never know, I know, and I say, Dear Kenneth Blake, I say it anyway, if your feet hurt you take off your shoes and put them in the dirt. I ask for nothing else. Just that.

(He crosses to her, sits, and takes off his shoes. He puts his feet in the dirt. He feels relief as his feet feel better.)

KENNETH: I'm not talking about marrying you, I'm just—. I'm not good at talking. I don't get along with people when I talk. How about you? How about your feet?

TINA: No. My eyes. My eyes.

KENNETH: What?

TINA: They cry and sometimes I can barely see. Look, see they cry.

KENNETH: Oh.

TINA: Look, I cry. *(She laughs.)* Even if I am happy, I cry.

KENNETH: Oh...Tina.

(She wipes the tears from her eyes, then drips them onto the dirt covering his feet.)

TINA: My tears water your feet.

KENNETH: Yeah. Huh.

TINA: Is it ok if we just sit here? We just sit here in your house. I like your house.

KENNETH: Uh, sure.

TINA: I like the view. And the furniture.

KENNETH: Sure.

TINA: I've come a long way to get to your house.

KENNETH: Uh huh.

TINA: I brought food.

KENNETH: Oh.

TINA: We can sit here. My tears drip onto your feet and we can see what will grow.

(They sit. She leans over to cry onto the soil that covers his feet.)

END

The Falling Man

by Will Scheffer

To Fred Einhorn and the fabulous falling people.

THE FALLING MAN was originally presented by The Ensemble Studio Theater, in New York City, in May 1994. It was directed by David Briggs. The cast was as follows:

FALLING MAN . . . . Will Scheffer
MAN IN BLACK . . . . Kevin Weldon

THE FALLING MAN was presented by HBO New Writer's Project and Wavy Line Productions, in Los Angeles, in October, 1994. It was directed by Beth Milles. The cast was as follows:

FALLING MAN . . . . Michael Malone Starr

THE FALLING MAN by Will Scheffer. © 1994 by Will Scheffer. All rights reserved. All inquiries should be addressed to the playwright's agent, Judy Boals, Berman, Boals & Flynn, Inc., 225 Lafayette Street, #1207, New York, NY 10012. No amateur or professional performance or reading of the play may be given without obtaining, in advance, the written permission.

WILL SCHEFFER is an award-winning playwright, screenwriter and actor. His one-act play FALLING MAN was produced in Spring, 1994, as part of Ensemble Studio Theater's Marathon. FALLING MAN AND OTHER MONOLOGUES was produced as part of HBO'S NEW WRITERS PROJECT after Scheffer was selected as one of ten new writers of exceptional promise. His play, MULTIPLE PERSONALITY was presented as part of New Works Now at the Public Theater, where Mr. Scheffer is a member of the Emerging Playwrights' Lab. His play EASTER has generated wide interest and has received staged readings at The Actors Studio, Ensemble Studio Theater, Stonehill Theater Project, and the Art and Work Ensemble. In 1994, Easter was staged at The Mojo Ensemble in L.A., and a production is planned for 1995. EASTER is currently being produced as a feature film. The musical WATERCOLOR GIRL, which he co-wrote with collaborator Mark Victor Olsen, is under option with plans for a 1995 production. Mr. Scheffer is also a member of the Ensemble Studio Theater and of The Actors Studio. He is a recipient of a Pilgrim Project Grant for his play EASTER. FALLING MAN was originally commissioned by Red Earth Ensemble. He received his B.F.A. from S.U.N.Y. Purchase. Currently, he teaches at C.U.N.Y., Ensemble Studio Theater, and for Lewis and Clark College.

AUTHOR'S NOTE

In 1993, a month after my HIV diagnosis, the love of my life took me on a trip to Guatemala, where he had lived for the seven years before we met. By the time we arrived in Antigua, Guatemala, I was both figuratively and literally in a strange and foreign land. I was unsure of my footing, desperately trying to get my bearings — and determined to appear cool (after all, this was only three months into our relationship). While having tea one day at the house of our friend, Marybelle, a trusted confidant and a kind of witch-doctor, I explained to her my hopes for the future, my writing projects and, most of all, my earnest and ardent desire to be of service to others and to do something important with my life. After listening to my lofty ambitions, she smiled at me slyly and while wagging her finger, she laughed: *"No te expliques, no te expliques, no te expliques!"* which loosely translated means: "But darling, don't you know, it is always better never to explain!" Needless to say I felt like a fool, as if she were piercing through my veneer to what felt like a dark and fearful core. Sensing my discomfort she quickly suggested that I make a brief excursion to the village of Totonicapan, in order to visit the Church of San Miguel the Archangel. I assumed this suggestion was her spiritual prescription, a pilgrimage that would hopefully make sense of the growing bewilderment I was feeling.

The next day, Mark and I set out on the road to Totonicapan. The further we traveled on the winding roads through the highlands, the further I felt myself falling into a place of confusion and darkness. I found it difficult to talk, my feelings and thoughts were disorganized, I seemed to be struggling for air. We arrived in Quezaltenango and rested for the night in a dirty and dingy hotel. That night, I had a kind of reverse epiphany — perhaps anxiety attack would be another way to describe it — and I found myself a complete fetal mess as I hid under the covers. The music and voices from the city mixed with the wind and created a kind of nightmare music. I thought I heard Marybelle's laughter, as images from my past mixed with strange visions. I felt I was falling, as if there were no longer a bottom, no longer a ground on which I could stand and say "This is me. This is who I am." I took a picture of myself in the morning. I looked like a ghost.

The next day, Mark deposited me on the steps of the Church of San Miguel the Archangel. He bought me some peanuts and told me he'd wait for me while I went inside. In a small side chapel I knelt before an image of San Miguel, and asked for an answer, an explanation. I heard nothing by way of response. I sat on a pew and cried for a long time. Then I walked out into the sun. When we returned to New York, there was something waiting for me. I had received a commission from the Red Earth Ensemble to write a short play about AIDS. FALLING MAN was the result of that commission. I tell this story not to illustrate how the play came into being, nor to supplement what the play is about. I haven't learned yet, why I write plays. I tell it to remind myself that I have only learned one thing in life: *"No te expliques."*

—*Will Scheffer*

CHARACTERS

Falling Man
Man in Black

THE FALLING MAN

*Wind. The sound of air, as it rushes past ears. Lights come up
on a Falling Man. His hair flies up in the wind. He is thin and his
skin is very white. He wears underwear. He is falling. White clouds
float behind him.*

FALLING MAN: You get used to the sound of the wind as it rushes past
your ears. And the ominous sense of velocity becomes familiar
after a while. You watch as the stars whiz by you like flying can-
dles. You listen to the planets as they sing their songs. You think
to yourself, at any moment I am going to come crashing down into
the Earth, but you never do. At least not yet.
(Wind)
You begin to wonder about gravity. You become obsessed
with it. You say to yourself over and over: I'm falling, I'm falling,
but soon you get used to not having your feet on the ground anymore. In fact, ground itself becomes a concept that no longer has
any meaning to you.
(Wind)
For some reason you can't seem to stop talking, as if talking
were the only action that could give you your bearings in a con-
stantly shifting environment without recognizable landmarks. You
convince yourself that if you are talking, if someone can hear you,
you must still be alive. You scream: I'm alive, I'm alive, to no one
in particular. You discover that you don't like to look down, but
prefer to look up, for obvious reasons. And then quite suddenly,
for a moment, without warning: you have this unbearable urge to
Cha Cha once more.
(Black out.)
*(Cha Cha Music. When the lights come up again the Falling Man
sits on a chair in a pool of light. He wears a hospital gown and ad-
dresses the audience. Occasionally he operates a slide projector.)*
Before I started falling, I was a Ballroom Dancing Champion,

expert at ten dances. They were, in order of my expertise and preference: Cha Cha, Salsa, Mambo, Samba, Paso Doble, Rhumba, Tango, Slow Waltz, Quick Waltz and Fox Trot. On a perfect night in 1983, at the age of 22, I became the Cha Cha champion of the world. *(Slide: Falling Man at 22. TA DA!)* No one much remembers that now, but it's true. Even before this, however, I was famous for my Cha Cha. My dancing partner Svetlana defected from the former Soviet Union in 1981, specifically to dance the Cha Cha with me. And, at that time, we were legendary. You would have loved Svetlana. *(Slide: Svetlana, a big Soviet girl!)* She had an accent just like Norma Shearer in Idiot's Delight. You know, all Vonderfuls and Werys. "I am so Wery Wery crazy about you" she would often say to me. Sometimes I wondered if she had actually defected from Russia or if she hadn't really just hitchhiked to Manhattan from Duluth and made the whole thing up. But she was acknowledged to be the Soviet Champion of the Jive-Rock step, *(Slide: Svetlana dancing!)* a dance step that for some reason only Baltic women could master. This and the fact that only Svetlana could really look sexy in Jordache Jeans, wearing a shade of lipstick that was five times too red for even the most fabulous 1940's movie star, proved to me, at least, that she was genuinely Eastern European.

(The Man in Black enters, wheeling an intravenous stand and proceeds to attach the hook up to the Falling Man's arm. Falling Man pauses for a moment and then continues.)

As I said before, we won the title of Cha Cha champions of the world on a perfect night in January of 1983. *(Slide: Falling Man and Svetlana. The winners!)* And we indeed ourselves were perfect that night, as we moved across the dance floor of the Cincinnati Hilton Hotel. The floor was so highly polished that a few couples actually fell that evening. But not us. My strong arms that night supported Svetlana in poses of inspired and delirious sexuality. *(Slide: Dancing!)* Our footwork was impeccable and unrivaled. We glittered and sparkled and shined. And of course, although the steps we navigated on that mirror smooth floor were uncompromisingly difficult— we did not once stumble or trip, or even slip or falter.

(Inspired, the Falling Man rises to his feet.)

Perhaps there could have been more of a natural passion

between us, yes, but our acting was flawless and inspired. Not for a second was there a false move to our grace, to our speed and authority. And I now realize that in my life up until that moment there had never ever been even the remotest possibility of falling, on the dance floor or off. It wasn't even a question. I would not have allowed it. I was not that kind of a person. No.

(Music fades up as the Falling Man dances with the intravenous stand.)

That night we floated, Svetlana and I. We glided. We dazzled. And for a moment, at the very climax of our passionate Cha Cha embrace, when I heard the entire crowd gasp together at our impossible beauty— I was almost happy.

(Applause. The Man in Black enters and escorts him back to the chair. Man in Black removes the intravenous hook-up.)

You must forgive me for talking so much. It's just that since I— started falling— I don't dance anymore. And so it seems I'm endlessly talking, endlessly meandering on about my past as a dancer. I hope I'm not boring you. Really all I'd like to do is to entertain you. You see, that's what Ballroom Dancing is really about, it's— entertainment and— it makes people feel good about life, about living, about being alive, do you know? And I am a born entertainer. I even used to dance to West Side Story, as a child, for the relatives. My mother encouraged me. As a matter of fact, I'd like to entertain you right now, even in my condition, as it were. Yes! That's what I'd really like to do, more than anything else. "Oh, I'd like to do a Cha Cha but the lesions hurt my feet!" *(He laughs.)* Only kidding. Sorry. Bad joke. Anyway. That night, Svetlana and I celebrated in my hotel room.

(Man in Black gives Falling Man a sip of water from a glass with a straw.)

We drank champagne from Svetlana's silver Cha Cha slipper, which she stained red with her lips. We got drunk, and before Svetlana could stain me red, I convinced her that we should make an appearance at the post-competition party in the Buck Eye Room of the Cincinnati Hilton.

(Man in Black escorts the Falling Man to another chair, lights shift. There is a basin beneath the chair. Throughout the following, the Man in Black will gently and delicately sponge bathe the Falling Man. The action should be slow and intimate.)

When we made our entrance the party was in full swing and the waves seemed to part for us, as we made our way into the room. Compliments flowed endlessly along with the alcohol but I felt vaguely uncomfortable that night with Svetlana on my arm. Sometimes it seems to me that Destiny has a way of making you ready for her arrival. Of creating the conditions necessary for her to be able to play out her cards. Because I can't explain why I felt, as I did at that moment, at that exact moment in the Buck Eye Room of the Cincinnati Hilton Hotel on the night of my triumphant Cha Cha, that my young life until then had been nothing more than a championship performance— a perfect ten absolutely, but just a performance nonetheless. A graceful, well-choreographed, impeccable dance for the relatives. And no sooner than I had this impression, or rather as I was having it, I saw an enchanting stranger from across the room, the crowded room as it were, and our eyes locked. He was not precisely a stranger, for I recognized him, although I had never met him, as Paolo, a Brazilian Dancer, whose Mambo I had appreciated. You might find this hard to believe, but I must admit to you now, that at the ripe age of 22 and even in that day and time, I was still a virgin on that fateful night in Cincinnati, in 1983. And as Paolo and I slowly and inexorably made our way towards each other, my heart beat with a fear experienced perhaps only by 22-year-old virgins, who have never entirely admitted to themselves that they are homosexual— and their mothers. But there was no turning back. Destiny had opened her arms wide to greet me and soon so had Paolo, who kissed me warmly on both cheeks with congratulations. This action on his part caused an immediate and uncontrollable erection on my part, so to speak. And I understood by the look in Paolo's eyes that indeed he had coveted my Cha Cha as much as I had admired his Mambo.

(The Man in Black comes around and lifts Falling Man to his feet.)

Quickly and without too much effort I lost Svetlana, who was demonstrating the Jive-Rock step to a group of enthusiastic older men, and made my way to Paolo's room.

(As the lights shift, The Man in Black lights a candle and puts a record on a small record player. A very romantic Brazilian Samba begins to play softly. The Falling Man continues to speak to the audience.)

I don't really know how to put into words what happened

next. If I could I would dance it for you; I would dance that night for you and not trivialize it with words. After all, Paolo and I barely spoke ourselves. Sometimes I think love is about inventing a private language, an intricate intoxicating language that you have forgotten and now you must remember. But surely you understand what I am saying? That night almost immediately upon entering his room, I fell into Paolo's arms and we began to dance.

(Falling Man dances with the Man in Black.)

That was the language we spoke all that night. A language that was all our own. We danced our words as if our tongues had been burned from out mouths.

(Falling Man removes Man in Black's shirt.)

I wonder if you can understand what that felt like to me— please try to understand because tonight I want us to be like lovers. But I wonder if you can, can know what it felt like for me to dance the Cha Cha with him. I who was the champion of the world in that dance. To dance the Samba, the Mambo, the Tango with him. To dance with a man. For me, who had danced a thousand sambas, with a thousand lovely women, in a thousand sparkling rooms, for me, to dance with a man for the first time in my life.

(Falling Man lets his robe fall to the ground.)

How can I explain it to you. How can I describe it as I fell. As I fell for the first time in my young life. As I fell into the eyes of him, as I fell into the deep of his smell, into the strong arms of him, into his mouth. As we fell into each other.

(They kiss.)

As we danced.

(After a moment, the Falling Man removes the record with a scratch and they freeze. Falling Man puts on his robe and comes down to talk to the audience. The Man in Black stands behind him.)

You must forgive me. You must forgive me for talking so much. I know it's silly but sometimes I think if I stop talking I'll die. That you will forget me. That you will forget that I was a champion dancer, expert at ten dances: Cha Cha, Salsa, Mambo, Samba, Paso Doble, Rhumba, Tango, Slow Waltz, Quick Waltz and Fox Trot, in order of my preference. I am afraid you will forget me and my Cha Cha. I am afraid that you will judge me. That you will condemn me for falling that night. That astonishing night in 1983.

I want so much to entertain you, but you must understand that night, it was as if I had to fall. As if a person like me had just been waiting to fall all his life. And it felt not so much as if I were falling, but more like I was being born. But of course you understand that, don't you?

(Pause.)

I'm afraid I must be boring you. I'm afraid I'm running out of time. I'll just tell you this. Paolo died a year later.

(Man in Black exits.)

It was so fast. I didn't even have a chance to learn Portuguese. Not long after that, Svetlana took me to the clinic to get tested. And I've been falling ever since.

(Black out.)

(Wind. Gentle Cha Cha music from West Side Story. Lights come up again on the Falling Man. Stars twinkle behind him.)

You know, sometimes I see the other falling people around me and I want to grab onto them as we fall. I want to dance with them up here in the sky. I want to choreograph some fabulous Busby Berkley type number up here in the sky. So everyone can look up and just see these fabulous falling people. I think that would be terrific, but it's so hard to organize.

(Wind)

I have to stop talking. I do have one thing to ask of you, though. When I am finished talking, remember that I used to dance the Cha Cha, that I was the Cha Cha champion of the world. And remember the sound of my voice— so that all of this talking will not have been in vain. Remember my Cha Cha. Remember my voice. Remember me.

(The sound of the wind rises. The Man in Black turns and the Falling Man appears to fall into his arms.)

(Black out.)

END

Extensions

by Murray Schisgal

EXTENSIONS was first presented by The Ensemble Studio Theatre (Curt Dempster, Artistic Director) in New York City in May, 1994. It was directed by Lee Costello; and the production stage manager was Ken Stuart with the following cast:

Marcia Jean Kurtz . . . . Betsy Abbott
Peter Maloney . . . . Bob Abbott

EXTENSIONS by Murray Schisgal. © 1991 by Murray Schisgal. All rights reserved. Reprinted by permission of International Creative Management, Inc. Caution: Professionals and amateurs are hereby warned that EXTENSIONS is subject to a royalty. It is fully protected under the copyright laws of the United States of America, and of all countries covered by the International Copyright Union (including the Dominion of Canada and the rest of the British Commonwealth), and of all countries covered by the Pan-American Copyright Convention and the Universal Copyright Convention, and of all countries with which the United States has reciprocal copyright relations. All rights, including professional, amateur, motion picture, recitation, lecturing, public reading, radio broadcasting, television, video or sound taping, all other forms of mechanical or electronic reproduction, such as information storage and retrieval systems and photocopying, and the rights of translation into foreign languages, are strictly reserved. Particular emphasis is laid upon the question of readings, permission for which must be secured from the author's agent in writing.

All inquiries concerning rights should be addressed to the playwright's representative: International Creative Management, Inc., 40 West 57th Street, New York, NY 10019, Attn: Bridget Aschenberg.

MURRAY SCHISGAL was born in New York City in 1926, attended Thomas Jefferson High School and then continued his education at the Brooklyn Conservatory of Music, Brooklyn Law School, New School for Social Research, and New York University Graduate School. He served in the United States Navy, played saxophone and clarinet in a small jazz band in New York City, practiced law from 1953 to 1956 and taught English in private and public schools. His initial experience in the professional theater came in 1960 when three of his one-act plays were presented abroad, soon followed by the very successful off-Broadway production in 1963 of THE TYPISTS AND THE TIGER, starring Anne Jackson and Eli Wallach. This production won for Schisgal considerable recognition with both the Vernon Rice and the Outer Critics Circle Awards, but the next production won him everlasting fame. In November, 1964, LUV, directed by Mike Nichols and starring Anne Jackson, Eli Wallach, and Alan Arkin, opened at the Booth Theater on Broadway. His subsequent Broadway productions have been: TWICE AROUND THE PARK, JIMMY SHINE, (starring Dustin Hoffman), ALL OVER TOWN, AN AMERICAN MILLIONAIRE, THE CHINESE, and DR. FISH.

Mr. Schisgal was nominated for an Academy Award for his screenplay TOOTSIE, starring Dustin Hoffman. He also wrote the film scenario for THE TIGER MAKES OUT (starring Anne Jackson and Eli Wallach) and an original television play, THE LOVE SONG OF BARNEY KEMPINSKI, staring Alan Arkin. His novel *Days And Nights Of A French Horn Player* was published by Little, Brown and will soon be produced as a film. His play, SONGS OF WAR premiered in Los Angeles in 1989; his play POPKINS was presented in Paris at Théâtre L'Atelier in 1990; and his play THEATRICAL RELEASE opened in Paris during the 1991/1992 season. Mr. Schisgal lives with his wife, Reene, and his two children, Jane and Zachary, in New York City and Easthampton.

For the past several years I've taken to writing down what can be loosely described as aphorisms. They've been published in the Dramatists Guild Quarterly. I list a few of them to offer a clue as to the genesis of Extensions.

"My work is like my life: panic-stricken."

"When a new play is recommended to me, I always ask: Do the actors sit down, stand up and talk? If the answer is yes, I don't go."

"It is not the desire to tell a story that brings me to the typewriter. It is rather to communicate to you the location of a bothersome itch that lies somewhere between the top of my head and the soles of my feet."

"We dramatists are at a great advantage. Our audience is not required to lift a book from the coffee table. We can shout right into their faces. Strings of saliva are our most powerful resource."

"Can one throw up a play? I'd like to try it. I imagine one has to first stuff one's mouth and throat and stomach with rotten experiences."

"Often, when I'm in the theater, waiting for a play to begin, I have the irresistible urge to stand up and say, "Ladies and gentlemen, I have something of the utmost importance to tell you."

"Why am I always out of breath when I write? Is there a medical reason for it? I do know the lungs are the most vital organ in the act of writing. Are my lungs in some way deficient? I must see a doctor or ask my playwright friend to watch me while I work. Perhaps one of them can come up with an answer."

"Kafka thinks of writing as a prayer. I think of it as a race. It pleases me to know that we're of the same mind."

"There is only theater. All else is vanity."

—*Murray Schisgal*

CHARACTERS

Bob

Betsy

TIME

Now

LOCATION

A place to put your hat

SOUND

No music either before or after the play

EXTENSIONS

A black void. To the left, slightly upstage, a small, round wooden table and two armless, mismatched chairs, all brought in from a second-hand furniture store. A yellow push-button telephone on a wooden column, angled, downstage, left. An old rectangular mirror on a wooden column, angled, downstage, right. A trunk, large enough for two people to sit on, upstage, right. To the left of the trunk, a Thornet bentwood coat stand with a black bowler hat on one of its top pegs, centered. At rise: Bob and Betsy are seated at table, playing gin rummy. They are performers, dressed in their costumes. They're wearing make-up. It's as if they're ready to be called on stage at any moment. Bob wears a short cutaway jacket; complimentary pants, a garish vest, black butterfly tie, ankle-high shoes, a fake carnation in lapel. Betsy wears a vintage sailor-style skirt and blouse: a white skirt, pleated, a blue naval blouse, a narrow ribbon with bow in her hair, beige shoes with an ankle strap.

BOB: Betsy? *(Betsy is preoccupied with her cards. Bob shouts in a panic.)* Betsy!

BETSY: *(Startled.)* What? What is it?

(The actors perform, self-dramatize the following lines, to get one another's sympathy, approval, interest, affection, concern, etc. The lines are not said in anger or confrontationally.)

BOB: Why didn't you answer me the first time? Why do I have to repeat everything twice? Do you get pleasure out of ignoring me? filling me with anxiety? apprehension? insecurity? Is this some kind of new sadistic game you're playing?

BETSY: I didn't hear you, Bob. I was concentrating on the cards. It's as simple as that. Don't complicate things, please. Now what do you want?

BOB: *(Sighs.)* What are we gonna do?

BETSY: I don't know what we're gonna do. How am I supposed to know? We have to pass the time; we have to keep busy; we have to be helpful and supportive; we have to be considerate and affectionate; we have to observe the amenities; that's all I know.

BOB: Can we do this forever? Aren't there limitations? When do we reach a point where we collapse? suffer an emotional breakdown? fall prey to various nervous disorders or worse?

BETSY: Don't ask me. You're asking the wrong person. I don't have the faintest idea. Don't forget, I haven't had this experience before either.

BOB: *(Moves downstage, right of table, to phone.)* It's like we dropped out of life.

BETSY: That's what it's like.

BOB: It's like the earth swallowed us up and nobody knows we're still alive.

BETSY: I never thought it would happen, not in a million years.

BOB: Who could have imagined it?

BETSY: No one. Absolutely no one.

BOB: *(Moves upstage, left of table, to his chair.)* I'm humiliated. I'm embarrassed. I'm ashamed to walk out the door. What if I run into somebody I know? What if he asks me what I've been doing with myself? How do I explain it to him?

BETSY: Don't even try.

BOB: He wouldn't believe me.

BETSY: He wouldn't. Practically speaking, though, the chances of you running into anyone we know is practically nil.

BOB: That's true. They're all gone. Vanished. Disappeared. *(He sits in his chair.)* But we used to know a lot of people, didn't we?

BETSY: Are you kidding? Are *you* kidding? We used to know thousands of people, literally and actually thousands of people.

(They pronounce each name with exaggeration, reverentially.)

BOB: Do you remember Mr. and Mrs. Françoise De Pre Labouchere?

BETSY: Of course I remember the De Pre Laboucheres. They owned a rooming house in Charleston, South Carolina. We used to play badminton with them every afternoon. Do you remember Josiah Burbank Skeffington Bixbie?

BOB: The juggler with the Canadian circus. He taught me to catch steelhead trout in that lake near Toronto. *(Relishing each syllable.)* Josiah Burbank Skeffington Bixbie.

BETSY: There was a Mr. and Mrs. Raymond Buttenwiser.

BOB: From Mapleville, Indiana. *(Pronouncing another name from the past.)* Mrs. Cassandra Cartwright Cederquist.

BETSY: From Topeka, Kansas. She taught me applique and how to braise a leg of lamb. I believe she was a friend of... Sir Cedric Percival Lumpkin.

BOB/BETSY: *(Simultaneously.)* From Sherman Oaks, California!

BOB: I once played baseball with Sir Cedric in a nudist camp in Topanga Canyon.

BETSY: I didn't know that.

BOB: That I was in a nudist camp?

BETSY: No, that you played baseball.

BOB: I didn't really play. *(Rises.)* I just stood in the outfield, sunning myself. *(Expansively; moves downstage, right, to mirror.)* What a day it was. What a gorgeous day. It made a person feel good to be alive.

BETSY: We knew thousands of people, thousands of them. We were so popular.

BOB: *(Turns to her after a glance in the mirror.)* I couldn't walk down the street without bumping into somebody I knew.

BETSY: I couldn't stick my head out the window without someone yelling, "Hey, Betsy, how you doin', honey?"

BOB: "Hey, how's it goin' there, Bobby? How are tricks?" They used to yell at me from their cars, from their...

BETSY: "Yoo-hoo, Betsy, yoo-hoo! Remember me from the Players Club in Philadelphia?"

BOB: "How about a drink with us after the show, Bobby-old-boy?" They were always buying me drinks. I used to say to them, I'd say, "Hey, fellows, I don't drink. Stop wasting your money!" But they wouldn't listen to me!

BETSY: The same with me! They'd buy me gifts and presents and almost every morning I'd wake up and find outside my door flowers and boxes of chocolate-covered strawberries.

BOB: You know, when we first started out together...

BETSY: Seventeen years ago. The same year we were married.

BOB: *(Moves upstage to take hat from coat stand.)* The only vaudeville act in the country. *(Moves downstage, center.)*

BETSY: The last of a long theatrical tradition. *(She moves to stand beside Bob, shoulder-to-shoulder. They do a bit of their act, out front to an imaginary audience.)*

BOB: What did you do yesterday, Betsy?

BETSY: Oh, we had a lovely time. We all went over to my cousin's pool.

BOB: Your cousin's pool? That does sound like fun.

BETSY: Oh, yes, we went swimming and diving...

BOB: Swimming and diving, huh?

BETSY: And we'll have even more fun tomorrow.

BOB: Why will you have more fun tomorrow?

BETSY: Because that's when they put the water in the pool! *(They take bows, wave; Bob tips his hat to imaginary audience, loops his arm for Betsy to take hold of it as they move upstage, making their exit, upstage, center, with Betsy throwing kisses to her "fans.")*

BOB: *(During above; filling in for "audience.")* Laughter, laughter, laughter, laughter, laughter, laughter, the audience is laughing, keeps laughing, they can't stop laughing... *(Betsy moves to sit on right end of trunk as Bob tosses his hat on coat stand, turns to her and speaks at once after last "laughing" word.)*

BOB: For cryin'-out-loud, we used to turn down jobs!

BETSY: We couldn't keep up with them. The phone was ringing from the minute we got up!

BOB: *(Sits next to Betsy on trunk.)* All day, whether we were in or not!

BETSY: The phone would ring and ring, ring and ring...

BOB: *(Picks up imaginary phone from his lap; holds fist to ear to represent phone.)* "Hello, who is this? Why the hell are you calling me so damn early in the morning?" *(They play at being awakened by the "ringing phone": they speak drowsily, yawn; Betsy wraps her arm around Bob's shoulder, drapes her leg between his thighs, presses her head to him.)*

BETSY: *(Takes "phone" from him.)* "Do you know what time it is? This is un-for-giveable."

BOB: *(Leans over to speak into the "phone" which she holds out to him.)* "We worked until four in the A.M., for cryin'-out-loud!"

BETSY: "We're unavailable, Liebling. Get the Cunninghams."

BOB: *(Takes the "phone" from her.)* "How about the Pappadellas? Use them. We're exhausted!" *(Holds out "phone" to her.)*

BETSY: "It's no use begging. We can't do it.." *(And Bob returns "phone" to cradle" on his lap.)*

BOB: Incredible.

BETSY: It's incredible.

BOB: *(Moves to phone.)* Not to hear from Liebling...How long is it?

BETSY: *(Moves to her chair at table.)* Weeks, months, years...I don't know anymore. The last job we got from him was the Resorts

Lounge. In Atlantic City.

BOB: Were we bad there?

BETSY: Bad? What are you talking about? We were wonderful! Fantastic!

BOB: And before that? In Miami?

BETSY: We got a standing ovation, for God sakes!

BOB: *(Moves upstage, left; sits in his chair.)* And...Reno? How were we in Reno?

BETSY: *(Sits in her chair.)* Are you losing your mind? The owner himself came over to us and said, "I want you guys back. Tell Liebling to call me."

BOB: *(Looking off.)* The owner himself said, "Tell Liebling to call me. I want you guys back."

BETSY: Bob? *(No response from him. In a panic:)* Bob!

BOB: *(Now hears her.)* Yeah?

BETSY: What was that for? Are you trying to get even with me because I didn't hear you before? Are you being spiteful? vindictive? deliberately and ruthlessly cruel? If I call your name, if I seek your attention, it seems to me a simple act of courtesy to respond without scaring me to death!

BOB: I didn't hear you. I did not hear you. Why are you making such a big deal out of it? Now whatta you want?

BETSY: Why don't we get out of these costumes and get into something more comfortable?

BOB: And if Liebling calls?

BETSY: We'll get back into our costumes.

BOB: But what if he calls and has a job for us and we have to be on a bus or a plane or a train in five, ten, twenty minutes? Whatta we do then?

BETSY: The chances of that happening are so... *("remote"... She decides not to disagree.)* You're right. It doesn't hurt to be ready.

BOB: You never know in this business.

BETSY: You don't know.

BOB: Would you be surprised if you learned that at this very minute Liebling is negotiating a deal for us to play two weeks in Acapulco?

BETSY: Not at all. Why should I be surprised? That's what the man does for a living.

BOB: We still have a reputation.

BETSY: Are you kidding? Are *you* kidding? We walk on the stage now, right now, and there'll be people in the audience who'll stand up on their feet and yell for all they're worth, "Bravo! Bravo! We love you, Betsy and Bob!"

BOB: They would. I know they would. *(Rises.)* "Bravo! Bravo! We love you…" *(Points to himself.)* "Bob and Betsy!" *(He grabs his hat, puts it on, moves downstage, center. Betsy joins him. They stand shoulder-to-shoulder; do a bit of their act, out front to an imaginary audience.)* So how's your cousin feeling these days?

BETSY: Oh, fine. Only the other night she was sleeping and in the middle of the night, she let out an awful scream.

BOB: What happened?

BETSY: Well, she looked down and saw that her feet were all black. *(Looks down at her feet.)*

BOB: Her feet were all black? What did you do?

BETSY: We sent for the doctor.

BOB: And what did he do?

BETSY: He took off her socks!

BOB: *(Points at her.)* Ohhhhh… *(Segues into "Ain't She Sweet" or some other such standard tune. After he sings the first line Betsy joins singing, does a little soft-shoe dance step. They sing the next two lines and Bob joins Betsy in soft-shoe move, possibly a "grapevine" set across the stage. They continue singing AABA of song. Still singing, humming, they move to table. Bob pulls out Betsy's chair for her; she sits. Bob moves upstage, puts hat on coat stand and sits in his chair. They resume playing cards. Humming the song, Betsy knocks on the table, emphatically, three times.)*

BETSY: Three points.
(She lays her cards faceup on the table and plucks Bob's cards from his hand. Bob stares at her, his mouth hanging open. Betsy counts points she has won from Bob's cards.)
Seven, twelve, fourteen, twenty-one… *(Continues murmuring the numbers.)*

BOB: Betsy? *(Betsy is writing the number of points she won on a pad. In a panic:)* Betsy!

BETSY: *(Now hears him.)* Yes?

BOB: Don't do this to me! It's unnerving. It's anxiety-provoking. It's a vicious cycle and there's gonna be no end to it if you don't answer when I call your name!

BETSY: How can I answer when I didn't hear you? I didn't literally and actually hear you. That's a physical fact.

BOB: *(Rises.)* Then see a doctor. Go to a hospital. Take care of your deficiencies so we can have some sanity in this household! *(Moves downstage, right.)*

BETSY: I will. I'll go to Doctor Barnes. Now what do you want?

BOB: *(Moves to left of table.)* I wanna know why you're knocking with three points! Why don't you play out your hand for gin rummy? *(Betsy shuffles cards. Bob moves upstage, left, to his chair.)* It's stupid to knock with three points after playing this lengthy period of time. If you want to win at this game, you go for gin rummy!

BETSY: May I speak without irritating you?

BOB: *(He sits.)* As you well know, irritation is not one of my foibles. *(He crosses his leg.)*

BETSY: I'll accept that, but let me make a personal, heartfelt plea. Let's not argue, sweetheart. I beg you. I beseech you. We're both very wrought up, very anxious, very at the end of our emotional tether. One of us could say the wrong word and we'll start yelling, we'll start fighting, we'll be vindictive, vicious, vituperative, and before you know it, we'll be utterly and irredeemably miserable. Besides... *(Tone changes to one of arrogance; puts pad in front of him.)* ...I have sixty-seven points and you have three points. I am winning. You are losing. Need more be said on the subject?

(Deeply offended, tight-lipped and grave, Bob picks up cards and deals out a new hand. Betsy continues humming, whistling "Ain't She Sweet" or some such tune. They spread their cards in their hands. Betsy picks up a card from desk, discards it. Bob picks up a card, discards another card; he spreads his cards faceup on the table.)

BOB: Gin Rummy. *(Bob plucks the cards out of Betsy's hand and counts them.)* Six, sixteen, twenty-four, twenty-eight... *(Continues murmuring the numbers before he writes the points he's won on pad.)* That gives me seventy-one points and you sixty-seven points. I am winning. You are losing. Need more be said on the subject? You deal.

BETSY: *(Stares front; folds arms.)* I'm not playing anymore.

BOB: Oh, when you're winning you'll play the whole night. But when you're losing, you sulk; you pout; you refuse to be a sportsman, a person who says win or lose I will play the game with dignity and sophistication. You're a baby, do you know that? You're a big, spoiled baby!

BETSY: *(Turns to him.)* I'm a big, spoiled baby! What do you call yourself?

BOB: A decent human being. *(Folds arms; stares front.)*

BETSY: Ha! Don't make me laugh! Your mother spoiled you so badly...

BOB: *(Through clenched teeth; points finger at her.)* Watch... Watch what you're saying. You are opening up a Pandora's box when you bring *my mother* into our discussions!

BETSY: *(He's right.)* I...I'm sorry. I apologize. I lost my head. I... I just... *(Looks to phone; in despair.)* Why doesn't the phone ring? Why doesn't Liebling call us? Why doesn't anyone call us?

BOB: *(She's right.)* It's amazing.

BETSY: And you know what hurts? You know what really hurts? We don't even get wrong numbers anymore!

BOB: It's positively amazing: It defies understanding. It... *(A thought.)* Wait a second. Wait...one...second.

BETSY: What? What is it?

BOB: When was the last time we checked the phone... *(Said quickly.)* ...to see if it was working?

BETSY: *(Looking at wristwatch.)* Sixteen minutes and nine seconds ago.

BOB: Betwixt and between, one doesn't know. A lot could have happened in sixteen minutes and nine seconds. I'll check it out. *(Moves to coat stand; puts on hat; breathes deeply; crosses with resolution to phone; breathes deeply, his face tense and flushed; he snaps up the phone; presses it to his ear.)*

BETSY: Is it working? Do you get a dial tone? Do you hear any voices? Any buzzes or static? Is there any indication that it's operational, functioning-wise? *(Bob moves to the far right; the extension cord trails after him. Betsy rises. In a panic:)* Bob, answer me! For God sakes, why don't you answer me? Why do you persist in torturing me? What pleasure could you possibly... *(Bob waves for her to be quiet.)*

BOB: *(Puffed up; loudly; into phone.)* Is there anyone who would like to talk to me? *(A beat.)* Is there anyone out there who has anything to say to me? *(A beat.)* My name is Bob Abbott. *(He opens up his arm for Betsy to join him. She moves to him. His arm presses her to him.)* I'm with Betsy Abbott. We are entertainers. Of some reputation. *(A beat.)* I am waiting for a reply. *(A few beats and, deflated, he walks around Betsy to return phone to cradle, inadvertently wrapping extension cord around her. The extension cord doesn't permit him to reach the cradle after moving approximately six feet past her. He turns, walks around Betsy. and crosses downstage to put phone into cradle.)*

BETSY: Was the phone working?

BOB: *(Faces front, turning hat in hand, looking at it.)* It's working.

BETSY: Someone picked up at the other end?

BOB: No. No one picked up.

BETSY: Who were you talking to?

BOB: The dial tone. *(Bob moves upstage, puts hat on table, sits in his chair. Betsy follows him upstage.)*

BETSY: Bob, sweetheart, I know we discussed this before. *(She gets down on her knees to right of Bob, holds his hands.)* I know your reservations, but...in view of the prevailing circumstances, why don't you let me call Liebling? I'm not as superstitious as you are. I don't have your mystical leanings, your...

BOB: *(Gets down on his knees, holds Betsy's hands.)* It's not a question of superstition or mystical leanings. It's a question of logic, of science, of mathematical probabilities. In all the years Liebling has been our agent, have we ever called him out of the blue, of our own free will and volition, and did we ever get a job as a result of that call?

BETSY: Uh-uh.

BOB: Or has he ever said when we called him, "You can't imagine how happy I am you called me."

BETSY: Uh-uh.

BOB: What has he said when we called him of our own free will and volition?

BETSY: "What was that name again?"

BOB: After being his client for how long?

BETSY: Seventeen years. The same year we were married.

BOB: Did he say anything else to us?

BETSY: Yes.

BOB: What?

BETSY: "We overpaid you on your last check."

BOB: And?

BETSY: "Send us the difference. Immediately."

BOB: That's what he said. After seventeen years. *(Bob helps Betsy to her feet.)* You look at our history with that man and you'll see that logically and mathematically, we never got a job when we called him first. *(He moves downstage, putting his hat on the toe of his raised shoe, balancing himself on one foot.)*

BETSY: It's true. Unfortunately, it's true. *(A beat.)* Bob? *(Bob kicks his foot up, sending the hat flying above his head, meaning for it to land perfectly on his head. But Betsy throws him off with a shout of panic.)* Bob! *(And Bob cowers and winces as the brim of the hat bounces off his head; he catches it as it falls.)* There! You're doing it again! You're deliberately causing me unnecessary stress and apprehension and...

BOB: All right, all right, don't make a federal case out of it! I didn't hear you. Whatta you want?

BETSY: I agree with you about not calling Liebling. But when it comes to our relatives and what few friends we have left...Would it hurt if I gave one of them a ring? As a reminder we're still alive? *(Bob puts his hat back on the coat stand. Betsy follows him upstage; sits on trunk.)*

BOB: Oh, they're quite a bunch, our relatives and so-called friends, including our so-called best friends, George and Maryann Eigenberg. When we were working, when we could give them free tickets to shows and pick up their tabs for dinner and hotel rooms, they were there, they were all around us, like flies, like bees, like locusts; we couldn't get rid of them.

BETSY: It's true. The Eigenbergs only call when we're working.

BOB: But now...now that we're on a slide, now that we're scrounging for a job, a gig, a walk-on, anything, anything we can get our hands on...Not a word. Not a single, isolated word from any of them!

BETSY: It's reprehensible, I know, but Bob, your mother...Don't you think I should call your mother? If only to see if she continues to disapprove of my sleeping with her son?

BOB: I warned you before. That's a subject we've been over many times with drastic consequences. Let's drop it. The question is... *(Turns to phone; shouts in total frustration.)* When is the phone gonna ring? When is somebody gonna call us of their own free will and volition, for cryin' out loud!

BETSY: *(Rises from trunk; moves around Bob to her chair; patting him comfortingly.)* Come on, let's play another game of gin rummy.

BOB: *(Seated in his chair.)* Tell me, and be honest, Betsy, was I nasty to Liebling? Was I rude to him? Did I say anything at any time that could be construed as mean-spirited, demeaning to his position?

BETSY: Never. Not once. You always said what was on your mind and he respected you for it. He...
(The phone rings. They both jump up, scream in terror at the ringing phone.)

BETSY: *(A whisper.)* Should I...? *(Bob nods. Taking a deep breath, Betsy moves to phone; hand trembling, she lifts it from cradle. Into phone, "tiny" voice.)*

Hello? *(A beat.)* Yes, it is. *(Presses phone to chest.)* It's...Liebling. Do you wanna...? *("take the phone?" Bob wags his head and hand, furiously: no! no!)*

(Into phone; one eye on Bob.) Liebling? Is that you, Liebling? We're...fine. *(Bob mimes that she's to say they're happy. Into phone:)* We're happy. *(Bob runs to upstage to stand on trunk.)* We're extraordinarily happy. *(Forces a laugh.)* You're extraordinarily happy, too? That's extraordinary. What? What was that? A job? *(She gestures: does Bob want the phone? Bob shakes his head. She's to continue.)*

(Into phone; enthusiastically.) That'd be great! What kind of job is it? Where is it? When do we start...?

(Bob mimes that she's not to show enthusiasm.)

(Into phone:) Weeell, on second thought, I don't know, Liebling. We've been... *(Bob mimes how busy they've been.)* ...so busy. I don't think we can accept.

(Bob nods approvingly.)

(Into phone.) No, I'm sorry. Bob's not in now. He went out. I have no idea when he'll be back.

(Bob mimes that he's there; he'll take the phone. He steps down from trunk and moves to Betsy.)

(Into phone) Ah, he came back. He just walked in. Just this minute. Here's Bob. *(Bob takes the phone out of her hand as Betsy continues talking, moving away.)* He just came back.

BOB: *(Into phone; breathing heavily as if he had been running.)* Liebling? Is that you? What? We heard you went out of business. What? We heard you went bankrupt. Sold you agency to a chain of funeral parlors. *(And they laugh heartily.)* No, I'm not kidding. That's what Betsy and me heard. *(Betsy gestures for him not to say anything rude or offensive, but he ignores her advice.)*

(Into phone) What do you want? You have a job for us? Columbia Pictures wants Betsy and me for a feature film?

(He wags his hand excitedly. Betsy jumps up and down, hand over mouth.)

(Presses phone to chest. To Betsy:) Ten days. *(Phone to ear a beat; then to chest.)* Santa Fe. *(Phone to ear; then to chest.)* Twenty-five thousand!

(Barely can contain his excitement. More jumping up and down by Betsy.)

(Into phone; rejecting the offer nonetheless.) It sounds... all right. But I'm afraid Betsy and I have to pass.

(Betsy frantically writes a note to Bob on pad: Don't blow it. She tears off page and hands it to him. He doesn't look at it, stuffs it into his pants pocket.)

(Into phone) Liebling, we have other commitments! We can't get out of them! I promised...All right, all right! If they better the deal we have, we'll try to get out of it.

(Betsy removes note from Bob's pocket, gives it to him. He glances at it, returns it to pants pocket.)

(Into phone) Now are they flying us out there first-class? Two room suite at the best hotel in town? Is there a mid-size car at our disposal? *(A beat; to Betsy, pointing at her with each negotiated agreement.)* Flying first-class, okay! *(A beat.)* Two-room suite, okay! *(A beat.)* Mid-size car, okay! By the way, what's the per-diem? *(A beat.)* Eight hundred a week, okay! *(A beat.)* For the both of us? That is rude, Liebling. That is rude and offensive! Forget it! *(Moves to replace phone in cradle.)* You can take your whole deal and... *(A beat.)* What? *(A beat.)* Eight hundred and ten dollars a week for the both of us is acceptable! *(A beat.)* You got it, Liebling. It's a deal! I love you, too! *(And he hangs up. Turns to Betsy, arms wide open.)*

We're going back to work.

BETSY: *(Arms wide open.)* Ohhh. I am so happy. *(They move towards each other; embrace. The phone rings. They both turn to it, faces filled with uncertainty, consternation. Softly:)* Who...?

BOB: I don't know.

BETSY: Should I...?

BOB: I'll get it. *(A breath; moves to phone and snaps it up.)* Hello? *(A beat; face breaking in a smile.)* George Eigenberg, is that you? *(To Betsy; glowing.)* It's George Eigenberg! *(Into phone.)* How have you been, George? And Maryann? Where have you guys been hiding? It's been... *(A beat; to Betsy.)* He heard we're doing a picture for Columbia! *(Into phone.)* How the hell did you find out so soon? I just got off the phone with...this is incredible. *(Laughing.)* It's true. We just made the deal. Thank you. No, we'd love to see you. *(Betsy motions that she'll phone them.)* I'll have Betsy call Maryann. Take care of yourself, buddy. *(He hangs up.)* How do you like that? After so many years...

BETSY: We'll invite them up and we'll have... *(The phone rings. Buoyantly; into phone.)* Betsy Abbott speaking. *(A beat.)* Who? *(To Bob.)* Do you know a man named Monte Goober?

BOB: Ask him what he wants.

BETSY: *(Into phone.)* What is it about, Mr. Goober? *(A beat; to Bob.)* Did you put money on the horses yesterday?

BOB: How does he sound?

BETSY: Depressed.

BOB: *(Encouraged.)* I'll take it. *(Into phone.)* Monte? Bob. How'd I do? *(Aghast.)* You're kidding. Yeah, I'll be there. I'll pick it up. *(Phone into cradle; beaming at Betsy.)* I won four hundred and sixty-two dollars. *(Moves to coat stand to get his hat.)*

BETSY: You're fantastic!

BOB: *(Hat on head; performing voice.)* May I say something to you, Miss Honicutt?

BETSY: *(Performing voice.)* Oh, please, Sir. My father will be disappointed if you don't.

BOB: *(Puts hand in pocket, takes it out, gestures that he has a roll of money; sings* Ain't She Sweet *or a similar song.)*
(Bob sings, very slowly, the first line. Betsy joins him and they sing, very slowly, the second line. Then they sing together, picking up the beat, linking arms, circling; jubilantly. They sing the first A, four lines, change arms, move in opposite direction, singing the next four lines, the second A. The phone rings. Betsy moves to it; Bob to mirror to adjust his tie; they both continue singing until Betsy picks up the phone.)

BETSY: *(Into phone; brightly.)* Abbott Entertainment here. *(Concerned.)* What is it, Sally? What's wrong?
(Bob removes his hat; his face anxious, apprehensive; he hangs onto each word.)
(Into phone.) I'm sorry. Yes. We'll be there. Call if there's a change. I'll tell him. *(She hangs up, turns to Bob.)*

BOB: My mother? Is it...?

BETSY: A minor coronary. I repeat, a minor coronary. She's in the hospital. They're taking tests. No one can see her until six. I told your sister we'd be there. She... *(The phone rings. Betsy snaps it up; into phone.)* Yes? *(Bob moves to sit in his chair, putting hat on table; he is lost inside himself. Into phone:)* What number did you want? *(A beat.)* You have the wrong number! *(Slams phone into cradle. She starts to move away. The phone rings.)* What's in the world's going on here! *(Into phone; shouts.)* Yes! *(A beat.)* We didn't ask for any newspaper delivery. We're not… *(A beat.)* No, we're not interested! *(Phone into cradle.)* I can't believe this. It's like an epidemic. It's like… *(Takes in Bob's forlorn expression as she moves to her chair.)* Do you wanna speak to your sister? I can call her back at the hospital.

BOB: She'd call. If there's anything we have to know. She did say…

BETSY: A minor coronary. We have every reason to be optimistic. When we go, we'll bring your mother… *("flowers." The phone rings. As she moves to it:)* Do you believe this? Can you believe it? *(Into phone, sharply.)* Yes, what is it? *(A beat; to Bob.)* It's a Mr. Louis Guardino. He says he's a friend of… Josiah. Burbank. Skeffington. Bixbie.

BOB: *(Rises; takes phone from her; Betsy sits.)* Mr. Guardino? Bob Abbott here. What can I… *(A beat.)* I see. Yes. We did know him. Years ago. He taught me how to catch steelhead trout in that lake near Toronto. When's the funeral? *(A beat.)* I'll do everything humanly possible to be there. Thank you for calling. *(Slowly, he hangs up. The phone rings at once.)*

BETSY: Bob, let it ring. It's a joke. Someone's playing a joke on us!

BOB: Who would be playing a joke on us?

BETSY: *(A beat.)* I don't know.

BOB: *(A beat.)* It could be…

BETSY: Who?

BOB: *(A beat.)* I don't know. *(He picks up phone.)* Who is it? *(A beat; irritatedly.)* I didn't ask for any weather report. What kind of service? We didn't subscribe to any such… *(Angrily.)* I don't want it, mister! You take our name off that list! Immediately! *(And he slams phone into cradle. He stares at phone, challenging it to ring. It doesn't. He starts walking away. The phone rings.)*

BETSY: Don't pick it up! Don't pick it up!

BOB: *(Can't resist; snaps it up.)* Now you listen to me! Enough is enough! I won't…! *("tolerate…")* Say that again? *(Phone pressed to chest.)* Did you order a lamp from a department store?

BETSY: *(Rises.)* Let me have it. *(Into phone.)* Did you get the lamp in? You didn't get the lamp in? Then why did you call? To tell me you didn't get the lamp in? *(A longer beat; angrily.)* Miss… Miss Stupido, it did not require a call to tell me you didn't get the lamp in! People have a right to their privacy! People have the right not to be disturbed by their phone ringing, intruding on their lives, intruding on their...

(Gently Bob takes the phone from her hand, pointedly disconnects line by pressing cradle-bar. Betsy continues talking nonetheless.) ...peace of mind...

BOB: *(Lowers the phone on its extension cord to the floor.)* That's it. No more. That's all the calls we're taking today. And maybe tomorrow, too. *(Helps her to her chair; then he sits in his chair.)* Let's play gin rummy. Let's try to have some fun. *(Deals out cards.)*

BETSY: I'd like that more than anything else in the world. *(They pick up their cards.)* When did Liebling say we go to work?

BOB: In about three weeks. We'll know definitely as soon as he gets the schedule. *(The off-the-hook sound beeps eerily from the phone on the floor. There is no intervening operator's voice. They slowly turn to look down at the phone, balefully, hypnotically. Several long beats. Bob returns to his cards, but Betsy can't tear her eyes away from the beeping phone.)* Betsy. *(No response from Betsy. In a panic:)*

Betsy!

BETSY: *(Startled.)* What? What is it?

BOB: You're pretending, aren't you? You're doing it on purpose. You wanna scare me! You wanna make me feel that I'm alone in this universe, that I have nobody, that all those seventeen years we've been together have been a sham, a fraud, an exercise in futility, a...

BETSY: *(Grabbing and holding tightly onto his hands.)* No, no, no, no, no. We are together. We are. We'll always be together. This is a given. We've been wedded. Until death do us part. And I'm not so sure it ends there. We are bound as one in so many ways: socially, emotionally, professionally, economically. Don't you agree? Don't you believe... *(The off-the-hook beeping suddenly stops, mysteriously, so it seems. They both turn to stare at the silent phone lying on the floor. Several long beats of silence.)* Bob?

BOB: Huh?

BETSY: What do we do?

BOB: I don't know.

BETSY: *(Turns to him.)* How long can we go on like this?

BOB: I don't know. The silence is unbearable.

BETSY: It is unbearable.

BOB: Can one live without a telephone?

BETSY: I don't know.

BOB: Should we...?

BETSY: Yes! Yes! We're being adolescent. A little while ago we were complaining that nobody was calling us and now... *(Rises, moves to phone.)* What are we afraid of? We don't owe anybody any money! *(She returns phone to cradle. It rings at once.)*

BETSY: *(Into phone; defiantly.)* Yes! Who is it? What stationery store? *(A beat.)* I'm Betsy Abbott. *(A beat.)* I have it right here. *(She removes a lottery ticket protruding from the middle of the pad on table. Bob rises. Into phone:)* It's six; eighteen; twenty-three; twenty-nine; thirty; thirty-four. *(Gasps.)* I am? *(To Bob.)* I'm an alternate state lottery winner.

BOB: How, how, how much is it?

BETSY: *(Into phone:)* How, how, how much is it, Mr. Farkas. *(Repeats what she hears for Bob's attention.)* We won't know until the winners are announced. But you believe it'll be in the vicinity of several thousand dollars. *(A beat.)* Thank you, Mr. Farkas. You'll be rewarded for your efforts after the formalities. *(She hangs up; excitedly.)* You see! You see! And you think we're unlucky! We happen to be extraordinarily lucky!

BOB: I can't believe it. That's two winners in one day. First the horses and now...

(The phone rings. Bob raises his hand, indicating that he'll answer it. He walks confidently to the phone. Into phone.) Bob Abbott of Bob and Betsy here. *(A long, sad beat; to Betsy.)* Did you see Doctor Barnes this week?

BETSY: *(Faintly.)* Monday.

BOB: It's his nurse. Is anything wrong?

BETSY: Why should there be anything wrong? Let me... *(She moves to take the phone, but he holds onto it, turns away form her.)*

BOB: *(Into phone:)* Can you tell me what the problem is? *(A beat.)* I know. She had it for... *(A beat. Betsy sits in her chair, facing front; she stares down at her clasped hands. Into phone:)* Is Doctor Barnes himself available? I'd like to... *(A beat.)* All right. I'll be there. With my wife. *(He hangs up; turns to Betsy.)* Why didn't you tell me you went to Doctor Barnes?

BETSY: *(Looks up at him.)* It was just for a checkup.

BOB: He removed the mole, the wart, the birthmark, whatever that thing was on your arm.

BETSY: It was routine.

BOB: But he did a biopsy.

BETSY: That's the very point I'm making. It was done as a normal procedure. What did the nurse say?

BOB: *(Steps towards Betsy; he wants to touch her but doesn't.)* We have an appointment with the doctor. Tomorrow at eleven. You should have told me. You should have said something. You should have… *(Realizing he might be upsetting her.)* Forget it. Forget it. *(Moves to right of table.)* It's nothing to fret about. If it was anything serious, Doctor Barnes would have been on the phone, filling us in, telling us all the details.

BETSY: He certainly would have. If it was really important, he wouldn't wait until tomorrow morning.

BOB: Absolutely not. But let's not conjecture. Let's not speculate. Let's not let our imaginations… *(The phone rings. Betsy stares at it. Bob stares at Betsy. One, two, three, perhaps four rings. Betsy slowly rises, takes a step towards the phone.)*

BOB: *(Softly; pleadingly.)* Don't answer. *(Betsy turns her head to stare at him.)* Please. Please. Don't answer. *(Betsy looks back at phone.)*

BETSY: *(A whisper.)* Bob. *(She turns, takes a few steps towards him, downstage. Emotionally.)* Bob, I'm afraid. *(Body bent almost in half; voice rising to a heart-breaking sob.)* I'm so afraid.

(Her hands cover her face, Bob moves to her; he raises her up towards him; slowly removes her hands from her face.

He speaks the words of "Ain't She Sweet" or some such standard tune. Pauses between words, slowly, didactically, as if he's trying to get Betsy to commit the words to memory.

Betsy joins in after he sings the first A of chorus. We can barely hear them. There is only a hint of the melody. It's as if they're hanging on to each word as if each word was a raft.

The phone rings relentlessly.

They sing the second A of the first chorus together, arms around each other, their faces pressed together, staring out front.

Lights begin to fade, congeal on their faces.

They sing the first B of first chorus.

Lights almost out.

Telephone ringing fainter.

They sing the song, the last A of first chorus.

Lights out. Sound out.

They sing the last line or two in darkness.)

END

Mudtracks

by Regina Taylor

MUDTRACKS was directed by Woodie King, Jr. and stage managed by Dwight R.B. Cook with the following cast:

Alma	Mary Alice
Sister Evelyn	Trazana Beverly
Ben	Leon Addison Brown
Charlie	Clebert Ford
Pearl	Frances Foster
Henry	Arthur French
Jessie	Mone Walton

MUDTRACKS by Regina Taylor. © 1994 by Regina Taylor. All rights reserved. Reprinted by permission of the playwright. Caution: Professionals and amateurs are hereby warned that MUDTRACKS is subject to a royalty. It is fully protected under the copyright laws of the United States of America, and of all countries covered by the International Copyright Union (including the Dominion of Canada and the rest of the British Commonwealth), and of all countries covered by the Pan-American Copyright Convention and the Universal Copyright Convention, and of all countries with which the United States has reciprocal copyright relations. All rights, including professional, amateur, motion picture, recitation, lecturing, public reading, radio broadcasting, television, video or sound taping, all other forms of mechanical or electronic reproduction, such as information storage and retrieval systems and photocopying, and the rights of translation into foreign languages, are strictly reserved. Particular emphasis is laid upon the question of readings, permission for which must be secured from the author's agent in writing.

All inquiries concerning rights should be addressed to the playwright's representative: The William Morris Agency, Inc., 1350 Avenue of the Americas, New York, NY 10019, Attn: Joan Fields.

REGINA TAYLOR is an associate artist of the Goodman Theatre where her one-act INSIDE THE BELLY OF THE BEAST opened recently along with WATERMELON RINDS, which premiered in the '93 Actor's Theatre of Louisville. Ms. Taylor has performed her solo piece, ESCAPE FROM PARADISE, at Circle Rep. and adapted two one-acts by Franz Xavier-Kroetz—GHOST TRAIN and STY FARM (translated by Mario Emes)—workshopped at the Public Theater. The '95 Actors Theater of Louisville presents her full-length play BETWEEN THE LINES. Ms. Taylor has been commissioned to write a musical at the Alliance Theatre.

CHARACTERS

Alma

Sister Evelyn

Ben

Charlie

Pearl

Henry

Jessie

MUDTRACKS

PRELUDE
As Alma crosses the stage she passes...
Lights up on Pearl falling asleep in a rocker.

RADIO: ...forecast is clear and sunny skies today and tomorrow. Low
nineties, expected high of 110. Wear your sunbonnets ladies...
(Radio voice bleeds into sound of ticking clock as Alma continues
past...)
(Lights up on Ben and Jessie in bed. Ben sleeps. Jessie turns—eyes
open.)
(Lights up on Alma washing her face in bathroom sink.)
ALMA: I used to dream. I don't dream anymore...no. No more.
(As man in white enters. He takes Pearl up into a dance. A tango.
It is alternately sensual and cruel.)
(Alma in the mirror...)
ALMA: These lines. When did these lines grow across my face. Like a
map... A mole... a scar... a blemish... Hardly recognize myself. No.
Used to dream about him all the time. He was my blood, my
breath. Even after he left for good a part of him grew inside me.
Bloated. Stinking of his seed. I tried pushing him out. There he
was cradling me in my dreams. Even awake. I looked at myself
and there he was smiling around my eyes. Perched on my lip like
if I would open my mouth—his voice would speak... No.
(The dance continues... then...)

SCENE I
(Ben and Jessie)
BEN: It was her legs that caught my eye. It was the legs I fell in love
with. Strong, quick-footed—and I followed.
JESSIE: Tell me...now, tell me...can you tell me something if I asked you?
Suppose I asked you...that is, suppose I told you... Tell me—
would you still love me if, say, for instance, I was one of those

women with perfect hair like in the magazines kind of women with perfect teeth and hair and skin, smooth skin, no blemishes, no scars, no ash, no black on the elbow and knees type of women. The kind of women with manicures and pedicures who don't sweat, who wake up in the morning with sweet breath, everything in place all the time. Their lips never peel, never chap. Everything smooth, smooth hands, smooth nylons that don't ever sag or run. Always smelling of Chanel even after making love. The kind of woman who doesn't bite her nails or spill spaghetti sauce on just-pressed fresh white blouses—silk blouses. Who know how to cross their legs just a certain way and hold their arms just so and hands moving like poetry through the air as she speaks with those lips, you know that mouth, speaking with sweet-smelling breath wrapped around ten dollar words with lots of syllables. Those women who, even without having something to say, hold their lips parted just so much, parted and moist with the color of peach or passion flower purple. Their mouths are parted and they breathe through flared nostrils with always a glint in their eye as you peer under their heavy eyelids, a twinkle that says that there's something going on up under there that she may, if she's in the mood, allow you to experience with her. Would you love me if I was one of those women. You know the women I'm talking about. Would you love me even more—or less than now—if I were?

BEN: Somehow I knew when I first saw her... I knew how those legs would fit around.

JESSIE: Of if I were a bag, an old dried-out bag, you know, just the opposite... If I were different...just simply different than who you love now...would you still love me?

BEN: I had to follow where she led. I loved her from the tips of her toes, the smooth heels of her arched feet and those sinewy vines that lead up to that place where a man could get lost in. I lost myself in her.

JESSIE: If I were different than the woman you love, as you see me now...if... See, Ben, the leaves are falling. Why? Because it's autumn. Things change color, it gets darker later. I get somber this time of year. I love the fall but my mood changes...it's not like spring. I love the spring, too—what I'm trying to say is—The tree. That's the same tree that it's always been. In a few weeks it will be completely naked and then snow will cling to it's branches. It's the same tree but it's not how I used to see it. But I love that tree in all it's changes...not more or less—just different. You can't expect spring when it's autumn. Sometimes, though, in the middle of winter I wake up in the morning and I can go out in shorts and a T-shirt and it feels like spring. Not that it's trying to be deceptive. It's not a lie. It's very real. What's deceptive is for me to expect it to stay that way all the time. You deceive yourself.

BEN: You know how I feel about you. You're perfect the way you are— just like you are. No need to change. I'll always love you perfect the way you are.

SCENE II

(Alma in mirror...)

ALMA: No more dreams.

(Alma smashes her head into mirror.)

SCENE III

(A motel room. Furniture is overturned. Clothes are scattered. Jessica tries to shield herself with a piece of a chair. Ben stands in front of the busted door and holds the leg of the chair in his hand.)

BEN: Who loves you, baby, who loves you, baby, who loves you more than anyone could ever love you, more than you can ever love yourself, baby? Who's baby are you, sweetheart, who's heart? Who whispers in your ear at night and rocks you to sleep, who's lover, who's heart, who's child, who's woman are you? Bitch, I could kill you. Before you could take in another breath to speak another word, I could be across this room and split your skull wide open. Split your skull wide open. I could split your crack wide open. Shove it up your crack, baby, shove it all the way up into your throat before you could open your mouth to scream. I could cut you into little pieces. Chop you up and put you in a suitcase, throw you in the trunk of the car and just drive away. *(Pause.)* And you know why? Because I love you. *(Looks out window.)* Yeah. Yeah. *(Paces around the room as if looking for something.)* Yeah. Yeah. *(He catches Jessie staring at the broken entrance door.)* Try it. *(Looking under the bed.)* Maybe you could make it to the door. *(Looking in closets.)* Maybe all the way to the car. *(Looking in the bathroom.)* If you're fast. If you're real fast, you can make it all the way to the border. Are you scared, Jessie? Are you scared that I might kill you? Because I could. I could kill you. *(He charges, throwing himself against the wall.)* I could kill you. *(Throws himself against the walls.)* I could—I could kill—

JESSIE: You're going to hurt yourself....

BEN: *(Stops)* Who told you to move? Sit down. Sit. Don't move until I tell you. Don't do nothing until I tell you.

(She sits.)

Where are we? Where's this? Between what and what?

JESSIE: Just outside of Greenville.

BEN: Nowhere. The middle of nowhere, that's where we are. Where were you headed? Going to Mexico?—Cross over to Mexico. Got some refried Mexican waiting for you across the border, the Rio Grande. Some Mucho grando, spic dick—some hot and spicy enchilada, coochy coochy frito, ole—baby. Where were you going, baby, sweetheart my precious my one, lovely baby, baby, oh, baby. Don't you know it's dangerous when you cross over the border. It's not safe. Wars going on. You could get shot crossing the border. Some cigar-smoking guerrilla could just shoot you between the eyes. Pow. Pow. You could step on a bomb. No one could piece enough of you together to send back home to your loved one. Not safe. Good thing I caught up with you when I did. Huh, baby?

JESSIE: I think you should leave, Ben.

BEN: You think I should leave.

JESSIE: The police—

BEN: Nobody's called the police. People don't want to get involved these days. That's the problem, these days. Nobody wants to make a commitment.

JESSIE: You broke the door. The manager... he'll be by—

BEN: That manager, he's a nice ole boy. Lyle, I believe. Clyde?—no, Lyle. When I drove up I had a little talk with Ole Lyle. I told him I was looking for my woman. He was behind the desk watching Starsky and Hutch. He said he didn't much like being disturbed while he was watching Starsky and Hutch. I told him I could understand that. A man has a something he enjoys but I was looking for my woman, my baby, how you were expecting me, we hadn't seen each other in—how long has it been?—Way too long. And we have a tendency to get a little frisky especially after being separate for so long, we get a bit loud but to never mind. I slipped him some lunch money. He assured me that us honeymooners would not be disturbed. We can take our time. *(He takes up remote control.)* What's this? *(He clicks it. The bed begins to vibrate.)* Ha! *(Clicks again. Lights turn off and on.)* Haa! *(Clicks again. Television comes on.)* Haa! *(Click...click...click...the television channels switch, lights brighten and dim, the bed shakes at different speeds, raises and lowers... Ben rides the bed.)* HAA! *(Ben points the switch at Jessica, clicking.)* Bang. Bang. Bang.

SCENE IV

(Lights out. In the darkness we hear Voice singing.)

VOICE: Some men like me cause I'm happy

Some because I'm snappy

Some call me honey

Other's think I got money

Some say, baby, oooh, you're built for speed

Put them all together

Makes me everything a good man needs.

(Lights up on motel. Ben has tied Jessica to a chair.)

JESSIE: Please, Ben, stop.

BEN: *(Puts tape over her mouth.)* Who said something? Must have been a ghost. *(Then)* They found her tied to the chair, her body mangled beyond recognition. *(Then)* Three weeks. Seems like years. Three weeks ago I walk in the house—"Jessie, I'm home." No answer. Maybe she's working late. No note on the refrigerator, nothing on the machine. Maybe she's just busy, she'll call later... No, something is wrong, here. The bathroom. I go into the bathroom. Something is missing. Her creams aren't in the cabinet, her soaps aren't on the counter—check the drawers. Check the closets— GONE. Somebody took all her things. Somebody—some pervert came in and snatched all my baby's stuff. Some filthy pervert is smoothing himself with her creams, feeling her blouses, wearing her shoes, jacking off in her underwear—maybe he took her with him. He kidnapped my Jessie. Ran into the yard, screaming. Somebody must have seen something. "Hey! Have you seen my baby? Anybody seen my baby. You see the filthy dope fiend that snatched my love? Hey, you, did you see—No. No, you're wrong. You're lying. I'll break your head, man. Rip your tongue out of your mouth. Shut up. Just shut up." I ran back to the house. It still smells of her. She's still here in the sofa, the kitchen, our bed. She couldn't have left me. Couldn't have left without leaving a note a god damn note—a word—a nod...a... We had something. Two years...we had something. Didn't we? Just disappeared like she never... like we never... Maybe she never—maybe not—maybe she didn't. *(Then)* She wouldn't let me in. Break down the fucking door. She looks at me like she doesn't recognize me. Baby it's me. Don't you recognize me? She runs around the room. Baby, it's me. She runs around the room knocking over shit like I must be some-body else. *(Searching.)* What am I looking for? Evidence, yeah, proof. Right here. *(Picks up pictures from the floor.)* Exhibit A... ex-hibit B...C...D... Here, that's you, isn't it? It's you sitting on the sofa in the house we lived in together. We're holding each other, see. Herbert took this picture. Remember Herbert? We used to go bowl-ing together every Tuesday with Sarah, his wife. Herbert loved that eggplant stuff you used to fix, remember. *(He rips the picture.)* Here we are again. In front of the Carousel at the State Park. How many times did you want to go around on that damn thing... See how I'm holding you. See how you're smiling at me, how you're looking at me. *(He rips the picture.)* This one is of the Bar-B-Q last summer... *(He cuts a circle in the picture.)* They found her head tossed in a field. Miles away they found her body floating down-stream.

(Lights out.)

SCENE V

(Spotlight comes up on Sister Evelyn. She stands in front of a mike with red underwear.)

SIS EVELYN: *(Singing.)* I ain't good looking
And my hair ain't curled
I ain't good looking
And my hair ain't curled
But my mama give me something
Gonna carry me through this world.
(She dresses—each layer of clothing makes her heavier, older, more worn.)

Scene VI

(Lights come up on the backyard clothesline. Alma with basket of sheets. She wrings out sheet, snaps it and throws it on the line... Sis Evelyn enters.)

SIS EVELYN: Just a flapping

ALMA: Afternoon, Sis Evelyn.

SIS EVELYN: Sis Alma. So white, your sheets. Flapping. You must use a scrub board.

ALMA: Yes ma'am.

SIS EVELYN: So white. Some folks are ashamed to put their white sheets on the line. Soiled. Stains. Machine won't do it. Stains encrusted forever. They hide them in the dryer. Flapping. Flapping.

ALMA: Hot out today.

SIS EVELYN: Yes ma'am. *(Then)* I heard about your daughter.

ALMA: It's been a long hot spell this summer.

SIS EVELYN: Read about it in the papers—found in that motel room.

ALMA: Yes, ma'am, it's a good day for washing.

SIS EVELYN: Poor thing. Poor, poor thing. Flapping like wings. Yes ma'am. You have a nice day, Sis Alma.

ALMA: You too, Sis Evelyn.

SIS EVELYN: See you come Sunday.

ALMA: Come Sunday.

(Lights fade on yard—rise as Alma takes the empty basket into the kitchen. Pearl sits rubbing her feet.)

PEARL: What did that nosy heifer want?

ALMA: She was just concerned.

PEARL: Concerned about what don't concern her. You may as well bring those sheets right back in. It's going to rain.

ALMA: Mama, the skies are clear.

PEARL: I can feel it.

ALMA: Doesn't smell of rain.

PEARL: My feet say rain. I know what I feel.

ALMA: The weatherman said—

PEARL: By suppertime it will be downpouring.

ALMA: No clouds. No, not a cloud in the—

PEARL: I know what I feel. *(Then)* This heat.

ALMA: Yes. That's probably what it is. The heat.

PEARL: I know what I feel.

ALMA: Take a good bath, have a nice rest. You'll feel better after a rest.

PEARL: It's my legs. Up and down. My knees never lie.

ALMA: Want me to fix you some tea?

PEARL: Fix me some tea.

(Alma puts the kettle on.)

Get my salve from my purse in the living room.

(Alma exits to the living room.)

A nose can fool you. Weathermen lie all the time. Science. My knees never lie. I know what I feel.

ALMA'S VOICE: It's not in the living room.

PEARL: It's on the edge of the divan.

ALMA'S VOICE: It's not here.

PEARL: Are you looking?

ALMA'S VOICE: I'm looking. It's not here.

PEARL: Someone must have moved it.

ALMA'S VOICE: I haven't touched your purse, mama.

PEARL: Look in the bedroom. It must be in the bedroom if you're positive it's not on the divan where I left it. *(To herself.)* I didn't put it in the bedroom. I left it on the edge of the divan. *(She tries to get up. Groans. Sits back down.)* She says she didn't see it. She must have moved it. Always putting things away. Can't just let things sit where a body puts them. She always has to pick it up and carry it some place else so a body can't find it when they come back for it. Then she forgets that she moved it. Enough to make a body old.

(Alma enters.)

It's suffocating.

ALMA: It's not in the bedroom either. I looked.

PEARL: Under the bed?

ALMA: I looked.

PEARL: Could be anywhere. I don't know where you put it if it's not there. Always fixing things, rearranging, picking up—hiding things.

ALMA: I haven't moved your purse.

PEARL: Then you forget. Forget. My knees hurt on account of the rain. I need my salve that's in my purse and you pretend that you can't remember. Stand there watching your mama hurt.

ALMA: The water's ready.

PEARL: Ice tea.

ALMA: I could rub some ice on.

PEARL: I'm all swollen.

(Alma wraps ice in a cloth and applies the ice to Pearl's knee.)

PEARL: AAAEEE! It's too cold.

ALMA: I'm sorry.

PEARL: Like a knife.

ALMA: I didn't mean to.

PEARL: Like a knife.

ALMA: Your purse. It's under the table.

PEARL: How did it get there? *(Pearl gets the salve from her purse and rubs her legs and feet.)* I'll feel better when it comes down. When it all comes down. Get some Epsom salt and pour me a tub of hot water. Hot. I like it as hot as I can stand it.

(Alma brings her a glass of tea. Pearl strokes her daughter's head.) Remember when I'd wash your hair in rainwater? Rainwater is the best to make your hair soft. Like cotton. I'd put pails out on the windowsill to catch it. That old house. It always smelled of fried potatoes, dried herbs and stanky children. Friday night was bath night. I'd be chasing all my dusky children through the field. Willy was the only one that didn't mind bathing. Soft as... I imagine I put a thousand pigtails on your head. Feels like wire now. Put a pail out and catch some water this evening it will do you good.

(Alma moves away. Goes to prepare the foot bath.) You didn't like the rain. You used to come screaming.

ALMA: I didn't like the sound. That noise.

PEARL: Running around like a scared chicken. "It's gonna get me, mama. It's gonna get me and carry me away." *(Then)* The papers said he must have been half crazy. I almost died when I read about my granddaughter in the papers. She sent me a picture once of them together. Did she send you one?

ALMA: No.

PEARL: He looked crazy. Looked like he could do something like that. Looked like he had a streak in him. Your daddy looked like that. Sometimes, old Henry, he got drunk and got those same eyes. Nothing to do but stay away from him then. *(She winces in pain.)* Aah! Rain for sure. Thunderstorm. Remember that time you hid up under the bed and we didn't know it.

ALMA: I don't remember.

PEARL: We didn't know you were up under there. The sky was clapping and banging and me and old Henry were doing the dog when all of a sudden we heard your voice coming out of—don't know where— "Don't you kill my mama." And—WHACK—across the back of old Henry, you brought down that broom. "Don't you be killing my mama." Lord, if I hadn't got you out of that room pepper fast, girl—Hiding up under the bed like that.

ALMA: I don't remember.

PEARL: My girl thought old Henry was killing her mama. Though, sometimes when he was making love I couldn't tell the difference myself.

(Alma sets the basin down and begins washing and massaging Pearl's legs. Pearl moans, a mixture of pain and relief. Her moans mix with the sound of a bluesy saxophone as lights fade out and rise on motel room. Ben plays.)

SCENE VII

BEN: I dedicated that number to you, Jessie. Did you like it? I played it just for you. Put the reed in my mouth and played it like when I touch you. Remember how you used to say you felt when I touched you. Did you feel it Jessie? Did you feel me touching you? Do you love me, Jessie? Say it Jess. Say what you used to say. Let me hear the words.

(Ben untapes her mouth. Lights out.)

SCENE VIII

(Lights up on kitchen.)

PEARL: Suffocating in here.

ALMA: *(Turning the fan toward Pearl.)* The air conditioner is busted.

PEARL: Ought to get a new one. Saw a sale on air conditioners at K-mart.

ALMA: I'll look at them.

PEARL: You need to work your yard. Just wasted earth. Wasted. Back at the old place I could pick cotton like a man. Kept up with the best of them. Old Henry could never say I couldn't. The garden was mine. I'd grow some vegetables, squash, lettuce, tomatoes, onions, and my flowers bloomed all year round. Zinnias, buttercups, geraniums—everything I put down shot up. You never touch your yard. Wasted.

ALMA: Never cared for gardening much.

PEARL: *(Groans in pain.)* I loved the smell after a big storm. I'd go outside in my barefeet and walk around in the mud. Wet. Everything was sticky wet. I put my hands deep in it, the mud, and feel around in the earth. Covered myself in it. Smelled of— *(Smacks her lips.)* Each time I was carrying, I'd have a craving for red clay earth. I still remember the taste. *(Then)* I swear, Alma, it's clean. This kitchen's already clean. It's clean.

ALMA: Just tidying.

PEARL: Come talk to your mama. Sit down. My favorite daughter.

ALMA: Your only daughter.

PEARL: Sit down and chat. *(Pause.)* This place never changes. The furniture never changes.

ALMA: The furniture is fine. I don't need anything new.

PEARL: Maybe if you got a few new pieces. That living room furniture—

ALMA: I like my furniture like it is.

PEARL: You never draw your curtains open.

ALMA: So strangers can peep in.

PEARL: Suffocating. Middle of summer. You need to get out.

ALMA: I get out.

PEARL: Take in a movie.

ALMA: I go to church. Bazaars...

PEARL: I never get to see you.

ALMA: I visit you.

PEARL: You hardly ever come by.

ALMA: As often as I can.

PEARL: It's not as if I live so far away. I understand Byron lives in another state, but you—You can't take the time—

ALMA: At least once a month I take the bus out—

PEARL: Then you can't wait to hop back on. Can't wait. It shouldn't take a tragedy to get flesh and blood together. Shouldn't take a death to— *(Pause.)* Well, mama's here, now. Mama is here. Everything is going to be alright, baby, don't you worry. I'm here.

(Lights come up on motel as scenes overlap. Ben takes gun from his jacket and points it at Jessica.)

PEARL: I tried running away from old Henry once.

BEN: Where were you going?

PEARL: Just stopped one day and took off—

JESSIE: I don't know—

PEARL: —down the road. I ran and I ran...

BEN: Another man?

JESSIE: No.

PEARL: But it come to me that I had nowhere to go.

JESSIE: I had to get out.

PEARL: I'd left my children behind.

BEN: Why?

JESSIE: I don't know.

PEARL: Something in my blood just seized me that day and I was gone.

JESSIE: I don't know.

BEN: You would have come back.

PEARL: I had to go back.

BEN: You would have come back.

JESSIE: I don't know. When we touch, we hurt each other.

PEARL: I got home and he was there waiting. He knocked me across the room. Knocked me flat. Then he took me up in his arms and cried like a baby.

(Ben puts the gun into his mouth. We hear a clap of thunder. Alma drops a cup. It breaks. Black out.)

SCENE IX

(The rain comes down. There is a knocking on the door.)

JESSIE'S VOICE: Mama.

PEARL: Come in. You're soaking.

(Jessie enters. She is soaked and mud-splattered.)

ALMA: You're tracking.

PEARL: What happened?

JESSIE: The car stopped.

PEARL: Get out of them wet things.

JESSIE: I walked...the mud—I'm sorry. *(Taking off clothes.)* I fell in the mud. Ran...the thunder chased me...

(Alma exits.)

PEARL: *(Calling off.)* I said it would rain.

JESSIE: *(Remembering.)* —Your feet—

PEARL: —never lie.

JESSIE: The chair. The table. The plates. The wallpaper. The clock. The smell. *(Calls.)* Mama. *(Then)* My skin is all wet, soaked through. I rode through the night. The sun came up went back down again. I rode. I didn't stop. The rain came down. The car stopped. I got out and ran, ran all the way. The thunder chasing me all the way. Growling. I made it safe. Safe. No harm. Wind scratching at the door.

(Alma re-enters.)

Mama.

(Alma wraps Jessie in towel.)

Your hands are so cold. Smell of vanilla. Always smelled of vanilla.

ALMA: You cut your hair.

(Light follows Alma and Jessie downstage to bathtub.)

JESSIE: *(Steps in.)* So warm. I'll never come out until I'm all over wrinkled. Stay awhile. *(Pause.)* So dark. Night. I thought I'd lost the way. I couldn't figure out if I had lost the way or if the way had changed. If I couldn't find it, I'd have to turn back around and go all the way back where I came or a different way and end up somewhere else. I nearly missed the exit. But there it was in front of me. *(Pause.)* Your hair.

ALMA: Grey.

JESSIE: You look the same.

ALMA: I hardly recognize you. You cut your hair. *(She rises.)* I'll make some tea. You'll sleep. *(Alma exits to kitchen.)*

JESSIE: The highway was smooth. All night I rode and through the day again. Few cars passed. It carried me all night until this evening then just sputtered, stopped in the middle of the road. I coasted down... The rain came pouring down. I ran. Fell. Fell in the mud. Got back up and ran. Everything whirring fast past until I got to the house. The house was still. The white wood fence. The fence holds the house still. The rooms smell the same but—No. Smaller than I remember them. Did they shrink? Do they grow and shrink when we're not watching? My breasts shrank. *(Pause.)* He opened his mouth as if to speak. He opened his mouth as if to say—Put the barrel of the gun inside. His face flew apart. He opened his mouth and said—I heard him say... He put the gun in his mouth to stop the words...the words blew apart. Words flew all over the room...the floors...the walls...his words splattered all over me.

(Lights up on kitchen.)

PEARL: What did she say?

ALMA: She didn't say anything.

PEARL: She didn't say nothing?

ALMA: Mama—

PEARL: *(Sarcastic.)* I'm just an old woman who don't know nothing—

ALMA: Mama—

PEARL: But God didn't put me on this earth for so long and not have me pick up a few things.

ALMA: Mama—

PEARL: Thank you, missy. Thank you, missy. *(Then)* She's lost a lot of weight. Looks kind of frail. Remember when she was a baby—just the smilingest thing. Talk, talk, talk and got into anything and everything—wild child. That's what she was, and such fat cheeks. Though for a while we were worried about her in the beginning. You dried up so soon. She was allergic to that formula you gave her. I nursed all my children until they were old enough to ask for second helpings. Remember little Willy waddling up and talking about, "Give me some tiddy." I said—boy get away from me, you are just too grown. You were a blue baby. Didn't want to take that first intake. I nursed you until your first teeth came. You used to bite down and wouldn't let go. I'd jump up, hollering. You'd holler.

(The screen door begins banging. Jessie and Alma are startled by the noise.)

PEARL: *(Laughing.)* Come on in, Mr. Wind, and carry my baby away.

SCENE X

(Alma and Jessie)

JESSIE: *(In rocker.)* I kept having this dream last night.

ALMA: *(Looking out the window.)* Digging. What is she doing digging up my yard this time of the night.

JESSIE: I was in the eye of the hurricane.

ALMA: *(Calling outside.)* Mama! You're going to get yourself a back. Come on in.

PEARL'S VOICE: Here all them crickets?

ALMA: She knows her back. Her back could just give out.

PEARL'S VOICE: *(Singing)* Oh, Mr. Moon, Moon, bright and shiny moon
Won't you please shine down on me
Oh, Mr. Moon, moon, bright and shiny moon
Won't you come from behind that tree...

JESSIE: The eye, the center of the eye was filled with light. But all around was dark. Things whirl around and bumped into each other—uprooted things bang together. Bang, bang, bang—that's the thunder. The eye looks around and around as its body picks up everything the eye sees. It scatters everything, throws it about. But in the eye it's quiet, safe.

ALMA: Who's going to take care of her if she strained her back?

JESSIE: I tried to outrun it. I fell. It pulled me up inside. Things banged about. But inside the eye I was safe. I watched as the words flew about, banging into each other.

ALMA: It was just a dream. Just a dream.

JESSIE: In the eye, I watched him open his mouth—

ALMA: Hush, now. Just a dream.

JESSIE: He said—

ALMA: Hush. You don't have to talk about it. You don't have to remember it anymore. Like it never happened. A dream.

PEARL'S VOICE: *(Singing)* ...I ain't had no loving since

January, February, June or July

Snow time ain't no time to sit

Outdoor's and spoon

So shine on, shine on harvest moon

For me and my guy

ALMA: I swear, she's going to kill herself. Have a heart attack and fall flat over.

SCENE XI

(Kitchen. Jessie hums to herself. Alma is at the table snapping beans. Pearl enters wearing a wide straw hat.)

ALMA: You're gonna get yourself a stroke out in that sun.

PEARL: Give me some lemonade.

(Jessie pours a glass.)

I had a dream last night.

ALMA: You didn't dream last night. You didn't sleep.

PEARL: I had a dream.

ALMA: With your eyes wide open.

PEARL: Don't have to close your eyes to dream.

ALMA: You stayed up all night in that yard digging. You're digging up my whole yard, mama.

PEARL: Just turning the soil. And how do you know I was up all night?

ALMA: You were still out there when I got up this morning.

PEARL: Maybe I'm an early riser.

ALMA: I saw you off and on last night. I looked out the window and there you were digging and singing. It's a wonder you didn't keep the whole neighborhood awake.

(Pearl has been searching the kitchen.)

What are you looking for?

PEARL: I thought I left it in here. My hair, I left it in here.

ALMA: On top of the refrigerator, where you left it. It's too hot to be wearing that thing.

PEARL: *(Puts wig on her head.)* I can stand the heat.

ALMA: Tell me that when they're rushing you to the hospital with a stroke.

PEARL: You couldn't sleep because of my singing. It kept you awake?

ALMA: Just couldn't sleep.

PEARL: You have a bad dream?

ALMA: How could I dream. I said I couldn't sleep. You were digging and humming all night. How could I sleep?

PEARL: I'm just trying to make your yard look pretty. Get something to grow. How a body can neglect a garden so. You have some good soil, Alma, rich.

ALMA: It's too late in the season. The ground is too dry. Too hot.

PEARL: I'm planting on the side of the house where there'll be plenty of shade. Water in the evening and the rest takes care of itself. With or without my green thumb. You'll have flowers blooming in no time. You ought to put a sprig of mint in your lemonade, Alma. Give it some taste. Cowchips. Fertilize with some cowchips. *(Laughing.)* Fresh cow chips. I remember living with an aunt in Texas when I was eleven years old. She taught me about herbs. Bitterroot, chamomile, sage...dried them and sold them. And she made the best berry and peach preserves. She was a midwife too. Aunt Selest. One time, I had gotten sick, burning with fever and aching all over. Aunt Selest made me some cow chip tea—the nastiest stuff. I drank it though and I was cured. The fever broke. Home remedies. I've forgotten most of them. Turnip greens, the pot liquor of turnip greens is good for the circulation. Aunt Selest had the clearest skin, she used oatmeal scrubs. She lived to be one hundred and nine. Home remedies are the best. Take a heart condition, for instance. Plain old conversation stirs up the circulation. *(Pause)*

ALMA: She doesn't want to talk about.

PEARL: Is that what she said, Alma?

ALMA: It's all past and gone.

PEARL: Past and gone. Past and gone. Those are your words, Alma, remember when you would rock her in the cradle. That's what you'd sing to your baby girl.

ALMA: That's enough, mama.

PEARL: That's how you lived your life.

ALMA: Enough!

PEARL: I'm just an old woman that don't know nothing. Thank you, missy...

JESSIE: What did you dream last night, grandma?

PEARL: I'm tired. I had a dream last night about riding this long-legged stallion. Rode all night long. *(Then)* Did I have any calls today?

ALMA: No. Who were you expecting?

PEARL: A man. Charlie French. I told him I'd be staying here for a few days—

ALMA: Charlie French. Don't I know him?

PEARL: No. You don't know my Charlie.

ALMA: But I remember a Charlie from a long time ago. When we moved to East Greenfield Street. He used to ride by in a big maroon Cadillac with a tall blond woman at his side. Charlie. He had red conked hair.

PEARL: You don't know my Charlie. My Charlie is bald. He's bald all over like a newborn babe.

ALMA: They said he ran a brothel in Orange County.

PEARL: He don't have any teeth anymore either. He refuses to wear his false teeth. He carries them around in his pocket until he sees something he wants to bite into that he can't gum to death.

ALMA: When he calls, why don't you invite him over for dinner.

PEARL: I told you, he doesn't have any teeth. I don't like the way you season your vegetables. You use too much pepper. Charlie puts his teeth in just to eat my snap beans.

ALMA: Papa liked my vegetables.

PEARL: No he didn't. You used to like my singing. You used to ask me to sing to you. Now it disturbs your sleep.

(Knocking on the door.)

SIS EV: Sister Alma.

ALMA: Sister Evelyn.

SIS EV: Just dropped by to borrow a cup of sugar.

ALMA: Well. Come on in.

(Alma exits to kitchen as Pearl enters from bedroom.)

PEARL: Alma told you about letting in flies. Busy buzzing... *(She swats the air.)*

SIS EV: Mrs. Spears.

PEARL: umm-hmm.

SIS EV: And is this...no it can't be little Jessie.

JESSIE: Hello Miss Rogers.

SIS EV: You remember me?

JESSIE: Yes ma'am. You used to give me a nickel and say—"to buy some sweets for a sweet."

SIS EV: Did I do that?

JESSIE: Yes ma'am. And you'd always wear those silk blouses, tight skirts with a slit up the side...

SIS EV: Was that me?

JESSIE: ...high-heeled shoes—

SIS EV: *(Laughing.)* You sure that was me?

PEARL: Yes. I remember.

(Alma enters with a cup of sugar.)

ALMA: No. That's not our Sister Evelyn. No.

SIS EV: *(Shaking her head sadly.)* No.

PEARL: Why don't you get Evelyn a slice of that chocolate cake and get me some lemonade.

SIS EV: No, not anymore.

(Alma exits. We hear dogs barking.)

JESSIE: You always smelled of that...umm...—lilac—

Evelyn: —Jasmine water. Dabbed it on my handkerchief I kept tucked between my breasts.

PEARL: Yeah, you kept the men's noses wide open. They followed you around in packs.

Evelyn: Yes.

(Alma re-enters with cake and lemonade.)

ALMA: Sister.

SIS EV: Look at that. I came by for a cup of sugar and I get a piece of cake as well.

(We hear dog fight. The women look out the window.)

ALMA: Coming over my fence! *(She gets her broom.)* She's in heat.— Get!— *(as Alma exits)* Get out of my yard!

(Jessie, Pearl, and Sister Evelyn mock the dogs—they bark.)

SCENE XII

(Alma and Jessie)

ALMA: ...don't forget the corners. Wash up in the corners and under the tables... under the refrigerator... in between the crevices... under

counters... unseen places are just as important. When you're done it's like starting over again. Everything is like new. A new page.
(Then)

JESSIE: What was he like? Tell me about him.

ALMA: Nothing to tell.

JESSIE: Why didn't you marry him. Grandma said he asked.

ALMA: Is that what she said?

JESSIE: What did he look like?

(Alma looks hard at Jessie.)

ALMA: ...He was smart. Strong... A good dancer. When he took me up in his arms... *(She stops.)* You never even wrote. Not once. You walked out of my house and just disappeared. You were all I had and you left me.

JESSIE: I came back—

ALMA: You cut your hair. I hardly recognize you.

JESSIE: You could never touch me. You never wanted to touch me. You're my mama and you hated... holding me. All I wanted... I had to come back... WHY?—What do you see when you look in my face?

(Overlap.)

ALMA: You never wanted for anything—I saw to that—Cared for you— I loved you—you know that.

(Jessie tries to embrace Alma. It is an awkward painful dance. Sister Evelyn sings—Precious Lord...)

Scene XIII

(Alma and Sis Evelyn in kitchen.)

RADIO VOICE: ...as Psalm 57 says: Have mercy on me O God
Have mercy on me
For in you my soul takes refuge
I will take refuge in the shadow of your wings until the disaster is over

(Lights come up on the living room. Jessica watches Pearl and Charlie dancing to a Muddy Waters tune.)

CHARLIE: Come on now, little mama. Come on now. That's the way, uh-huh.

(We hear a knocking on the door. Jessie answers.)

HENRY: Pearl Morgan. I'm looking for my Pearl.

PEARL: Henry?

HENRY: Hello, Pearl.

PEARL: I thought you were long dead, Henry. What are you doing here?

HENRY: Man's got a right to see his wife every once in a while, don't he?

PEARL: Thirty-six years, Henry.

HENRY: Thirty-six years? Has it been that long. Thirty-six years.

PEARL: I thought you were dead.

HENRY: I guess you would. Thirty-six years.

PEARL: Well, come on in. Sit down.

(Alma enters.)

ALMA: Daddy?

HENRY: Who's that?

ALMA: Daddy, it's me—Alma.

HENRY: Alma?

ALMA: I guess I've changed. Years. Wrinkles...my nails—I don't bite my nails the way I used to. You used to put hot sauce on my fingers. And I wore a thousand pigtails on my head until I was at least sixteen. My hips...thighs...spreading all over. I'm old now.

HENRY: Alma?

PEARL: She came between Byron and Willy. Our only girl. Remember when she beat you with that broom?

ALMA: Mama—

HENRY: No, I don't remember no Alma.

PEARL: That's Alma's child, Jessie. My grandchild.

HENRY: My grandchild.

PEARL: And Charlie.

CHARLIE: It's getting late. I better be heading back.

HENRY: Don't leave on my account, Charlie.

CHARLIE: It's getting late.

HENRY: Don't leave. Not on my account.

CHARLIE: I guess I could stay awhile longer. Just a few more minutes...

HENRY: I heard the music. I stood out there on the porch for a while looking in the door. You didn't see me standing there looking in. You can still move, Pearl. Just like you used to.

PEARL: You're supposed to be dead.

HENRY: I've been driving around. Drove down to El Paso, up to Utah... California... Chicago... Birmingham... Nevada... Driving through, I heard the music, stood on the porch—looking. Been driving around for thirty-six years looking for you, Pearl, after you left me.

PEARL: You're the one that left. You walked out on a Saturday night going to play cards at Ray's. You never came back. You usually go out to Ray's on Saturday to play cards, drink, listen to some music. You didn't come back that Sunday. Finally on Monday morning I went over to Ray's and he said he hadn't seen you. Nobody had seen you. You didn't come back home. I thought—I thought a lot of things and finally I thought you must be dead.

HENRY: I went out for a drive. I told you I was going out for a drive. When I came home the house was boarded up and my wife and children were gone. Man goes out for a drive, he comes back home and there's nothing there. Like there was nothing ever there. Why did you leave me, Pearl?

PEARL: We waited a year. I looked up and down the country for a year. You went out for a drive? A year and two months.

HENRY: Thirty-six years? Seems like yesterday. You look the same today as the day I met you, Pearl.

CHARLIE: Maybe I should leave now. I should be heading back.

HENRY: Don't leave now, Charlie.

CHARLIE: Don't you think it's getting late?

PEARL: It is late—

HENRY: Just been introduced. Is it late? Thirty-six years. It's early yet.

CHARLIE: Maybe just a few minutes.

HENRY: I'll tell you how I met this fine little lady. It was at the church picnic on a fourth of July. Red soda pop, chicken wings, mashed potatoes, cut green beans and at the pie stand, there she was. I knew the first time I saw her that I'd follow. I'd follow her to the end of my days. Peach pies, rhubarb pies, blueberry pies...apple pie. I walked up to her and asked— "Did you bake that apple pie yourself?" She was wearing a yellow bonnet with pink flowers around the band. Her skin was like honey and her teeth, like her name, a string of pearls. She looked up at me and smiled, the prettiest smile. The angels were truly envious. "Did you bake that apple pie yourself?"

PEARL: I sure did, sir.

HENRY: And she cut me an extra thick slice and it was good.

PEARL: You ate the whole damn pie.

HENRY: Because I couldn't get enough. Didn't want no peach pie, lemon meringue, no strawberry, boysenberry pie. I didn't want nobody's pie but yours. I ate that whole pie and still wanted more.

PEARL: Thirty-six years.

CHARLIE: Her pie's still good. Just the right amount of nutmeg.

HENRY: I told you, I'd follow. Why did you want to leave the man that loved you?

PEARL: You the one that left me.

HENRY: You knew I'd come back. You ran off from me that time before.

PEARL: You were eating me up alive until there was nothing left for myself. Nothing left for me to love. One day I started running, running to try and catch up with myself—some piece, an arm a leg some piece of myself that I could hold on to and call my own. Everybody else had laid claim to me. I was field hand, mother, lover, wife, sister—I didn't recognize myself anymore. Like holding a stranger in my arms.

HENRY: I loved you more than anybody ever could. More than you could, even. Wasn't that enough?

PEARL: Thirty-six years.

HENRY: I told you I'd follow.

PEARL: I figured you'd catch up with me someday. Well, where's my purse—my hair—where's my purse? Why are you always moving things, Alma? Never mind. I'll get it. *(Pearl exits.)*

ALMA: I never wanted to be like her.

CHARLIE: Is it late?

HENRY: Early yet, Charlie. *(Looking at Jessie.)* Willy?

JESSIE: *(Correcting him.)* Jessie.

Henry: Jessie. I loved her more than myself. All I asked was the same in return. Women. Their sides can't hold in the amount of love a man can. A man is hungry, howling at the moon and would swallow that whole and still have an appetite. Such is the capacity of consumption of a man in love. A woman picks at a kernel and says she's full, pushing the whole meal aside—saying a full stomach displaces the heart. She would rather, like a cow, chew on the same cud for years rather than complain of indigestion. I pity the children who suck from her tits. They're bound to be sickly calves with big hearts and no appetite—they waste away.

ALMA: I promised myself to never be like her.

HENRY: Have you known the love of a woman yet, Jessie?

JESSIE: *(Looks at Alma.)* Once.

HENRY: To what conclusion?

JESSIE: Her appetite could outbest any man. But she starved of love—loving too much and never being able to put enough away. I promised myself never to be like her—to never feed on the love of any woman or man but myself to make me fat.

HENRY: That's why you're so skinny.

JESSIE: These are lean days.

HENRY: Ha—lean days you ain't seen. I could tell you about lean, man. What night is this? Friday? Tell Pearl I'm going for a drive. *(To Jessie.)* Want to keep me company?

(Jessie nods.)

Tell Pearl that I'll be back—don't go nowhere unless I follow.

(Jessie and Henry exit. Charlie is asleep.)

ALMA: He never came back. Left me fat bellied and sucking my own fingers. I tried pushing him out—pushing him out of me. And when she was born, she had his eyes, his mouth, the shape of his head—I named her after him. They looked so much alike. Jessie—he never came back—then she left. Left sucking my fingers. *(Then)* Who opened the window letting the hand of a forgotten memory come in to caress my cheek?

(Alma closes the window. Pearl enters.)

PEARL: Henry?—It's Friday night, isn't it. Ray's for some cards, beers. He'll be back. I'll just sit here awhile until— *(Seeing Charlie.)* Poor Charlie. It's so late. *(Trying to wake him.)* Charlie. Charlie...Charlie?

SCENE XIV

(Jessie behind the wheel of car.)

JESSIE: He opened his mouth...the words flew from his face...splattered all over me. *(She wipes her face with her hand.)* I tasted my fingers...licked myself with my tongue.

SCENE XV

(Pearl enters, her hands and feet are covered with mud. Alma stands in a gown.)

PEARL: I buried him in the bed on the side of the house.

ALMA: I had a dream last night.

PEARL: They'll take root. Any day you'll see their heads poking up above the ground.

SCENE XVI

(Jessie behind the wheel of car.)

JESSIE: *(Caressing her belly.)* Growing inside me...

END

Smith and Kraus *Books For Actors*

MONOLOGUE SERIES
The Best Men's / Women's Stage Monologues of 1993
The Best Men's / Women's Stage Monologues of 1992
The Best Men's / Women's Stage Monologues of 1991
The Best Men's / Women's Stage Monologues of 1990
One Hundred Men's / Women's Stage Monologues from the 1980's
2 Minutes and Under: Character Monologues for Actors
Street Talk: Character Monologues for Actors
Uptown: Character Monologues for Actors
Monologues from Contemporary Literature: Volume I
Monologues from Classic Plays

FESTIVAL MONOLOGUE SERIES
The Great Monologues from the Humana Festival
The Great Monologues from the EST Marathon
The Great Monologues from the Mark Taper Forum
The Great Monologues from the Women's Project

YOUNG ACTORS SERIES
Great Scenes and Monologues for Children
New Plays from A.C.T.'s Young Conservatory
Great Scenes for Young Actors from the Stage
Great Monologues for Young Actors
Multicultural Monologues for Young Actors
Multicultural Scenes for Young Actors
Villeggiature: The Trilogy Condensed, Goldoni, tr. by Robert Cornthwaite

SCENE STUDY SERIES
Scenes From Classic Plays 468 B.C. to 1960 A.D.
The Best Stage Scenes of 1993
The Best Stage Scenes of 1992
The Best Stage Scenes for Women from the 1980's
The Best Stage Scenes for Men from the 1980's

CONTEMPORARY PLAYWRIGHTS
Romulus Linney: 17 Short Plays
Eric Overmyer: Collected Plays
Lanford Wilson: 21 Short Plays
William Mastrosimone: Collected Plays
Horton Foote: 4 New Plays
Terrence McNally: 15 Short Plays
Women Playwrights: The Best Plays of 1992
Women Playwrights: The Best Plays of 1993
Humana Festival '93: The Complete Plays
Humana Festival '94: The Complete Plays

GREAT TRANSLATION FOR ACTORS SERIES
The Wood Demon: Anton Chekhov *translated by N. Saunders & F. Dwyer*
The Seagull: Anton Chekhov *translated by N. Saunders & F. Dwyer*
Three Sisters: Anton Chekhov *translated by Lanford Wilson*
Mercadet: Honoré de Balzac *translated by Robert Cornthwaite*

CAREER DEVELOPMENT BOOKS
The Actor's Chekhov
Kiss and Tell: Restoration Scenes, Monologues, & History
Cold Readings: Some Do's and Don'ts for Actors at Auditions
A Shakespearean Actor Prepares
Auditioning For Musical Theater
The Camera Smart Actor

If you require pre-publication information about upcoming Smith and Kraus books, you may receive our semi-annual catalogue, free of charge, by sending your name and address to *Smith and Kraus Catalogue, P.O. Box 127 One Main Street, Lyme, NH 03768 phone 1-800-895-4331, fax 1-603-795-4427.*